|| Shri Hari ||

1411

Śrīmad Bhagavadgītā

(With English Translation & Transliteration)

त्वमेव माता च पिता त्वमेव
त्वमेव बन्धुश्च सखा त्वमेव।
त्वमेव विद्या द्रविणं त्वमेव
त्वमेव सर्वं मम देवदेव॥

tvameva mātā ca pitā tvameva
tvameva bandhuśca sakhā tvameva
tvameva vidyā draviṇaṁ tvameva
tvameva sarvaṁ mama devadeva

Gita Press, Gorakhpur

First Edition to Five Reprints		27,500 Copies
Sixth Reprint	2006	5,000 Copies
	Total	32,500 Copies

Price

ISBN 81-293-0093-1

Printed & Published by **Gita Press, Gorakhpur—273005 (INDIA)**
(a unit of Gobind Bhavan-Karyalaya, Kolkata)
© (0551) 2334721; Fax : 2336997

website:**www.gitapress.org** | e-mail:**booksales@gitapress.org**

Publisher's Note

As a book of scripture, the Bhagavadgītā has assumed a position of universal interest. Its teachings have gained appreciation not only in India, but far beyond its borders. Our Gītā-Library alone comprises about 1400 editions of the Bhagavadgītā published in 34 different languages. We have brought out this new English edition in book form and we trust it will find favour with the English-reading public. The English translation of this edition has been based on the Hindi rendering of the Gītā made by Syt. Jayadayal Goyandka and appearing in the Gītā-Tattva Number of the Hindi monthly 'Kalyan', published by the Gita Press. In preparing the present English translation, the translators have made use, every now and then of other English translations of the Gītā, and express their grateful acknowledgement to the same.

An introduction by Syt. Jayadayal Goyandka is added to enhance further the utility of the book.

About the Fourth Edition

In this edition some suggestions given by Sri J. P. Agrawal (Ex. Controller of Examinations, Kurukshetra University) have been incorporated in order to improve certain expressions in translation originally given in the book.

—Publisher

GLORY OF THE GĪTĀ

The Bhagavadgītā contains divine words emanating from the lips of God Himself. Its glory is infinite, unlimited. None can really describe it. Even Śeṣa, the thousand-headed serpent-god, whose back forms the couch of God Viṣṇu, and Śiva and Gaṇeśa, cannot fully depict this glory. How can a puny mortal expect to do it? The Epics and Purāṇas etc., have sung the glory of the Gītā at many places; but if all those words of praise are brought together, even then it cannot be declared that the praise of the Gītā has been exhausted. The fact is that a full description of the glory of the Gītā is never possible. For how can a thing which can be fully described remain unlimited? It at once becomes finite and limited.

As a scripture, the Gītā embodies the supreme spiritual mystery and secret. It contains the essence of all the four Vedas. Its style is so simple and elegant that after a little study man can easily follow the structure of its words; but the thought behind those words is so deep and abstruse that even a lifelong, constant study does not show one the end of it. Everyday the book exhibits a new facet to thought, hence the Gītā remains eternally new. And deep reflection with reverence and faith will make it directly appear impregnated with deep meaning at every step. The virtues, glory, essential character, truth, mystery and worship of God as well as the topics of Action and Knowledge have been discussed in the Gītā in such a way that its parallel can hardly be found in any other book. As a scripture, the Gītā is so incomparable that there is no word in it which is free from some instructive thought. There is not a single word in the Gītā, which may be described as flattering. Whatever statements have been made in it are true to the very letter. Smelling overpraise in the words of God, the very embodiment of Truth, is to show disrespect to the divine words.

The Gītā is an epitome of all the scriptures. The essence of all the scriptures is to be found in it. And it would be no exaggeration, indeed, if it is called the very storehouse of all scriptural knowledge. For a mastery of the Gītā may lead one automatically to a comprehension of the truths contained in the other scriptures, and no separate study is required to obtain this knowledge.

The Mahābhārata also says: "सर्वशास्त्रमयी गीता" "The Gītā comprises all the scriptures" (Bhīṣma., 44. 4). But this statement too is inadequate. For all the scriptures have originated from the Vedas, the Vedas were revealed through Brahmā's mouths, and Brahmā himself took his descent from the Lord's navel. In this way, a great distance separates the scriptures from the Lord. But the Gītā has emanated directly from the lips of the Lord; hence there will be no exaggeration if it is declared as superior to all the scriptures. The divine sage Vedavyāsa himself says:—

गीता सुगीता कर्तव्या किमन्यैः शास्त्रसंग्रहैः।
या स्वयं पद्मनाभस्य मुखपद्माद्विनिःसृता॥

(Mahābhārata, Bhīṣmaparva 43.1)

"The Gītā alone should be sung, heard, recited, studied taught, pondered and assimilated properly and well. What is the use of collecting other scriptures? For the Gītā has emerged directly from the lotus-like lips of God Viṣṇu Himself."

Through the word 'Padmanābha' in the above verse, the author of the Mahābhārata has brought out the very idea expressed by us. That is to say, the Gītā has emanated from the lips of the same Lord from whose navel Brahmā took His birth; and the Vedas, which are the source of all the scriptures, were revealed through the mouths of Brahmā.

The Gītā is superior even to the Gaṅgā. In the scriptures, liberation has been declared to be the reward of a bath in the Gaṅgā. But he who bathes in the Gaṅgā, though he can obtain liberation himself, does not acquire the power of liberating others. He, however, who takes a dive into the Gītā not only gets liberated himself, but also gains the power of liberating others. The Gaṅgā has sprung from the feet of the Lord, whereas the Gītā has emanated directly from the divine lips. Again, while the Gaṅgā liberates him alone who goes to it and takes a plunge in its waters, the Gītā finds its way to every home, and shows the way to liberation to every individual. These are the reasons why the Gītā is declared as superior to the Gaṅgā.

The Gītā is superior even to the Gāyatrī. Through the practice of Japa of the Gāyatrī man attains liberation, no doubt. But he who practises Japa of the Gāyatrī secures liberation only for himself; whereas the student of the Gītā liberates not only himself but others as well. When the Dispenser of liberation, God Himself, becomes his own, Mukti becomes a trifling affair to him. It takes up its abode in the dust of his feet. He makes a gift of Mukti to anyone and everyone who asks for it.

If we declare the Gītā as greater even than God, there will be no exaggeration. The Lord Himself says:—

गीताश्रयेऽहं तिष्ठामि गीता मे चोत्तमं गृहम्।
गीताज्ञानमुपाश्रित्य त्रीँल्लोकान् पालयाम्यहम्॥

(Varāhapurāṇa)

"I take My stand on the Gītā, the Gītā is My supreme abode. I maintain the three worlds on the strength of the wisdom contained in the Gītā."

Apart from this, in the Gītā itself the Lord openly declares that he who follows His instructions in the shape of the Gītā will undoubtedly attain liberation. Not only this, He further says that even he who studies this scripture will have worshipped Him through wisdom-sacrifice. When such is the value of a mere study of the Gītā, what shall we say of the man who has moulded his life according to its teachings, initiates God's devotees into its secrets and disseminates and propagates its teachings among them. Referring to such a man, the Lord says that he is very dear to Him. It will be no exaggeration to say that he is dearer to God than His very life. The Lord subordinates Himself to the will of such devotees. Even in the case of noble souls, it is found that those who follow their teachings become dearer to them than their own life. The Gītā constitutes the Lord's principal mystic teachings. What wonder, then, that the follower of these teachings should be dearer to Him than even His life?

The Gītā is the very life-breath, the heart, and the verbal image of the Lord. He who has his heart, speech, body and all his senses and their functions imbued with the Gītā is the very embodiment of the Gītā. His very sight, touch, speech and thought lend supreme sanctity to others, to say nothing of those who follow his precept and example. Really speaking, no sacrifice, charity, austerity, pilgrimage, religious vow, self-restraint and fasting etc., stand comparison with the Gītā.

The Gītā contains words directly emanating from the lips of Bhagavān Śrī Kṛṣṇa. Its compiler is Maharṣi Vyāsa. The Lord uttered parts of His discourse in verse, which the compiler Vyāsa recorded exactly as they emanated from His lips. The part of it uttered in prose was versified by the compiler, and the words of Arjuna, Sañjaya and Dhṛtarāṣṭra were similarly versified by him in his own words, and dividing the book of seven hundred verses into eighteen chapters, he made it an organic part of the Mahābhārata. This is how the book has come down to us.

TABLE OF CONTENTS

ॐ श्रीपरमात्मने नमः

अथ श्रीमद्भगवद्गीता

अथ प्रथमोऽध्यायः

CHAPTER ONE

धृतराष्ट्र उवाच

धर्मक्षेत्रे कुरुक्षेत्रे समवेता युयुत्सवः।
मामकाः पाण्डवाश्चैव किमकुर्वत सञ्जय॥ १॥

dhṛtarāṣṭra uvāca

dharmakṣetre kurukṣetre samavetā yuyutsavaḥ
māmakāḥ pāṇḍavāścaiva kimakurvata sañjaya

Dhṛtarāṣṭra said: Sañjaya, gathered on the sacred soil of Kurukṣetra, eager to fight, what did my sons and the sons of Pāndu do? (1)

सञ्जय उवाच

दृष्ट्वा तु पाण्डवानीकं व्यूढं दुर्योधनस्तदा।
आचार्यमुपसङ्गम्य राजा वचनमब्रवीत्॥ २॥

sañjaya uvāca

dṛṣṭvā tu pāṇḍavānīkaṁ vyūḍhaṁ duryodhanastadā
ācāryamupasaṅgamya rājā vacanamabravīt

Sañjaya said: At that time, seeing the army of the Pāṇḍavas drawn up for battle and approaching Droṇācārya, King Duryodhana spoke the following words : (2)

पश्यैतां पाण्डुपुत्राणामाचार्य महतीं चमूम्।
व्यूढां द्रुपदपुत्रेण तव शिष्येण धीमता॥ ३॥

paśyaitāṁ pāṇḍuputrāṇāmācārya mahatīṁ camūm
vyūḍhāṁ drupadaputreṇa tava śiṣyeṇa dhīmatā

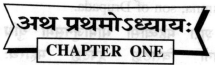

Behold, master, the mighty army of the sons of Pāṇḍu arrayed for battle by your talented pupil, Dhṛṣṭadyumna, son of Drupada. (3)

अत्र शूरा महेष्वासा भीमार्जुनसमा युधि।
युयुधानो विराटश्च द्रुपदश्च महारथः॥ ४॥
धृष्टकेतुश्चेकितानः काशिराजश्च वीर्यवान्।
पुरुजित्कुन्तिभोजश्च शैब्यश्च नरपुङ्गवः॥ ५॥
युधामन्युश्च विक्रान्त उत्तमौजाश्च वीर्यवान्।
सौभद्रो द्रौपदेयाश्च सर्व एव महारथाः॥ ६॥

atra śūrā maheṣvāsā bhīmārjunasamā yudhi
yuyudhāno virāṭaśca drupadaśca mahārathaḥ
dhṛṣṭaketuścekitānaḥ kāśirājaśca vīryavān
purujitkuntibhojaśca śaibyaśca narapuṅgavaḥ
yudhāmanyuśca vikrānta uttamaujāśca vīryavān
saubhadro draupadeyāśca sarva eva mahārathāḥ

There are in this army heroes wielding mighty bows and equal in military prowess to Bhīma and Arjuna—Sātyaki and Virāṭa and the Mahārathī (warrior chief) Drupada; Dhṛṣṭaketu, Cekitāna and the valiant King of Kāśī, and Purujit, Kuntibhoja, and Śaibya, the best of men, and mighty Yudhāmanyu, and valiant Uttamaujā, Abhimanyu, the son of Subhadrā, and the five sons of Draupadī—all of them Mahārathīs (warrior chiefs). (4—6)

अस्माकं तु विशिष्टा ये तान्निबोध द्विजोत्तम।
नायका मम सैन्यस्य सञ्ज्ञार्थं तान्ब्रवीमि ते॥ ७॥

asmākaṁ tu viśiṣṭā ye tānnibodha dvijottama
nāyakā mama sainyasya sañjñārthaṁ tānbravīmi te

O best of Brāhmaṇas, know them also who are the principal warriors on our side—the generals of my army. For your information I shall mention them. (7)

भवान्भीष्मश्च कर्णश्च कृपश्च समितिञ्जयः।
अश्वत्थामा विकर्णश्च सौमदत्तिस्तथैव च॥ ८ ॥

bhavānbhiṣmaśca karṇaśca kṛpaśca samitiñjayaḥ
aśvatthāmā vikarṇaśca saumadattistathaiva ca

"Yourself and Bhīṣma and Karṇa and Kṛpa, who is ever victorious in battle; and even so Aśvatthāmā, Vikarṇa and Bhūriśravā (the son of Somadatta); (8)

अन्ये च बहवः शूरा मदर्थे त्यक्तजीविताः।
नानाशस्त्रप्रहरणाः सर्वे युद्धविशारदाः॥ ९ ॥

anye ca bahavaḥ śūrā madarthe tyaktajīvitāḥ
nānāśastrapraharaṇāḥ sarve yuddhaviśāradāḥ

And there are many other heroes, equipped with various weapons and missiles, who have staked their lives for me, all skilled in warfare. (9)

अपर्याप्तं तदस्माकं बलं भीष्माभिरक्षितम्।
पर्याप्तं त्विदमेतेषां बलं भीमाभिरक्षितम्॥ १० ॥

aparyāptaṁ tadasmākaṁ balaṁ bhīṣmābhirakṣitam
paryāptaṁ tvidameteṣāṁ balaṁ bhīmābhirakṣitam

This army of ours, fully protected by Bhīṣma, is

unconquerable; while that army of theirs, guarded in everyway by Bhīma, is easy to conquer. (10)

अयनेषु च सर्वेषु यथाभागमवस्थिताः।
भीष्ममेवाभिरक्षन्तु भवन्तः सर्व एव हि॥ ११॥

ayaneṣu ca sarveṣu yathābhāgamavasthitāḥ
bhīṣmamevābhirakṣantu bhavantaḥ sarva eva hi

Therefore, stationed in your respective positions on all fronts, do you all guard Bhīṣma in particular on all sides. (11)

तस्य सञ्जनयन्हर्षं कुरुवृद्धः पितामहः।
सिंहनादं विनद्योच्चैः शङ्खं दध्मौ प्रतापवान्॥ १२॥

tasya sañjanayanharṣaṁ kuruvṛddhaḥ pitāmahaḥ
siṁhanādaṁ vinadyoccaiḥ śaṅkhaṁ dadhmau pratāpavān

The grand old man of the Kaurava race, their glorious grand-uncle Bhīṣma, cheering up Duryodhana, roared terribly like a lion and blew his conch. (12)

ततः शङ्खाश्च भेर्यश्च पणवानकगोमुखाः।
सहसैवाभ्यहन्यन्त स शब्दस्तुमुलोऽभवत्॥ १३॥

tataḥ śaṅkhāśca bheryaśca paṇavānakagomukhāḥ
sahasaivābhyahanyanta sa śabdastumulo'bhavat

Then conches, kettledrums, tabors, drums and trumpets suddenly blared forth and the noise was tumultuous. (13)

ततः श्वेतैर्हयैर्युक्ते महति स्यन्दने स्थितौ।
माधवः पाण्डवश्चैव दिव्यौ शङ्खौ प्रदध्मतुः॥ १४॥

tataḥ śvetairhayairyukte mahati syandane sthitau
mādhavaḥ pāṇḍavaścaiva divyau śaṅkhau pradadhmatuḥ

Then, seated in a glorious chariot drawn by white horses, Śrī Kṛṣṇa as well as Arjuna blew their celestial conches. (14)

पाञ्चजन्यं हृषीकेशो देवदत्तं धनञ्जयः।
पौण्ड्रं दध्मौ महाशङ्खं भीमकर्मा वृकोदरः ॥ १५ ॥

pāñcajanyaṁ hṛṣīkeśo devadattaṁ dhanañjayaḥ
pauṇḍraṁ dadhmau mahāśaṅkhaṁ bhīmakarmā vṛkodaraḥ

Śrī Kṛṣṇa blew His conch named Pāñcajanya; Arjuna, Devadatta; while Bhīma of terrible deeds blew his great conch Pauṇḍra. (15)

अनन्तविजयं राजा कुन्तीपुत्रो युधिष्ठिरः।
नकुलः सहदेवश्च सुघोषमणिपुष्पकौ ॥ १६ ॥

anantavijayaṁ rājā kuntīputro yudhiṣṭhiraḥ
nakulaḥ sahadevaśca sughoṣamaṇipuṣpakau

King Yudhiṣṭhira, son of Kuntī, blew his conch Anantavijaya, while Nakula and Sahadeva blew theirs, known as Sughoṣa and Maṇipuṣpaka respectively. (16)

काश्यश्च परमेष्वासः शिखण्डी च महारथः।
धृष्टद्युम्नो विराटश्च सात्यकिश्चापराजितः ॥ १७ ॥
द्रुपदो द्रौपदेयाश्च सर्वशः पृथिवीपते।
सौभद्रश्च महाबाहुः शङ्खान्दध्मुः पृथक् पृथक् ॥ १८ ॥

kāśyaśca parameṣvāsaḥ śikhaṇḍī ca mahārathaḥ
dhṛṣṭadyumno virāṭaśca sātyakiścāparājitaḥ

drupado draupadeyāśca sarvaśaḥ pṛthivīpate
saubhadraśca mahābāhuḥ śaṅkhāndadhmuḥ pṛthak pṛthak

And the excellent archer, the King of Kāśī, and Śikhaṇḍī the Mahārathī (great car-warrior), Dhṛṣṭadyumna and Virāṭa, and invincible Sātyaki, Drupada as well as the five sons of Draupadī, and the mighty-armed Abhimanyu, son of Subhadrā, all of them, O lord of the earth, severally blew their respective conches from all sides. (17-18)

स घोषो धार्तराष्ट्राणां हृदयानि व्यदारयत्।
नभश्च पृथिवीं चैव तुमुलो व्यनुनादयन्॥ १९॥

sa ghoṣo dhārtarāṣṭrāṇāṁ hṛdayāni vyadārayat
nabhaśca pṛthivīṁ caiva tumulo vyanunādayan

And the terrible sound, echoing through heaven and earth, rent the hearts of Dhṛtarāṣṭra's army. (19)

अथ व्यवस्थितान्दृष्ट्वा धार्तराष्ट्रान् कपिध्वजः।
प्रवृत्ते शस्त्रसम्पाते धनुरुद्यम्य पाण्डवः॥ २०॥
हृषीकेशं तदा वाक्यमिदमाह महीपते।

अर्जुन उवाच

सेनयोरुभयोर्मध्ये रथं स्थापय मेऽच्युत॥ २१॥

atha vyavasthitāndṛṣṭvā dhārtarāṣṭrān kapidhvajaḥ
pravṛtte śastrasampāte dhanurudyamya pāṇḍavaḥ
hṛṣīkeśaṁ tadā vākyamidamāha mahīpate

arjuna uvāca

senayorubhayormadhye rathaṁ sthāpaya me'cyuta

Now, O lord of the earth, seeing your sons arrayed against him and when missiles were ready to be hurled, Arjuna, who had the figure of Hanumān on the flag of his chariot, took up his bow and then addressed the following words to Śrī Kṛṣṇa; "Kṛṣṇa, place my chariot between the two armies. (20-21)

यावदेतान्निरीक्षेऽहं योद्धुकामानवस्थितान्।
कैर्मया सह योद्धव्यमस्मिन्रणसमुद्यमे॥ २२॥

yāvadetānnirīkṣe'haṁ yoddhukāmānavasthitān
kairmayā saha yoddhavyamasminraṇasamudyame

"And keep it there till I have carefully observed these warriors drawn up for battle, and have seen with whom I have to engage in this fight. (22)

योत्स्यमानानवेक्षेऽहं य एतेऽत्र समागताः।
धार्तराष्ट्रस्य दुर्बुद्धेर्युद्धे प्रियचिकीर्षवः॥ २३॥

yotsyamānānavekṣe'haṁ ya ete'tra samāgatāḥ
dhārtarāṣṭrasya durbuddheryuddhe priyacikīrṣavaḥ

"I shall scan the well-wishers in this war of evil-minded Duryodhana, whoever have assembled on his side and are ready for the fight." (23)

सञ्जय उवाच

एवमुक्तो हृषीकेशो गुडाकेशेन भारत।
सेनयोरुभयोर्मध्ये स्थापयित्वा रथोत्तमम्॥ २४॥
भीष्मद्रोणप्रमुखतः सर्वेषां च महीक्षिताम्।
उवाच पार्थ पश्यैतान्समवेतान्कुरूनिति॥ २५॥

sañjaya uvāca

evamukto hṛṣīkeśo guḍākeśena bhārata
senayorubhayormadhye sthāpayitvā rathottamam
bhīṣmadroṇapramukhataḥ sarveṣāṁ ca mahīkṣitām
uvāca pārtha paśyaitānsamavetānkurūniti

Sañjaya said: O king, thus addressed by Arjuna, Śrī Kṛṣṇa placed the magnificent chariot between the two armies in front of Bhīṣma, Droṇa and all the kings and said, "Arjuna, behold these Kauravas assembled here." (24-25)

तत्रापश्यत्स्थितान् पार्थः पितॄनथ पितामहान्।
आचार्यान्मातुलान्भ्रातॄन्पुत्रान्पौत्रान्सखींस्तथा ॥ २६ ॥
श्वशुरान्सुहृदश्चैव सेनयोरुभयोरपि।

tatrāpaśyatsthitān pārthaḥ pitṝnatha pitāmahān
ācāryānmātulānbhrātṝnputrānpautrānsakhīṁstathā
śvaśurānsuhṛdaścaiva senayorubhayorapi

Now Arjuna saw stationed there in both the armies his uncles, grand-uncles and teachers, even great grand-uncles, maternal uncles, brothers and cousins, sons and nephews, and grand-nephews, even so friends, fathers-in-law and well-wishers as well.(26 & first half of 27)

तान्समीक्ष्य स कौन्तेयः सर्वान्बन्धूनवस्थितान् ॥ २७ ॥
कृपया परयाविष्टो विषीदन्निदमब्रवीत्।

tānsamīkṣya sa kaunteyaḥ sarvānbandhūnavasthitān
kṛpayā parayāviṣṭo viṣīdannidamabravīt

Seeing all the relations present there, Arjuna was

overcome with deep compassion and spoke thus in sorrow. (Second half of 27 and first half of 28)

अर्जुन उवाच

दृष्ट्वेमं स्वजनं कृष्ण युयुत्सुं समुपस्थितम्॥ २८॥
सीदन्ति मम गात्राणि मुखं च परिशुष्यति।
वेपथुश्च शरीरे मे रोमहर्षश्च जायते॥ २९॥

arjuna uvāca

dṛṣṭvemaṁ svajanaṁ kṛṣṇa yuyutsuṁ samupasthitam
sīdanti mama gātrāṇi mukhaṁ ca pariśuṣyati
vepathuśca śarīre me romaharṣaśca jāyate

Arjuna said: Kṛṣṇa, as I see these kinsmen arrayed for battle, my limbs give way, and my mouth is getting parched; nay, a shiver runs through my body and hair stand on end. (Second half of 28 and 29)

गाण्डीवं स्रंसते हस्तात्त्वक्चैव परिदह्यते।
न च शक्नोम्यवस्थातुं भ्रमतीव च मे मनः॥ ३०॥

gāṇḍīvaṁ sraṁsate hastāttvakcaiva paridahyate
na ca śaknomyavasthātuṁ bhramatīva ca me manaḥ

The bow, Gāṇḍīva, slips from my hand and my skin too burns all over; my mind is whirling, as it were, and I can no longer hold myself steady. (30)

निमित्तानि च पश्यामि विपरीतानि केशव।
न च श्रेयोऽनुपश्यामि हत्वा स्वजनमाहवे॥ ३१॥

nimittāni ca paśyāmi viparītāni keśava
na ca śreyo'nupaśyāmi hatvā svajanamāhave

And, Keśava, I see such omens of evil, nor do I see any good in killing my kinsmen in battle. (31)

न काङ्क्षे विजयं कृष्ण न च राज्यं सुखानि च।
किं नो राज्येन गोविन्द किं भोगैर्जीवितेन वा॥ ३२॥

na kāṅkṣe vijayaṁ kṛṣṇa na ca rājyaṁ sukhāni ca
kiṁ no rājyena govinda kiṁ bhogairjīvitena vā

Kṛṣṇa, I do not covet victory, nor kingdom, nor pleasures. Govinda, of what use will kingdom, or luxuries, or even life be to us! (32)

येषामर्थे काङ्क्षितं नो राज्यं भोगाः सुखानि च।
त इमेऽवस्थिता युद्धे प्राणांस्त्यक्त्वा धनानि च॥ ३३॥
आचार्याः पितरः पुत्रास्तथैव च पितामहाः।
मातुलाः श्वशुराः पौत्राः श्यालाः सम्बन्धिनस्तथा॥ ३४॥

yeṣāmarthe kāṅkṣitaṁ no rājyaṁ bhogāḥ sukhāni ca
ta ime'vasthitā yuddhe prāṇāṁstyaktvā dhanāni ca
ācāryāḥ pitaraḥ putrāstathaiva ca pitāmahāḥ
mātulāḥ śvaśurāḥ pautrāḥ śyālāḥ sambandhinastathā

Those very persons for whose sake we covet the kingdom, luxuries and pleasures–teachers, uncles, sons and nephews and even so grand-uncles and great grand-uncles, maternal uncles, fathers-in-law, grand-nephews, brothers-in-law and other relations–are here arrayed on the battlefield staking their lives and wealth. (33-34)

एतान्न हन्तुमिच्छामि घ्नतोऽपि मधुसूदन।
अपि त्रैलोक्यराज्यस्य हेतोः किं नु महीकृते॥ ३५॥

etānna hantumicchāmi ghnato'pi madhusūdana
api trailokyarājyasya hetoḥ kiṁ nu mahīkṛte

O Slayer of Madhu, I do not want to kill them, even though they slay me, even for the sovereignty over the three worlds; how much the less for the kingdom here on earth. (35)

निहत्य धार्तराष्ट्रान्नः का प्रीतिः स्याज्जनार्दन।
पापमेवाश्रयेदस्मान्हत्वैतानाततायिनः ॥ ३६ ॥

nihatya dhārtarāṣṭrānnaḥ kā prītiḥ syājjanārdana
pāpamevāśrayedasmānhatvaitānātatāyinaḥ

Kṛṣṇa, how can we hope to be happy slaying the sons of Dhṛtarāṣṭra; by killing even these desperadoes, sin will surely accrue to us. (36)

तस्मान्नार्हा वयं हन्तुं धार्तराष्ट्रान्स्वबान्धवान्।
स्वजनं हि कथं हत्वा सुखिनः स्याम माधव ॥ ३७ ॥

tasmānnārhā vayaṁ hantuṁ dhārtarāṣṭrānsvabāndhavān
svajanaṁ hi kathaṁ hatvā sukhinaḥ syāma mādhava

Therefore, Kṛṣṇa, it does not behove us to kill our relations, the sons of Dhṛtarāṣṭra. For, how can we be happy after killing our own kinsmen? (37)

यद्यप्येते न पश्यन्ति लोभोपहतचेतसः।
कुलक्षयकृतं दोषं मित्रद्रोहे च पातकम् ॥ ३८ ॥
कथं न ज्ञेयमस्माभिः पापादस्मान्निवर्तितुम्।
कुलक्षयकृतं दोषं प्रपश्यद्भिर्जनार्दन ॥ ३९ ॥

yadyapyete na paśyanti lobhopahatacetasaḥ
kulakṣayakṛtaṁ doṣaṁ mitradrohe ca pātakam

kathaṁ na jñeyamasmābhiḥ pāpādasmānnivartitum
kulakṣayakṛtaṁ doṣaṁ prapaśyadbhirjanārdana

Even if these people, with their mind blinded by greed, perceive no evil in destroying their own race and no sin in treason to friends, why should not we, O Kṛṣṇa, who see clearly the sin accruing from the destruction of one's family, think of desisting from committing this foul deed. (38-39)

कुलक्षये प्रणश्यन्ति कुलधर्माः सनातनाः।
धर्मे नष्टे कुलं कृत्स्नमधर्मोऽभिभवत्युत ॥ ४० ॥

kulakṣaye praṇaśyanti kuladharmāḥ sanātanāḥ
dharme naṣṭe kulaṁ kṛtsnamadharmo'bhibhavatyuta

Age-long family traditions disappear with the destruction of a family; and virtue having been lost, vice takes hold of the entire race. (40)

अधर्माभिभवात्कृष्ण प्रदुष्यन्ति कुलस्त्रियः।
स्त्रीषु दुष्टासु वार्ष्णेय जायते वर्णसङ्करः ॥ ४१ ॥

adharmābhibhavātkṛṣṇa praduṣyanti kulastriyaḥ
strīṣu duṣṭāsu vārṣṇeya jāyate varṇasaṅkaraḥ

With the preponderance of vice, Kṛṣṇa, the women of the family become corrupt; and with the corruption of women, O descendant of Vṛṣṇi, there ensues an intermixture of castes. (41)

सङ्करो नरकायैव कुलघ्नानां कुलस्य च।
पतन्ति पितरो ह्येषां लुप्तपिण्डोदकक्रियाः ॥ ४२ ॥

saṅkaro narakāyaiva kulaghnānāṁ kulasya ca
patanti pitaro hyeṣāṁ luptapiṇḍodakakriyāḥ

Promiscuity damns the destroyers of the race as well as the race itself. Deprived of the offerings of rice and water (Śrāddha, Tarpaṇa etc.,) the manes of their race also fall. (42)

दोषैरेतैः कुलघ्नानां वर्णसङ्करकारकैः।
उत्साद्यन्ते जातिधर्माः कुलधर्माश्च शाश्वताः॥ ४३॥

doṣairetaiḥ kulaghnānāṁ varṇasaṅkarakārakaiḥ
utsādyante jātidharmāḥ kuladharmāśca śāśvatāḥ

Through these evils bringing about an intermixture of castes, the age-long caste traditions and family customs of the killers of kinsmen get extinct. (43)

उत्सन्नकुलधर्माणां मनुष्याणां जनार्दन।
नरकेऽनियतं वासो भवतीत्यनुशुश्रुम॥ ४४॥

utsannakuladharmāṇāṁ manuṣyāṇāṁ janārdana
narake'niyataṁ vāso bhavatītyanuśuśruma

Kṛṣṇa, we hear that men who have lost their family traditions dwell in hell for an indefinite period of time. (44)

अहो बत महत्पापं कर्तुं व्यवसिता वयम्।
यद्राज्यसुखलोभेन हन्तुं स्वजनमुद्यताः॥ ४५॥

aho bata mahatpāpaṁ kartuṁ vyavasitā vayam
yadrājyasukhalobhena hantuṁ svajanamudyatāḥ

Oh what a pity! Though possessed of intelligence we have set our mind on the commission of a great sin;

that due to lust for throne and enjoyment we are intent on killing our own kinsmen. (45)

यदि मामप्रतीकारमशस्त्रं शस्त्रपाणयः।
धार्तराष्ट्रा रणे हन्युस्तन्मे क्षेमतरं भवेत्॥ ४६॥

yadi māmapratīkāramaśastraṁ śastrapāṇayaḥ
dhārtarāṣṭrā raṇe hanyustanme kṣemataraṁ bhavet

It would be better for me if the sons of Dhṛtarāṣṭra, armed with weapons, kill me in battle, while I am unarmed and unresisting. (46)

सञ्जय उवाच

एवमुक्त्वार्जुनः सङ्ख्ये रथोपस्थ उपाविशत्।
विसृज्य सशरं चापं शोकसंविग्नमानसः॥ ४७॥

sañjaya uvāca

evamuktvārjunaḥ saṅkhye rathopastha upāviśat
visṛjya saśaraṁ cāpaṁ śokasaṁvignamānasaḥ

Sañjaya said: Arjuna, whose mind was agitated by grief on the battlefield, having spoken thus, and having cast aside his bow and arrows, sank into the hinder part of his chariot. (47)

ॐ तत्सदिति श्रीमद्भगवद्गीतासूपनिषत्सु ब्रह्मविद्यायां योगशास्त्रे श्रीकृष्णार्जुनसंवादेऽर्जुनविषादयोगो नाम प्रथमोऽध्यायः॥ १॥

Thus, in the Upaniṣad sung by the Lord, the Science of Brahma, the scripture of Yoga, the dialogue between Śrī Kṛṣṇa and Arjuna, ends the first chapter entitled "The Yoga of Dejection of Arjuna."

ॐ श्रीपरमात्मने नमः

अथ द्वितीयोऽध्यायः

CHAPTER TWO

सञ्जय उवाच

तं तथा कृपयाविष्टमश्रुपूर्णाकुलेक्षणम्।
विषीदन्तमिदं वाक्यमुवाच मधुसूदनः ॥ १ ॥

sañjaya uvāca

taṁ tathā kṛpayāviṣṭamaśrupūrṇākulekṣaṇam
viṣīdantamidaṁ vākyamuvāca madhusūdanaḥ

Sañjaya said : Śrī Kṛṣṇa then addressed the following words to Arjuna, who was, as mentioned before, overwhelmed with pity, whose eyes were filled with tears and agitated, and who was full of sorrow. (1)

श्रीभगवानुवाच

कुतस्त्वा कश्मलमिदं विषमे समुपस्थितम्।
अनार्यजुष्टमस्वर्ग्यमकीर्तिकरमर्जुन ॥ २ ॥

śrībhagavānuvāca

kutastvā kaśmalamidaṁ viṣame samupasthitam
anāryajuṣṭamasvargyamakīrtikaramarjuna

Śrī Bhagavān said : Arjuna, how has this infatuation overtaken you at this odd hour? It is shunned by noble souls; neither will it bring heaven, nor fame, to you. (2)

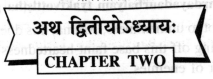

क्लैब्यं मा स्म गमः पार्थ नैतत्त्वय्युपपद्यते।
क्षुद्रं हृदयदौर्बल्यं त्यक्त्वोत्तिष्ठ परन्तप॥ ३॥

klaibyaṁ mā sma gamaḥ pārtha naitattvayyupapadyate
kṣudraṁ hṛdayadaurbalyaṁ tyaktvottiṣṭha parantapa

Yield not to unmanliness, Arjuna; this does not befit you. Shaking off this base faint-heartedness stand-up, O scorcher of enemies. (3)

अर्जुन उवाच

कथं भीष्ममहं सङ्ख्ये द्रोणं च मधुसूदन।
इषुभिः प्रतियोत्स्यामि पूजार्हावरिसूदन॥ ४॥

arjuna uvāca

kathaṁ bhīṣmamahaṁ saṅkhye droṇaṁ ca madhusūdana
iṣubhiḥ pratiyotsyāmi pūjārhāvarisūdana

Arjuna said : How Kṛṣṇa, shall I fight Bhīṣma and Droṇa with arrows on the battlefield? They are worthy of deepest reverence, O destroyer of foes. (4)

गुरूनहत्वा हि महानुभावान्
श्रेयो भोक्तुं भैक्ष्यमपीह लोके।
हत्वार्थकामांस्तु गुरूनिहैव
भुञ्जीय भोगान्रुधिरप्रदिग्धान्॥ ५॥

gurūnahatvā hi mahānubhāvān
śreyo bhoktuṁ bhaikṣyamapīha loke
hatvārthakāmāṁstu gurūnihaiva
bhuñjīya bhogānrudhirapradigdhān

It is better to live on alms in this world without

slaying these noble elders, because even after killing them we shall after all enjoy only bloodstained pleasures in the form of wealth and sense-enjoyments. (5)

न चैतद्विद्मः कतरन्नो गरीयो-
यद्वा जयेम यदि वा नो जयेयुः।
यानेव हत्वा न जिजीविषाम-
स्तेऽवस्थिताः प्रमुखे धार्तराष्ट्राः॥ ६॥

na caitadvidmaḥ kataranno garīyo-
yadvā jayema yadi vā no jayeyuḥ
yāneva hatvā na jijīviṣāma-
ste'vasthitāḥ pramukhe dhārtarāṣṭrāḥ

We do not even know which is preferable for us—to fight or not to fight; nor do we know whether we shall win or whether they will conquer us. Those very sons of Dhṛtarāṣṭra, killing whom we do not even wish to live, stand in the enemy ranks. (6)

कार्पण्यदोषोपहतस्वभावः
पृच्छामि त्वां धर्मसम्मूढचेताः।
यच्छ्रेयः स्यान्निश्चितं ब्रूहि तन्मे
शिष्यस्तेऽहं शाधि मां त्वां प्रपन्नम्॥ ७॥

kārpaṇyadoṣopahatasvabhāvaḥ
pṛcchāmi tvāṁ dharmasammūḍhacetāḥ
yacchreyaḥ syānniścitaṁ brūhi tanme
śiṣyaste'haṁ śādhi māṁ tvāṁ prapannam

With my very being smitten by the vice of faint-heartedness and my mind puzzled with regard to duty, I beseech You, tell me that which is decidedly good; I am your disciple. Pray, instruct me, who have taken refuge in you. (7)

न हि प्रपश्यामि ममापनुद्याद्
यच्छोकमुच्छोषणमिन्द्रियाणाम् ।
अवाप्य भूमावसपत्नमृद्धं-
राज्यं सुराणामपि चाधिपत्यम् ॥ ८ ॥

na hi prapaśyāmi mamāpanudyād
yacchokamucchoṣaṇamindriyāṇām
avāpya bhūmāvasapatnamṛddhaṁ-
rājyaṁ surāṇāmapi cādhipatyam

For even on obtaining undisputed sovereignty and an affluent kingdom on this earth and lordship over the gods, I do not see any means that can drive away the grief which is drying up my senses. (8)

सञ्जय उवाच

एवमुक्त्वा हृषीकेशं गुडाकेशः परन्तप।
न योत्स्य इति गोविन्दमुक्त्वा तूष्णीं बभूव ह॥ ९ ॥

sañjaya uvāca

evamuktvā hṛṣīkeśaṁ guḍākeśaḥ parantapa
na yotsya iti govindamuktvā tūṣṇīṁ babhūva ha

Sañjaya said : O King, having thus spoken to Śrī Kṛṣṇa, Arjuna again said to Him, "I will not fight," and became silent. (9)

तमुवाच हृषीकेशः प्रहसन्निव भारत।
सेनयोरुभयोर्मध्ये विषीदन्तमिदं वचः॥ १०॥

tamuvāca hṛṣīkeśaḥ prahasanniva bhārata
senayorubhayormadhye viṣīdantamidaṁ vacaḥ

Then, O Dhṛtarāṣṭra, Śrī Kṛṣṇa, as if smiling addressed the following words to grieving Arjuna in the midst of the two armies. (10)

श्रीभगवानुवाच

अशोच्यानन्वशोचस्त्वं प्रज्ञावादांश्च भाषसे।
गतासूनगतासूंश्च नानुशोचन्ति पण्डिताः॥ ११॥

śrībhagavānuvāca

aśocyānanvaśocastvaṁ prajñāvādāṁśca bhāṣase
gatāsūnagatāsūṁśca nānuśocanti paṇḍitāḥ

Śrī Bhagavān said: Arjuna, you grieve over those who should not be grieved for and yet speak like the learned; wise men do not sorrow over the dead or the living. (11)

न त्वेवाहं जातु नासं न त्वं नेमे जनाधिपाः।
न चैव न भविष्यामः सर्वे वयमतः परम्॥ १२॥

na tvevāhaṁ jātu nāsaṁ na tvaṁ neme janādhipāḥ
na caiva na bhaviṣyāmaḥ sarve vayamataḥ param

In fact, there was never a time when I was not, or when you or these kings were not. Nor is it a fact that hereafter we shall all cease to be. (12)

देहिनोऽस्मिन्यथा देहे कौमारं यौवनं जरा।
तथा देहान्तरप्राप्तिर्धीरस्तत्र न मुह्यति॥ १३॥

dehino'sminyathā dehe kaumāraṁ yauvanaṁ jarā
tathā dehāntaraprāptirdhīrastatra na muhyati

Just as boyhood, youth and old age are attributed to the soul through this body, even so it attains another body. The wise man does not get deluded about this. (13)

मात्रास्पर्शास्तु कौन्तेय शीतोष्णसुखदुःखदाः।
आगमापायिनोऽनित्यास्तांस्तितिक्षस्व भारत॥ १४॥

mātrāsparśāstu kaunteya śītoṣṇasukhaduḥkhadāḥ
āgamāpāyino'nityāstāṁstitikṣasva bhārata

O son of Kuntī, the contact between the senses and their objects, which give rise to the feelings of heat and cold, pleasure and pain etc., are transitory and fleeting; therefore, Arjuna, ignore them. (14)

यं हि न व्यथयन्त्येते पुरुषं पुरुषर्षभ।
समदुःखसुखं धीरं सोऽमृतत्वाय कल्पते॥ १५॥

yaṁ hi na vyathayantyete puruṣaṁ puruṣarṣabha
samaduḥkhasukhaṁ dhīraṁ so'mṛtatvāya kalpate

Arjuna, the wise man to whom pain and pleasure are alike, and who is not tormented by these contacts, becomes eligible for immortality. (15)

नासतो विद्यते भावो नाभावो विद्यते सतः।
उभयोरपि दृष्टोऽन्तस्त्वनयोस्तत्त्वदर्शिभिः॥ १६॥

nāsato vidyate bhāvo nābhāvo vidyate sataḥ
ubhayorapi dṛṣṭo'ntastvanayostattvadarśibhiḥ

The unreal has no existence, and the Real never ceases to be; the reality of both has thus been perceived by the seers of Truth. (16)

अविनाशि तु तद्विद्धि येन सर्वमिदं ततम्।
विनाशमव्ययस्यास्य न कश्चित्कर्तुमर्हति॥ १७॥

avināśi tu tadviddhi yena sarvamidaṁ tatam
vināśamavyayasyāsya na kaścitkartumarhati

Know That alone to be imperishable which pervades this universe; for no one has power to destroy this indestructible substance. (17)

अन्तवन्त इमे देहा नित्यस्योक्ताः शरीरिणः।
अनाशिनोऽप्रमेयस्य तस्माद्युध्यस्व भारत॥ १८॥

antavanta ime dehā nityasyoktāḥ śarīriṇaḥ
anāśino'prameyasya tasmādyudhyasva bhārata

All these bodies pertaining to the imperishable, indefinable and eternal soul are spoken of as perishable; therefore, Arjuna, fight. (18)

य एनं वेत्ति हन्तारं यश्चैनं मन्यते हतम्।
उभौ तौ न विजानीतो नायं हन्ति न हन्यते॥ १९॥

ya enaṁ vetti hantāraṁ yaścainaṁ manyate hatam
ubhau tau na vijānīto nāyaṁ hanti na hanyate

Both of them are ignorant, he who considers the soul to be capable of killing and he who takes it as killed; for verily the soul neither kills, nor is killed. (19)

न जायते म्रियते वा कदाचि-
न्नायं भूत्वा भविता वा न भूयः।
अजो नित्यः शाश्वतोऽयं पुराणो-
न हन्यते हन्यमाने शरीरे॥ २०॥

na jāyate mriyate vā kadāci-
nnāyaṁ bhūtvā bhavitā vā na bhūyaḥ
ajo nityaḥ śāśvato'yaṁ purāṇo-
na hanyate hanyamāne śarīre

The soul is never born nor dies; nor does it become only after being born. For it is unborn, eternal, everlasting and primeval; even though the body is slain, the soul is not. (20)

वेदाविनाशिनं नित्यं य एनमजमव्ययम्।
कथं स पुरुषः पार्थ कं घातयति हन्ति कम्॥ २१॥

vedāvināśinaṁ nityaṁ ya enamajamavyayam
kathaṁ sa puruṣaḥ pārtha kaṁ ghātayati hanti kam

Arjuna, the man who knows this soul to be imperishable; eternal and free from birth and decay—how and whom will he cause to be killed, how and whom will he kill? (21)

वासांसि जीर्णानि यथा विहाय
नवानि गृह्णाति नरोऽपराणि।
तथा शरीराणि विहाय जीर्णा-
न्यन्यानि संयाति नवानि देही॥ २२॥

vāsāṁsi jīrṇāni yathā vihāya
navāni gṛhṇāti naro'parāṇi
tathā śarīrāṇi vihāya jīrṇā-
nyanyāni saṁyāti navāni dehī

As a man shedding worn-out garments, takes other new ones, likewise the embodied soul, casting off worn-out bodies, enters into others which are new. (22)

नैनं छिन्दन्ति शस्त्राणि नैनं दहति पावकः।
न चैनं क्लेदयन्त्यापो न शोषयति मारुतः॥ २३॥

nainaṁ chindanti śastrāṇi nainaṁ dahati pāvakaḥ
na cainaṁ kledayantyāpo na śoṣayati mārutaḥ

Weapons cannot cut it nor can fire burn it; water cannot wet it nor can wind dry it. (23)

अच्छेद्योऽयमदाह्योऽयमक्लेद्योऽशोष्य एव च।
नित्यः सर्वगतः स्थाणुरचलोऽयं सनातनः॥ २४॥

acchedyo'yamadāhyo'yamakledyo'śoṣya eva ca
nityaḥ sarvagataḥ sthāṇuracalo'yaṁ sanātanaḥ

For this soul is incapable of being cut; it is proof against fire, impervious to water and undriable as well. This soul is eternal, omnipresent, immovable, constant and everlasting. (24)

अव्यक्तोऽयमचिन्त्योऽयमविकार्योऽयमुच्यते ।
तस्मादेवं विदित्वैनं नानुशोचितुमर्हसि॥ २५॥

avyakto'yamacintyo'yamavikāryo'yamucyate
tasmādevaṁ viditvainaṁ nānuśocitumarhasi

This soul is unmanifest; it is incomprehensible and it is spoken of as immutable. Therefore, knowing it as such, you should not grieve. (25)

अथ चैनं नित्यजातं नित्यं वा मन्यसे मृतम्।
तथापि त्वं महाबाहो नैवं शोचितुमर्हसि॥ २६॥

atha cainaṁ nityajātaṁ nityaṁ vā manyase mṛtam
tathāpi tvaṁ mahābāho naivaṁ śocitumarhasi

And, Arjuna, if you should suppose this soul to be subject to constant birth and death, even then you should not grieve like this. (26)

जातस्य हि ध्रुवो मृत्युर्ध्रुवं जन्म मृतस्य च।
तस्मादपरिहार्येऽर्थे न त्वं शोचितुमर्हसि॥ २७॥

jātasya hi dhruvo mṛtyurdhruvaṁ janma mṛtasya ca
tasmādaparihārye'rthe na tvaṁ śocitumarhasi

For in that case death is certain for the born, and rebirth is inevitable for the dead. You should not, therefore, grieve over the inevitable. (27)

अव्यक्तादीनि भूतानि व्यक्तमध्यानि भारत।
अव्यक्तनिधनान्येव तत्र का परिदेवना॥ २८॥

avyaktādīni bhūtāni vyaktamadhyāni bhārata
avyaktanidhanānyeva tatra kā paridevanā

Arjuna, before birth beings are not manifest to our human senses; at death they return to the unmanifest again. They are manifest only in the interim between birth and death. What occasion, then, for lamentation? (28)

आश्चर्यवत्पश्यति कश्चिदेन-
माश्चर्यवद्वदति तथैव चान्यः।
आश्चर्यवच्चैनमन्यः शृणोति
श्रुत्वाप्येनं वेद न चैव कश्चित्॥ २९॥

āścaryavatpaśyati kaścidena-
māścaryavadvadati tathaiva cānyaḥ
āścaryavaccainamanyaḥ śṛṇoti
śrutvāpyenaṁ veda na caiva kaścit

Hardly anyone perceives this soul as marvellous, scarce another likewise speaks thereof as marvellous, and scarce another hears of it as marvellous, while there are some who know it not even on hearing of it. (29)

देही नित्यमवध्योऽयं देहे सर्वस्य भारत।
तस्मात्सर्वाणि भूतानि न त्वं शोचितुमर्हसि॥ ३०॥

dehī nityamavadhyo'yaṁ dehe sarvasya bhārata
tasmātsarvāṇi bhūtāni na tvaṁ śocitumarhasi

Arjuna, this soul dwelling in the bodies of all can never be slain; therefore, you should not mourn for anyone. (30)

स्वधर्ममपि चावेक्ष्य न विकम्पितुमर्हसि।
धर्म्याद्धि युद्धाच्छ्रेयोऽन्यत्क्षत्रियस्य न विद्यते॥ ३१॥

svadharmamapi cāvekṣya na vikampitumarhasi
dharmyāddhi yuddhācchreyo'nyatkṣatriyasya na vidyate

Besides, considering your own duty too you should

not waver, for there is nothing more welcome for a man of the warrior class than a righteous war. (31)

यदृच्छया चोपपन्नं स्वर्गद्वारमपावृतम्।
सुखिनः क्षत्रियाः पार्थ लभन्ते युद्धमीदृशम्॥ ३२॥

yadṛcchayā copapannaṁ svargadvāramapāvṛtam
sukhinaḥ kṣatriyāḥ pārtha labhante yuddhamīdṛśam

Arjuna, happy are the Kṣatriyas who get such an unsolicited opportunity for war, which is an open gateway to heaven. (32)

अथ चेत्त्वमिमं धर्म्यं सङ्ग्रामं न करिष्यसि।
ततः स्वधर्मं कीर्तिं च हित्वा पापमवाप्स्यसि॥ ३३॥

atha cettvamimaṁ dharmyaṁ saṅgrāmaṁ na kariṣyasi
tataḥ svadharmaṁ kīrtiṁ ca hitvā pāpamavāpsyasi

Now, If you refuse to fight this righteous war, then, shirking your duty and losing your reputation, you will incur sin. (33)

अकीर्तिं चापि भूतानि कथयिष्यन्ति तेऽव्ययाम्।
सम्भावितस्य चाकीर्तिर्मरणादतिरिच्यते॥ ३४॥

akīrtiṁ cāpi bhūtāni kathayiṣyanti te'vyayām
sambhāvitasya cākīrtirmaraṇādatiricyate

Nay, people will also pour undying infamy on you; and infamy brought on a man enjoying popular esteem is worse than death. (34)

भयाद्रणादुपरतं मंस्यन्ते त्वां महारथाः।
येषां च त्वं बहुमतो भूत्वा यास्यसि लाघवम्॥ ३५॥

bhayādraṇāduparataṁ maṁsyante tvāṁ mahārathāḥ
yeṣāṁ ca tvaṁ bahumato bhūtvā yāsyasi lāghavam

And the warrior-chiefs who thought highly of you, will now despise you, thinking that it was fear which drove you from battle. (35)

अवाच्यवादांश्च बहून्वदिष्यन्ति तवाहिताः।
निन्दन्तस्तव सामर्थ्यं ततो दुःखतरं नु किम्॥ ३६॥

avācyavādāṁśca bahūnvadiṣyanti tavāhitāḥ
nindantastava sāmarthyaṁ tato duḥkhataraṁ nu kim

And your enemies, disparaging your might, will speak many unbecoming words; what can be more distressing than this? (36)

हतो वा प्राप्स्यसि स्वर्गं जित्वा वा भोक्ष्यसे महीम्।
तस्मादुत्तिष्ठ कौन्तेय युद्धाय कृतनिश्चयः॥ ३७॥

hato vā prāpsyasi svargaṁ jitvā vā bhokṣyase mahīm
tasmāduttiṣṭha kaunteya yuddhāya kṛtaniścayaḥ

Die, and you will win heaven; conquer, and you enjoy sovereignty of the earth; therefore, stand up, Arjuna, determined to fight. (37)

सुखदुःखे समे कृत्वा लाभालाभौ जयाजयौ।
ततो युद्धाय युज्यस्व नैवं पापमवाप्स्यसि॥ ३८॥

sukhaduḥkhe same kṛtvā lābhālābhau jayājayau
tato yuddhāya yujyasva naivaṁ pāpamavāpsyasi

Treating alike victory and defeat, gain and loss, pleasure and pain, get ready for the fight, then; fighting thus you will not incur sin. (38)

एषा तेऽभिहिता साङ्ख्ये बुद्धिर्योगे त्विमां शृणु।
बुद्ध्या युक्तो यया पार्थ कर्मबन्धं प्रहास्यसि॥ ३९॥

eṣā te'bhihitā sāṅkhye buddhiryoge tvimāṁ śṛṇu
buddhyā yukto yayā pārtha karmabandhaṁ prahāsyasi

Arjuna, this attitude of mind has been presented to you from the point of view of Jñānayoga; now hear the same as presented from the standpoint of Karmayoga (the Yoga of selfless action). Equipped with this attitude of mind, you will be able to throw off completely the shackles of Karma. (39)

नेहाभिक्रमनाशोऽस्ति प्रत्यवायो न विद्यते।
स्वल्पमप्यस्य धर्मस्य त्रायते महतो भयात्॥ ४०॥

nehābhikramanāśo'sti pratyavāyo na vidyate
svalpamapyasya dharmasya trāyate mahato bhayāt

In this path (of disinterested action) there is no loss of effort, nor is there fear of contrary result, even a little practice of this discipline saves one from the terrible fear of birth and death. (40)

व्यवसायात्मिका बुद्धिरेकेह कुरुनन्दन।
बहुशाखा ह्यनन्ताश्च बुद्धयोऽव्यवसायिनाम्॥ ४१॥

vyavasāyātmikā buddhirekeha kurunandana
bahuśākhā hyanantāśca buddhayo'vyavasāyinām

Arjuna, in this Yoga (of disinterested action) the intellect is determinate and directed singly towards one ideal; whereas the intellect of the undecided (ignorant men moved by desires) wanders in all directions, after innumerable aims. (41)

यामिमां पुष्पितां वाचं प्रवदन्त्यविपश्चितः।
वेदवादरताः पार्थ नान्यदस्तीति वादिनः॥ ४२॥
कामात्मानः स्वर्गपरा जन्मकर्मफलप्रदाम्।
क्रियाविशेषबहुलां भोगैश्वर्यगतिं प्रति॥ ४३॥
भोगैश्वर्यप्रसक्तानां तयापहृतचेतसाम्।
व्यवसायात्मिका बुद्धिः समाधौ न विधीयते॥ ४४॥

yāmimāṁ puṣpitāṁ vācaṁ pravadantyavipaścitaḥ
vedavādaratāḥ pārtha nānyadastīti vādinaḥ
kāmātmānaḥ svargaparā janmakarmaphalapradām
kriyāviśeṣabahulāṁ bhogaiśvaryagatiṁ prati
bhogaiśvaryaprasaktānāṁ tayāpahṛtacetasām
vyavasāyātmikā buddhiḥ samādhau na vidhīyate

Arjuna, those who are full of worldly desires and devoted to the letter of the Vedas, who look upon heaven, as the supreme goal and argue that there is nothing beyond heaven are unwise. They utter flowery speech recommending many rituals of various kinds for the attainment of pleasure and power with rebirth as their fruit. Those whose minds are carried away by such words, and who are deeply attached to pleasure and worldly power, cannot attain the determinate intellect concentrated on God. (42—44)

त्रैगुण्यविषया वेदा निस्त्रैगुण्यो भवार्जुन।
निर्द्वन्द्वो नित्यसत्त्वस्थो निर्योगक्षेम आत्मवान्॥ ४५॥

traiguṇyaviṣayā vedā nistraiguṇyo bhavārjuna
nirdvandvo nityasattvastho niryogakṣema ātmavān

Arjuna, the Vedas thus deal with the evolutes of the three Guṇas (modes of Prakṛti), viz., worldly enjoyments and the means of attaining such enjoyments; be thou indifferent to these enjoyments and their means, rising above pairs of opposites like pleasure and pain etc., established in the Eternal Existence (God), absolutely unconcerned about the fulfilment of wants and the preservation of what has been already attained, and self-controlled. (45)

यावानर्थ उदपाने सर्वतः सम्प्लुतोदके।
तावान्सर्वेषु वेदेषु ब्राह्मणस्य विजानतः॥ ४६॥

yāvānartha udapāne sarvataḥ samplutodake
tāvānsarveṣu vedeṣu brāhmaṇasya vijānataḥ

A Brāhmaṇa, who has obtained enlightenment, has the same use for all the Vedas as one who stands at the brink of a sheet of water overflowing on all sides has for a small reservoir of water. (46)

कर्मण्येवाधिकारस्ते मा फलेषु कदाचन।
मा कर्मफलहेतुर्भूर्मा ते सङ्गोऽस्त्वकर्मणि॥ ४७॥

karmaṇyevādhikāraste mā phaleṣu kadācana
mā karmaphalaheturbhūrmā te saṅgo'stvakarmaṇi

Your right is to work only and never to the fruit

thereof. Be not instrumental in making your actions bear fruit, nor let your attachment be to inaction. (47)

योगस्थः कुरु कर्माणि सङ्गं त्यक्त्वा धनञ्जय।
सिद्ध्यसिद्ध्योः समो भूत्वा समत्वं योग उच्यते ॥ ४८ ॥

yogasthaḥ kuru karmāṇi saṅgaṁ tyaktvā dhanañjaya
siddhyasiddhyoḥ samo bhūtvā samatvaṁ yoga ucyate

Arjuna, perform your duties established in Yoga, renouncing attachment, and be even-minded in success and failure; evenness of mind is called 'Yoga'. (48)

दूरेण ह्यवरं कर्म बुद्धियोगाद्धनञ्जय।
बुद्धौ शरणमन्विच्छ कृपणाः फलहेतवः ॥ ४९ ॥

dūreṇa hyavaraṁ karma buddhiyogāddhanañjaya
buddhau śaraṇamanviccha kṛpaṇāḥ phalahetavaḥ

Action (with a selfish motive) is far inferior to this Yoga in the form of equanimity. Do seek refuge in this equipoise of mind, Arjuna; for poor and wretched are those who are instrumental in making their actions bear fruit. (49)

बुद्धियुक्तो जहातीह उभे सुकृतदुष्कृते।
तस्माद्योगाय युज्यस्व योगः कर्मसु कौशलम् ॥ ५० ॥

buddhiyukto jahātīha ubhe sukṛtaduṣkṛte
tasmādyogāya yujyasva yogaḥ karmasu kauśalam

Endowed with equanimity, one sheds in this life both good and evil. Therefore, strive for the practice of this Yoga of equanimity. Skill in action lies in the practice of this Yoga. (50)

कर्मजं बुद्धियुक्ता हि फलं त्यक्त्वा मनीषिणः।
जन्मबन्धविनिर्मुक्ताः पदं गच्छन्त्यनामयम्॥ ५१॥

karmajaṁ buddhiyuktā hi phalaṁ tyaktvā manīṣiṇaḥ janmabandhavinirmuktāḥ padaṁ gacchantyanāmayam

For wise men possessing an equipoised mind, renouncing the fruit of actions and freed from the shackles of birth, attain the blissful supreme state. (51)

यदा ते मोहकलिलं बुद्धिर्व्यतितरिष्यति।
तदा गन्तासि निर्वेदं श्रोतव्यस्य श्रुतस्य च॥ ५२॥

yadā te mohakalilaṁ buddhirvyatitariṣyati tadā gantāsi nirvedaṁ śrotavyasya śrutasya ca

When your mind will have fully crossed the mire of delusion, you will then grow indifferent to the enjoyments of this world and the next that have been heard of as well as to those that are yet to be heard of. (52)

श्रुतिविप्रतिपन्ना ते यदा स्थास्यति निश्चला।
समाधावचला बुद्धिस्तदा योगमवाप्स्यसि॥ ५३॥

śrutivipratipannā te yadā sthāsyati niścalā samādhāvacalā buddhistadā yogamavāpsyasi

When your intellect, confused by hearing conflicting statements, will rest steady and undistracted in meditation on God, you will then attain Yoga (everlasting union with God). (53)

अर्जुन उवाच

स्थितप्रज्ञस्य का भाषा समाधिस्थस्य केशव।
स्थितधीः किं प्रभाषेत किमासीत व्रजेत किम्॥ ५४॥

arjuna uvāca

sthitaprajñasya kā bhāṣā samādhisthasya keśava
sthitadhīḥ kiṁ prabhāṣeta kimāsīta vrajeta kim

Arjuna said : Kṛṣṇa, what is the definition (mark) of a God-realized soul, stable of mind and established in Samādhi (perfect tranquillity of mind)? How does the man of stable mind speak, how does he sit, how does he walk? (54)

श्रीभगवानुवाच

प्रजहाति यदा कामान्सर्वान्पार्थ मनोगतान्।
आत्मन्येवात्मना तुष्टः स्थितप्रज्ञस्तदोच्यते॥ ५५॥

śrībhagavānuvāca

prajahāti yadā kāmānsarvānpārtha manogatān
ātmanyevātmanā tuṣṭaḥ sthitaprajñastadocyate

Śrī Bhagavān said: Arjuna, when one thoroughly casts off all cravings of the mind, and is satisfied in the Self through the joy of the Self, he is then called stable of mind. (55)

दुःखेष्वनुद्विग्नमनाः सुखेषु विगतस्पृहः।
वीतरागभयक्रोधः स्थितधीर्मुनिरुच्यते॥ ५६॥

duḥkheṣvanudvignamanāḥ sukheṣu vigataspṛhaḥ
vītarāgabhayakrodhaḥ sthitadhīrmunirucyate

The sage, whose mind remains unperturbed amid sorrows, whose thirst for pleasures has altogether disappeared, and who is free from passion, fear and anger, is called stable of mind. (56)

यः सर्वत्रानभिस्नेहस्तत्तत्प्राप्य शुभाशुभम्।
नाभिनन्दति न द्वेष्टि तस्य प्रज्ञा प्रतिष्ठिता॥ ५७॥

yaḥ sarvatrānabhisnehastattatprāpya śubhāśubham
nābhinandati na dveṣṭi tasya prajñā pratiṣṭhitā

He who is unattached to everything, and meeting with good and evil, neither rejoices nor recoils, his mind is stable. (57)

यदा संहरते चायं कूर्मोऽङ्गानीव सर्वशः।
इन्द्रियाणीन्द्रियार्थेभ्यस्तस्य प्रज्ञा प्रतिष्ठिता॥ ५८॥

yadā saṁharate cāyaṁ kūrmo'ṅgānīva sarvaśaḥ
indriyāṇīndriyārthebhyastasya prajñā pratiṣṭhitā

When, like a tortoise, that draws in its limbs from all directions, he withdraws all his senses from the sense-objects, his mind becomes steady. (58)

विषया विनिवर्तन्ते निराहारस्य देहिनः।
रसवर्जं रसोऽप्यस्य परं दृष्ट्वा निवर्तते॥ ५९॥

viṣayā vinivartante nirāhārasya dehinaḥ
rasavarjaṁ raso'pyasya paraṁ dṛṣṭvā nivartate

Sense-objects turn away from him, who does not

enjoy them with his senses; but the taste for them persists. This relish also disappears in the case of the man of stable mind when he realizes the Supreme. (59)

यततो ह्यपि कौन्तेय पुरुषस्य विपश्चितः।
इन्द्रियाणि प्रमाथीनि हरन्ति प्रसभं मनः॥ ६०॥

yatato hyapi kaunteya puruṣasya vipaścitaḥ
indriyāṇi pramāthīni haranti prasabhaṁ manaḥ

Turbulent by nature, the senses even of a wise man, who is practising self-control, forcibly carry away his mind, Arjuna. (60)

तानि सर्वाणि संयम्य युक्त आसीत मत्परः।
वशे हि यस्येन्द्रियाणि तस्य प्रज्ञा प्रतिष्ठिता॥ ६१॥

tāni sarvāṇi saṁyamya yukta āsīta matparaḥ
vaśe hi yasyendriyāṇi tasya prajñā pratiṣṭhitā

Therefore, having controlled all the senses and concentrating his mind, he should sit for meditation, devoting himself heart and soul to Me. For, he whose senses are mastered, is known to have a stable mind. (61)

ध्यायतो विषयान्पुंसः सङ्गस्तेषूपजायते।
सङ्गात्सञ्जायते कामः कामात्क्रोधोऽभिजायते॥ ६२॥

dhyāyato viṣayānpuṁsaḥ saṅgasteṣūpajāyate
saṅgātsañjāyate kāmaḥ kāmātkrodho'bhijāyate

The man dwelling on sense-objects develops attachment for them; from attachment springs up desire, and from desire (unfulfilled) ensues anger. (62)

क्रोधाद्भवति सम्मोहः सम्मोहात्स्मृतिविभ्रमः।
स्मृतिभ्रंशाद् बुद्धिनाशो बुद्धिनाशात्प्रणश्यति ॥ ६३ ॥

krodhādbhavati sammohaḥ sammohātsmṛtivibhramaḥ
smṛtibhraṁśād buddhināśo buddhināśātpraṇaśyati

From anger arises infatuation; from infatuation, confusion of memory; from confusion of memory, loss of reason; and from loss of reason one goes to complete ruin. (63)

रागद्वेषवियुक्तैस्तु विषयानिन्द्रियैश्चरन्।
आत्मवश्यैर्विधेयात्मा प्रसादमधिगच्छति ॥ ६४ ॥

rāgadveṣaviyuktaistu viṣayānindriyaiścaran
ātmavaśyairvidheyātmā prasādamadhigacchati

But the self-controlled Sādhaka, while enjoying the various sense-objects through his senses, which are disciplined and free from likes and dislikes, attains placidity of mind. (64)

प्रसादे सर्वदुःखानां हानिरस्योपजायते।
प्रसन्नचेतसो ह्याशु बुद्धिः पर्यवतिष्ठते ॥ ६५ ॥

prasāde sarvaduḥkhānāṁ hānirasyopajāyate
prasannacetaso hyāśu buddhiḥ paryavatiṣṭhate

With the attainment of such placidity of mind, all his sorrows come to an end; and the intellect of such a person of tranquil mind soon withdrawing itself from all sides, becomes firmly established in God. (65)

नास्ति बुद्धिरयुक्तस्य न चायुक्तस्य भावना।
न चाभावयतः शान्तिरशान्तस्य कुतः सुखम्॥ ६६॥

nāsti buddhirayuktasya na cāyuktasya bhāvanā
na cābhāvayataḥ śāntiraśāntasya kutaḥ sukham

He who has not controlled his mind and senses can have no reason; nor can such an undisciplined man think of God. The unthinking man can have no peace; and how can there be happiness for one lacking peace of mind? (66)

इन्द्रियाणां हि चरतां यन्मनोऽनुविधीयते।
तदस्य हरति प्रज्ञां वायुर्नावमिवाम्भसि॥ ६७॥

indriyāṇāṁ hi caratāṁ yanmano'nuvidhīyate
tadasya harati prajñāṁ vāyurnāvamivāmbhasi

As the wind carries away a boat upon the waters, even so of the senses moving among sense-objects, the one to which the mind is attached takes away his discrimination. (67)

तस्माद्यस्य महाबाहो निगृहीतानि सर्वशः।
इन्द्रियाणीन्द्रियार्थेभ्यस्तस्य प्रज्ञा प्रतिष्ठिता॥ ६८॥

tasmādyasya mahābāho nigṛhītāni sarvaśaḥ
indriyāṇīndriyārthebhyastasya prajñā pratiṣṭhitā

Therefore, Arjuna, he, whose senses are completely restrained from their objects, is said to have a stable mind. (68)

या निशा सर्वभूतानां तस्यां जागर्ति संयमी।
यस्यां जाग्रति भूतानि सा निशा पश्यतो मुनेः ॥ ६९ ॥

yā niśā sarvabhūtānāṁ tasyāṁ jāgarti saṁyamī
yasyāṁ jāgrati bhūtāni sā niśā paśyato muneḥ

That which is night to all beings, in that state of Divine Knowledge and Supreme Bliss the God-realized Yogī keeps awake, and that (the ever-changing, transient worldly happiness) in which all beings keep awake, is night to the seer. (69)

आपूर्यमाणमचलप्रतिष्ठं-
समुद्रमापः प्रविशन्ति यद्वत्।
तद्वत्कामा यं प्रविशन्ति सर्वे
स शान्तिमाप्नोति न कामकामी ॥ ७० ॥

āpūryamāṇamacalapratiṣṭhaṁ-
samudramāpaḥ praviśanti yadvat
tadvatkāmā yaṁ praviśanti sarve
sa śāntimāpnoti na kāmakāmī

As the waters of different rivers enter the ocean, which, though full on all sides, remains undisturbed; likewise, he, in whom all enjoyments merge themselves without causing disturbance, attains peace; not he who hankers after such enjoyments. (70)

विहाय कामान्यः सर्वान्पुमांश्चरति निःस्पृहः।
निर्ममो निरहङ्कारः स शान्तिमधिगच्छति ॥ ७१ ॥

vihāya kāmānyaḥ sarvānpumāṁścarati niḥspṛhaḥ
nirmamo nirahaṅkāraḥ sa śāntimadhigacchati

He who has given up all desires, and moves free from attachment, egoism and thirst for enjoyment attains peace. (71)

एषा ब्राह्मी स्थितिः पार्थ नैनां प्राप्य विमुह्यति।
स्थित्वास्यामन्तकालेऽपि ब्रह्मनिर्वाणमृच्छति॥ ७२॥

eṣā brāhmī sthitiḥ pārtha naināṁ prāpya vimuhyati sthitvāsyāmantakāle'pi brahmanirvāṇamṛcchati

Arjuna, such is the state of the God-realized soul; having reached this state, he overcomes delusion. And established in this state, even at the last moment, he attains Brahmic Bliss. (72)

ॐ तत्सदिति श्रीमद्भगवद्गीतासूपनिषत्सु ब्रह्मविद्यायां
योगशास्त्रे श्रीकृष्णार्जुनसंवादे साङ्ख्ययोगो
नाम द्वितीयोऽध्यायः॥ २॥

Thus, in the Upaniṣad sung by the Lord, the Science of Brahma, the scripture of Yoga, the dialogue between Śrī Kṛṣṇa and Arjuna, ends the second chapter entitled "Sāṅkhyayoga" (the Yoga of Knowledge).

ॐ श्रीपरमात्मने नमः

अथ तृतीयोऽध्यायः

CHAPTER THREE

अर्जुन उवाच

ज्यायसी चेत्कर्मणस्ते मता बुद्धिर्जनार्दन।
तत्किं कर्मणि घोरे मां नियोजयसि केशव॥ १॥

arjuna uvāca

jyāyasī cetkarmaṇaste matā buddhirjanārdana
tatkiṁ karmaṇi ghore māṁ niyojayasi keśava

Arjuna said : Kṛṣṇa if You consider Knowledge as superior to Action, why then do You urge me to this dreadful action, Keśava! (1)

व्यामिश्रेणेव वाक्येन बुद्धिं मोहयसीव मे।
तदेकं वद निश्चित्य येन श्रेयोऽहमाप्नुयाम्॥ २॥

vyāmiśreṇeva vākyena buddhiṁ mohayasīva me
tadekaṁ vada niścitya yena śreyo'hamāpnuyām

You are, as it were, puzzling my mind by these seemingly conflicting expressions; therefore, tell me the one definite discipline by which I may obtain the highest good. (2)

श्रीभगवानुवाच

लोकेऽस्मिन्द्विविधा निष्ठा पुरा प्रोक्ता मयानघ।
ज्ञानयोगेन साङ्ख्यानां कर्मयोगेन योगिनाम्॥ ३॥

śrībhagavānuvāca

loke'smindvividhā niṣṭhā purā proktā mayānagha
jñānayogena sāṅkhyānāṁ karmayogena yoginām

Śrī Bhagavān said: Arjuna, in this world two courses of Sādhanā (spiritual discipline) have been enunciated by Me in the past. In the case of the Sāṅkhyayogī, the Sādhanā proceeds along the path of Knowledge; whereas in the case of the Karmayogī, it proceeds along the path of Action. (3)

न कर्मणामनारम्भान्नैष्कर्म्यं पुरुषोऽश्नुते।
न च सन्न्यसनादेव सिद्धिं समधिगच्छति॥ ४॥

na karmaṇāmanārambhānnaiṣkarmyaṁ puruṣo'śnute
na ca sannyasanādeva siddhiṁ samadhigacchati

Man does not attain freedom from action (culmination of the discipline of Action) without entering upon action; nor does he reach perfection (culmination of the discipline of Knowledge) merely by ceasing to act. (4)

न हि कश्चित्क्षणमपि जातु तिष्ठत्यकर्मकृत्।
कार्यते ह्यवशः कर्म सर्वः प्रकृतिजैर्गुणैः॥ ५॥

na hi kaścitkṣaṇamapi jātu tiṣṭhatyakarmakṛt
kāryate hyavaśaḥ karma sarvaḥ prakṛtijairguṇaiḥ

Surely, none can ever remain inactive even for a moment; for, everyone is helplessly driven to action by nature-born qualities. (5)

कर्मेन्द्रियाणि संयम्य य आस्ते मनसा स्मरन्।
इन्द्रियार्थान्विमूढात्मा मिथ्याचारः स उच्यते॥ ६॥

karmendriyāṇi saṁyamya ya āste manasā smaran
indriyārthānvimūḍhātmā mithyācāraḥ sa ucyate

He who outwardly restraining the organs of sense and action, sits mentally dwelling on the objects of senses, that man of deluded intellect is called a hypocrite. (6)

यस्त्विन्द्रियाणि मनसा नियम्यारभतेऽर्जुन।
कर्मेन्द्रियैः कर्मयोगमसक्तः स विशिष्यते॥ ७ ॥

yastvindriyāṇi manasā niyamyārabhate'rjuna
karmendriyaiḥ karmayogamasaktaḥ sa viśiṣyate

On the other hand, he who controlling the organs of sense and action by the power of his will, and remaining unattached, undertakes the Yoga of Action through those organs, Arjuna, he excels. (7)

नियतं कुरु कर्म त्वं कर्म ज्यायो ह्यकर्मणः।
शरीरयात्रापि च ते न प्रसिद्ध्येदकर्मणः॥ ८ ॥

niyataṁ kuru karma tvaṁ karma jyāyo hyakarmaṇaḥ
śarīrayātrāpi ca te na prasiddhyedakarmaṇaḥ

Therefore, do you perform your allotted duty; for action is superior to inaction. Desisting from action, you cannot even maintain your body. (8)

यज्ञार्थात्कर्मणोऽन्यत्र लोकोऽयं कर्मबन्धनः।
तदर्थं कर्म कौन्तेय मुक्तसङ्गः समाचर॥ ९ ॥

yajñārthātkarmaṇo'nyatra loko'yaṁ karmabandhanaḥ
tadarthaṁ karma kaunteya muktasaṅgaḥ samācara

Man is bound by his own action except when it is performed for the sake of sacrifice. Therefore, Arjuna, do you efficiently perform your duty, free from attachment, for the sake of sacrifice alone. (9)

सहयज्ञाः प्रजाः सृष्ट्वा पुरोवाच प्रजापतिः।
अनेन प्रसविष्यध्वमेष वोऽस्त्विष्टकामधुक्॥ १०॥

sahayajñāḥ prajāḥ sṛṣṭvā purovāca prajāpatiḥ
anena prasaviṣyadhvameṣa vo'stviṣṭakāmadhuk

Having created mankind along with (the spirit of) sacrifice at the beginning of creation, the Creator, Brahmā, said to them, "You shall prosper by this; may this yield the enjoyment you seek. (10)

देवान्भावयतानेन ते देवा भावयन्तु वः।
परस्परं भावयन्तः श्रेयः परमवाप्स्यथ॥ ११॥

devānbhāvayatānena te devā bhāvayantu vaḥ
parasparaṁ bhāvayantaḥ śreyaḥ paramavāpsyatha

Foster the gods through this sacrifice, and let the gods be gracious to you. Thus, each fostering the other selflessly, you will attain the highest good. (11)

इष्टान्भोगान्हि वो देवा दास्यन्ते यज्ञभाविताः।
तैर्दत्तानप्रदायैभ्यो यो भुङ्क्ते स्तेन एव सः॥ १२॥

iṣṭānbhogānhi vo devā dāsyante yajñabhāvitāḥ
tairdattānapradāyaibhyo yo bhuṅkte stena eva saḥ

Fostered by sacrifice, the gods will surely bestow

on you unasked all the desired enjoyments. He who enjoys the gifts bestowed by them without offering anything to them in return, is undoubtedly a thief. (12)

यज्ञशिष्टाशिनः सन्तो मुच्यन्ते सर्वकिल्बिषैः।
भुञ्जते ते त्वघं पापा ये पचन्त्यात्मकारणात्॥ १३॥

yajñaśiṣṭāśinaḥ santo mucyante sarvakilbiṣaiḥ
bhuñjate te tvaghaṁ pāpā ye pacantyātmakāraṇāt

The virtuous who partake of what is left over after sacrifice, are absolved of all sins. Those sinful ones who cook for the sake of nourishing their bodies alone, eat only sin. (13)

अन्नाद्भवन्ति भूतानि पर्जन्यादन्नसम्भवः।
यज्ञाद्भवति पर्जन्यो यज्ञः कर्मसमुद्भवः॥ १४॥
कर्म ब्रह्मोद्भवं विद्धि ब्रह्माक्षरसमुद्भवम्।
तस्मात्सर्वगतं ब्रह्म नित्यं यज्ञे प्रतिष्ठितम्॥ १५॥

annādbhavanti bhūtāni parjanyādannasambhavaḥ
yajñādbhavati parjanyo yajñaḥ karmasamudbhavaḥ
karma brahmodbhavaṁ viddhi brahmākṣarasamudbhavam
tasmātsarvagataṁ brahma nityaṁ yajñe pratiṣṭhitam

All beings are evolved from food; production of food is dependent on rain; rain ensues from sacrifice, and sacrifice is rooted in prescribed action. Know that prescribed action has its origin in the Vedas, and the Vedas proceed from the Indestructible (God); hence the all-pervading Infinite is always present in sacrifice. (14-15)

एवं प्रवर्तितं चक्रं नानुवर्तयतीह यः।
अघायुरिन्द्रियारामो मोघं पार्थ स जीवति॥ १६॥

evaṁ pravartitaṁ cakraṁ nānuvartayatīha yaḥ
aghāyurindriyārāmo moghaṁ pārtha sa jīvati

Arjuna, he who does not follow the wheel of creation thus set going in this world i.e., does not perform his duties, sinful and sensual, he lives in vain. (16)

यस्त्वात्मरतिरेव स्यादात्मतृप्तश्च मानवः।
आत्मन्येव च सन्तुष्टस्तस्य कार्यं न विद्यते॥ १७॥

yastvātmaratireva syādātmatṛptaśca mānavaḥ
ātmanyeva ca santuṣṭastasya kāryaṁ na vidyate

He, however, who takes delight in the Self alone and is gratified with the Self, and is contented in the Self, has no duty. (17)

नैव तस्य कृतेनार्थो नाकृतेनेह कश्चन।
न चास्य सर्वभूतेषु कश्चिदर्थव्यपाश्रयः॥ १८॥

naiva tasya kṛtenārtho nākṛteneha kaścana
na cāsya sarvabhūteṣu kaścidarthavyapāśrayaḥ

In this world that great soul has nothing to gain by action nor by abstaining from action; nor has he selfish dependence of any kind on any creature. (18)

तस्मादसक्तः सततं कार्यं कर्म समाचर।
असक्तो ह्याचरन्कर्म परमाप्नोति पूरुषः॥ १९॥

tasmādasaktaḥ satataṁ kāryaṁ karma samācara
asakto hyācarankarma paramāpnoti pūruṣaḥ

Therefore, go on efficiently doing your duty without attachment. Doing work without attachment man attains the Supreme. (19)

कर्मणैव हि संसिद्धिमास्थिता जनकादयः।
लोकसङ्ग्रहमेवापि सम्पश्यन्कर्तुमर्हसि॥ २०॥

karmaṇaiva hi saṁsiddhimāsthitā janakādayaḥ
lokasaṅgrahamevāpi sampaśyankartumarhasi

It is through action (without attachment) alone that Janaka and other wise men reached perfection. Having an eye to maintenance of the world order too you should take to action. (20)

यद्यदाचरति श्रेष्ठस्तत्तदेवेतरो जनः।
स यत्प्रमाणं कुरुते लोकस्तदनुवर्तते॥ २१॥

yadyadācarati śreṣṭhastattadevetaro janaḥ
sa yatpramāṇaṁ kurute lokastadanuvartate

For whatever a great man does, that very thing other men also do; whatever standard he sets up, the generality of men follow the same. (21)

न मे पार्थास्ति कर्तव्यं त्रिषु लोकेषु किञ्चन।
नानवाप्तमवाप्तव्यं वर्त एव च कर्मणि॥ २२॥

na me pārthāsti kartavyaṁ triṣu lokeṣu kiñcana
nānavāptamavāptavyaṁ varta eva ca karmaṇi

Arjuna, there is no duty in all the three worlds for Me to perform, nor is there anything worth attaining, unattained by Me; yet I continue to work. (22)

यदि ह्यहं न वर्तेयं जातु कर्मण्यतन्द्रितः।
मम वर्त्मानुवर्तन्ते मनुष्याः पार्थ सर्वशः॥ २३॥

yadi hyahaṁ na varteyaṁ jātu karmaṇyatandritaḥ
mama vartmānuvartante manuṣyāḥ pārtha sarvaśaḥ

Should I not engage in action, scrupulously at any time, great harm will come to the world; for, Arjuna, men follow My way in all matters. (23)

उत्सीदेयुरिमे लोका न कुर्यां कर्म चेदहम्।
सङ्करस्य च कर्ता स्यामुपहन्यामिमाः प्रजाः॥ २४॥

utsīdeyurime lokā na kuryāṁ karma cedaham
saṅkarasya ca kartā syāmupahanyāmimāḥ prajāḥ

If I ever cease to act, these worlds would perish; nay, I should prove to be the cause of confusion, and of the destruction of these people. (24)

सक्ताः कर्मण्यविद्वांसो यथा कुर्वन्ति भारत।
कुर्याद्विद्वांस्तथासक्तश्चिकीर्षुर्लोकसङ्ग्रहम् ॥ २५॥

saktāḥ karmaṇyavidvāṁso yathā kurvanti bhārata
kuryādvidvāṁstathāsaktaścikīrṣurlokasaṅgraham

Arjuna, as the unwise act with attachment, so should the wise man, with a view to maintain the world order, act without attachment. (25)

न बुद्धिभेदं जनयेदज्ञानां कर्मसङ्गिनाम्।
जोषयेत्सर्वकर्माणि विद्वान्युक्तः समाचरन्॥ २६॥

na buddhibhedaṁ janayedajñānāṁ karmasaṅginām
joṣayetsarvakarmāṇi vidvānyuktaḥ samācaran

A wise man established in the Self should not unsettle the mind of the ignorant attached to action, but should get them to perform all their duties, duly performing his own duties. (26)

प्रकृतेः क्रियमाणानि गुणैः कर्माणि सर्वशः ।
अहङ्कारविमूढात्मा कर्ताहमिति मन्यते ॥ २७ ॥

prakṛteḥ kriyamāṇāni guṇaiḥ karmāṇi sarvaśaḥ
ahaṅkāravimūḍhātmā kartāhamiti manyate

All actions are being performed by the modes of Prakṛti (Primordial Matter). The fool, whose mind is deluded by egoism, thinks: "I am the doer." (27)

तत्त्ववित्तु महाबाहो गुणकर्मविभागयोः ।
गुणा गुणेषु वर्तन्त इति मत्वा न सज्जते ॥ २८ ॥

tattvavittu mahābāho guṇakarmavibhāgayoḥ
guṇā guṇeṣu vartanta iti matvā na sajjate

He, however, who has true insight into the respective spheres of Guṇas (modes of Prakṛti) and their actions, holding that it is the Guṇas (in the shape of the senses, mind, etc.,) that move among the Guṇas (objects of perception), does not get attached to them, Arjuna. (28)

प्रकृतेर्गुणसम्मूढाः सज्जन्ते गुणकर्मसु ।
तानकृत्स्नविदो मन्दान्कृत्स्नविन्न विचालयेत् ॥ २९ ॥

prakṛterguṇasammūḍhāḥ sajjante guṇakarmasu
tānakṛtsnavido mandānkṛtsnavinna vicālayet

Those who are completely deluded by the Guṇas

(modes) of Prakṛti remain attached to those Guṇas and actions; the man of perfect Knowledge should not unsettle the mind of those insufficiently knowing ignorants. (29)

मयि सर्वाणि कर्माणि सन्न्यस्याध्यात्मचेतसा।
निराशीर्निर्ममो भूत्वा युध्यस्व विगतज्वरः॥ ३०॥

mayi sarvāṇi karmāṇi sannyasyādhyātmacetasā
nirāśīrnirmamo bhūtvā yudhyasva vigatajvaraḥ

Therefore, dedicating all actions to Me with your mind fixed on Me, the Self of all, freed from desire and the feeling of meum and cured of mental agitation, fight. (30)

ये मे मतमिदं नित्यमनुतिष्ठन्ति मानवाः।
श्रद्धावन्तोऽनसूयन्तो मुच्यन्ते तेऽपि कर्मभिः॥ ३१॥

ye me matamidaṁ nityamanutiṣṭhanti mānavāḥ
śraddhāvanto'nasūyanto mucyante te'pi karmabhiḥ

Even those men who, with an uncavilling and devout mind, always follow this teaching of Mine are released from the bondage of all actions. (31)

ये त्वेतदभ्यसूयन्तो नानुतिष्ठन्ति मे मतम्।
सर्वज्ञानविमूढांस्तान्विद्धि नष्टानचेतसः॥ ३२॥

ye tvetadabhyasūyanto nānutiṣṭhanti me matam
sarvajñānavimūḍhāṁstānviddhi naṣṭānacetasaḥ

They, however, who, finding fault with this teaching of Mine, do not follow it, take those fools to be deluded in the matter of all knowledge, and lost. (32)

सदृशं चेष्टते स्वस्याः प्रकृतेर्ज्ञानवानपि।
प्रकृतिं यान्ति भूतानि निग्रहः किं करिष्यति॥ ३३॥

sadṛśaṁ ceṣṭate svasyāḥ prakṛterjñānavānapi
prakṛtiṁ yānti bhūtāni nigrahaḥ kiṁ kariṣyati

All living creatures follow their tendencies; even the wise man acts according to the tendencies of his own nature. Of what use is any external restraint? (33)

इन्द्रियस्येन्द्रियस्यार्थे रागद्वेषौ व्यवस्थितौ।
तयोर्न वशमागच्छेत्तौ ह्यस्य परिपन्थिनौ॥ ३४॥

indriyasyendriyasyārthe rāgadveṣau vyavasthitau
tayorna vaśamāgacchettau hyasya paripanthinau

Attraction and repulsion are rooted in all sense-objects. Man should never allow himself to be swayed by them, because they are the two principal enemies standing in the way of his redemption. (34)

श्रेयान्स्वधर्मो विगुणः परधर्मात्स्वनुष्ठितात्।
स्वधर्मे निधनं श्रेयः परधर्मो भयावहः॥ ३५॥

śreyānsvadharmo viguṇaḥ paradharmātsvanuṣṭhitāt
svadharme nidhanaṁ śreyaḥ paradharmo bhayāvahaḥ

One's own duty, though devoid of merit, is preferable to the duty of another well performed. Even death in the performance of one's own duty brings blessedness; another's duty is fraught with fear. (35)

अर्जुन उवाच

अथ केन प्रयुक्तोऽयं पापं चरति पूरुषः।
अनिच्छन्नपि वार्ष्णेय बलादिव नियोजितः॥ ३६॥

arjuna uvāca

atha kena prayukto'yaṁ pāpaṁ carati pūruṣaḥ
anicchannapi vārṣṇeya balādiva niyojitaḥ

Arjuna said : Now impelled by what, Kṛṣṇa does this man commit sin even involuntarily, as though driven by force? (36)

श्रीभगवानुवाच

काम एष क्रोध एष रजोगुणसमुद्भवः।
महाशनो महापाप्मा विद्ध्येनमिह वैरिणम्॥ ३७॥

śrībhagavānuvāca

kāma eṣa krodha eṣa rajoguṇasamudbhavaḥ
mahāśano mahāpāpmā viddhyenamiha vairiṇam

Śrī Bhagavān said : It is desire begotten of the element of Rajas, which appears as wrath; nay, it is insatiable and grossly wicked. Know this to be the enemy in this case. (37)

धूमेनाव्रियते वह्निर्यथादर्शो मलेन च।
यथोल्बेनावृतो गर्भस्तथा तेनेदमावृतम्॥ ३८॥

dhūmenāvriyate vahniryathādarśo malena ca
yatholbenāvṛto garbhastathā tenedamāvṛtam

As fire is covered by smoke, mirror by dust, and embryo by the amnion, so is knowledge covered by desire. (38)

आवृतं ज्ञानमेतेन ज्ञानिनो नित्यवैरिणा।
कामरूपेण कौन्तेय दुष्पूरेणानलेन च॥ ३९॥

āvṛtaṁ jñānametena jñānino nityavairiṇā
kāmarūpeṇa kaunteya duṣpūreṇānalena ca

And, Arjuna, Knowledge stands covered by this eternal enemy of the wise known as desire, which is insatiable like fire. (39)

इन्द्रियाणि मनो बुद्धिरस्याधिष्ठानमुच्यते।
एतैर्विमोहयत्येष ज्ञानमावृत्य देहिनम्॥ ४०॥

indriyāṇi mano buddhirasyādhiṣṭhānamucyate
etairvimohayatyeṣa jñānamāvṛtya dehinam

The senses, the mind and the intellect are declared to be its seat; screening the light of Truth through these; it (desire) deludes the embodied soul. (40)

तस्मात्त्वमिन्द्रियाण्यादौ नियम्य भरतर्षभ।
पाप्मानं प्रजहि ह्येनं ज्ञानविज्ञाननाशनम्॥ ४१॥

tasmāttvamindriyāṇyādau niyamya bharatarṣabha
pāpmānaṁ prajahi hyenaṁ jñānavijñānanāśanam

Therefore, Arjuna, you must first control your senses, and then kill this evil thing which obstructs Jñāna (Knowledge of the Absolute or Nirguṇa Brahma) and Vijñāna (Knowledge of Sākāra Brahma or manifest Divinity). (41)

इन्द्रियाणि पराण्याहुरिन्द्रियेभ्यः परं मनः।
मनसस्तु परा बुद्धिर्यो बुद्धेः परतस्तु सः॥ ४२॥

indriyāṇi parāṇyāhurindriyebhyaḥ paraṁ manaḥ
manasastu parā buddhiryo buddheḥ paratastu saḥ

The senses are said to be greater than the body; but greater than the senses is the mind. Greater than the mind is the intellect; and what is greater than the intellect is He, the Self. (42)

एवं बुद्धेः परं बुद्ध्वा संस्तभ्यात्मानमात्मना।
जहि शत्रुं महाबाहो कामरूपं दुरासदम्॥ ४३॥

evaṁ buddheḥ paraṁ buddhvā saṁstabhyātmānamātmanā
jahi śatruṁ mahābāho kāmarūpaṁ durāsadam

Thus, Arjuna, knowing that which is higher than the intellect and subduing the mind by reason, kill this enemy in the form of desire that is hard to overcome. (43)

ॐ तत्सदिति श्रीमद्भगवद्गीतासूपनिषत्सु ब्रह्मविद्यायां
योगशास्त्रे श्रीकृष्णार्जुनसंवादे कर्मयोगो
नाम तृतीयोऽध्यायः॥ ३॥

Thus, in the Upaniṣad sung by the Lord, the Science of Brahma, the scripture of Yoga, the dialogue between Śrī Kṛṣṇa and Arjuna, ends the third chapter entitled "Karmayoga, or the Yoga of Action."

ॐ श्रीपरमात्मने नमः

अथ चतुर्थोऽध्यायः
CHAPTER FOUR

श्रीभगवानुवाच

इमं विवस्वते योगं प्रोक्तवानहमव्ययम्।
विवस्वान्मनवे प्राह मनुरिक्ष्वाकवेऽब्रवीत्॥ १॥

śrībhagavānuvāca

imaṁ vivasvate yogaṁ proktavānahamavyayam
vivasvānmanave prāha manurikṣvākave'bravīt

Śrī Bhagavān said: I revealed this immortal Yoga to Vivasvān (Sun-god); Vivasvān conveyed it to Manu (his son); and Manu imparted it to (his son) Ikṣvāku. (1)

एवं परम्पराप्राप्तमिमं राजर्षयो विदुः।
स कालेनेह महता योगो नष्टः परन्तप॥ २॥

evaṁ paramparāprāptamimaṁ rājarṣayo viduḥ
sa kāleneha mahatā yogo naṣṭaḥ parantapa

Thus transmitted in succession from father to son, Arjuna, this Yoga remained known to the Rājarṣis (royal sages). Through long lapse of time, this Yoga has got lost to the world. (2)

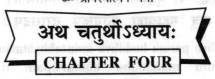

स एवायं मया तेऽद्य योगः प्रोक्तः पुरातनः।
भक्तोऽसि मे सखा चेति रहस्यं ह्येतदुत्तमम्॥ ३॥

sa evāyaṁ mayā te'dya yogaḥ proktaḥ purātanaḥ
bhakto'si me sakhā ceti rahasyaṁ hyetaduttamam

The same ancient Yoga, which is a supreme secret, has this day been imparted to you by Me, because you are My devotee and friend. (3)

अर्जुन उवाच

अपरं भवतो जन्म परं जन्म विवस्वतः।
कथमेतद्विजानीयां त्वमादौ प्रोक्तवानिति॥ ४॥

arjuna uvāca

aparaṁ bhavato janma paraṁ janma vivasvataḥ
kathametadvijānīyāṁ tvamādau proktavāniti

Arjuna said: You are of recent origin, while the birth of Vivasvān dates back to remote antiquity. How, then, am I to believe that You imparted this Yoga at the beginning of the creation! (4)

श्रीभगवानुवाच

बहूनि मे व्यतीतानि जन्मानि तव चार्जुन।
तान्यहं वेद सर्वाणि न त्वं वेत्थ परन्तप॥ ५॥

śrībhagavānuvāca

bahūni me vyatītāni janmāni tava cārjuna
tānyahaṁ veda sarvāṇi na tvaṁ vettha parantapa

Śrī Bhagavān said : Arjuna, you and I have passed

through many births, I remember them all; you do not remember, O chastiser of foes. (5)

अजोऽपि सन्नव्ययात्मा भूतानामीश्वरोऽपि सन्।
प्रकृतिं स्वामधिष्ठाय सम्भवाम्यात्ममायया॥ ६॥

ajo'pi sannavyayātmā bhūtānāmīśvaro'pi san
prakṛtiṁ svāmadhiṣṭhāya sambhavāmyātmamāyayā

Though birthless and immortal and the Lord of all beings, I manifest Myself through My own Yogamāyā (divine potency), keeping My nature (Prakṛti) under control. (6)

यदा यदा हि धर्मस्य ग्लानिर्भवति भारत।
अभ्युत्थानमधर्मस्य तदात्मानं सृजाम्यहम्॥ ७॥

yadā yadā hi dharmasya glānirbhavati bhārata
abhyutthānamadharmasya tadātmānaṁ sṛjāmyaham

Arjuna, whenever righteousness is on the decline, unrighteousness is in the ascendant, then I body Myself forth. (7)

परित्राणाय साधूनां विनाशाय च दुष्कृताम्।
धर्मसंस्थापनार्थाय सम्भवामि युगे युगे॥ ८॥

paritrāṇāya sādhūnāṁ vināśāya ca duṣkṛtām
dharmasaṁsthāpanārthāya sambhavāmi yuge yuge

For the protection of the virtuous, for the extirpation of evil-doers, and for establishing Dharma (righteousness) on a firm footing, I am born from age to age. (8)

जन्म कर्म च मे दिव्यमेवं यो वेत्ति तत्त्वतः।
त्यक्त्वा देहं पुनर्जन्म नैति मामेति सोऽर्जुन॥ ९॥

janma karma ca me divyamevaṁ yo vetti tattvataḥ
tyaktvā dehaṁ punarjanma naiti māmeti so'rjuna

Arjuna, My birth and activities are divine. He who knows this in reality is not reborn on leaving his body, but comes to Me. (9)

वीतरागभयक्रोधा मन्मया मामुपाश्रिताः।
बहवो ज्ञानतपसा पूता मद्भावमागताः॥ १०॥

vītarāgabhayakrodhā manmayā māmupāśritāḥ
bahavo jñānatapasā pūtā madbhāvamāgatāḥ

Completely rid of attachment, fear and anger, wholly absorbed in Me, depending on Me, and purified by the penance of wisdom, many have become one with Me even in the past. (10)

ये यथा मां प्रपद्यन्ते तांस्तथैव भजाम्यहम्।
मम वर्त्मानुवर्तन्ते मनुष्याः पार्थ सर्वशः॥ ११॥

ye yathā māṁ prapadyante tāṁstathaiva bhajāmyaham
mama vartmānuvartante manuṣyāḥ pārtha sarvaśaḥ

Arjuna, howsoever men seek Me, even so do I approach them; for all men follow My path in everyway. (11)

काङ्क्षन्तः कर्मणां सिद्धिं यजन्त इह देवताः।
क्षिप्रं हि मानुषे लोके सिद्धिर्भवति कर्मजा॥ १२॥

kāṅkṣantaḥ karmaṇāṁ siddhiṁ yajanta iha devatāḥ
kṣipraṁ hi mānuṣe loke siddhirbhavati karmajā

In this world of human beings, men seeking the fruition of their activities worship the gods; for success born of actions follows quickly. (12)

चातुर्वर्ण्यं मया सृष्टं गुणकर्मविभागशः।
तस्य कर्तारमपि मां विद्ध्यकर्तारमव्ययम्॥ १३॥

cāturvarṇyaṁ mayā sṛṣṭaṁ guṇakarmavibhāgaśaḥ
tasya kartāramapi māṁ viddhyakartāramavyayam

The four orders of society (viz., the Brāhmaṇa, the Kṣatriya, the Vaiśya and the Śūdra) were created by Me, classifying them according to the Guṇas predominant in each and apportioning corresponding duties to them; though the originator of this creation, know Me, the Immortal Lord, to be a non-doer. (13)

न मां कर्माणि लिम्पन्ति न मे कर्मफले स्पृहा।
इति मां योऽभिजानाति कर्मभिर्न स बध्यते॥ १४॥

na māṁ karmāṇi limpanti na me karmaphale spṛhā
iti māṁ yo'bhijānāti karmabhirna sa badhyate

Since I have no craving for the fruit of actions, actions do not contaminate Me. Even he who thus knows Me in reality is not bound by actions. (14)

एवं ज्ञात्वा कृतं कर्म पूर्वैरपि मुमुक्षुभिः।
कुरु कर्मैव तस्मात्त्वं पूर्वैः पूर्वतरं कृतम्॥ १५॥

evaṁ jñātvā kṛtaṁ karma pūrvairapi mumukṣubhiḥ
kuru karmaiva tasmāttvaṁ pūrvaiḥ pūrvataraṁ kṛtam

Having known thus, action was performed even by the ancient seekers for liberation; therefore, do you also perform actions as have been performed by the ancients from antiquity. (15)

किं कर्म किमकर्मेति कवयोऽप्यत्र मोहिताः।
तत्ते कर्म प्रवक्ष्यामि यज्ज्ञात्वा मोक्ष्यसेऽशुभात्॥ १६॥

kiṁ karma kimakarmeti kavayo'pyatra mohitāḥ
tatte karma pravakṣyāmi yajjñātvā mokṣyase'śubhāt

What is action and what is inaction? Even men of intelligence are puzzled over this question. Therefore, I shall expound to you the truth about action, knowing which you will be freed from its evil effect (binding nature). (16)

कर्मणो ह्यपि बोद्धव्यं बोद्धव्यं च विकर्मणः।
अकर्मणश्च बोद्धव्यं गहना कर्मणो गतिः॥ १७॥

karmaṇo hyapi boddhavyaṁ boddhavyaṁ ca vikarmaṇaḥ
akarmaṇaśca boddhavyaṁ gahanā karmaṇo gatiḥ

The truth about action must be known and the truth of inaction also must be known; even so the truth about prohibited action must be known. For mysterious are the ways of action. (17)

कर्मण्यकर्म यः पश्येदकर्मणि च कर्म यः।
स बुद्धिमान्मनुष्येषु स युक्तः कृत्स्नकर्मकृत्॥ १८॥

karmaṇyakarma yaḥ paśyedakarmaṇi ca karma yaḥ sa buddhimānmanuṣyeṣu sa yuktaḥ kṛtsnakarmakṛt

He who sees inaction in action, and action in inaction, is wise among men; he is a Yogī, who has performed all actions. (18)

यस्य सर्वे समारम्भाः कामसङ्कल्पवर्जिताः।
ज्ञानाग्निदग्धकर्माणं तमाहुः पण्डितं बुधाः॥ १९॥

yasya sarve samārambhāḥ kāmasaṅkalpavarjitāḥ jñānāgnidagdhakarmāṇaṁ tamāhuḥ paṇḍitaṁ budhāḥ

Even the wise call him a sage, whose undertakings are all free from desire and thoughts of the world, and whose actions are burnt up by the fire of wisdom. (19)

त्यक्त्वा कर्मफलासङ्गं नित्यतृप्तो निराश्रयः।
कर्मण्यभिप्रवृत्तोऽपि नैव किञ्चित्करोति सः॥ २०॥

tyaktvā karmaphalāsaṅgaṁ nityatṛpto nirāśrayaḥ karmaṇyabhipravṛtto'pi naiva kiñcitkaroti saḥ

He, who, having totally given up attachment to actions and their fruit, no longer depends on the world, and is ever content, does nothing at all, though fully engaged in action. (20)

निराशीर्यतचित्तात्मा त्यक्तसर्वपरिग्रहः।
शारीरं केवलं कर्म कुर्वन्नाप्नोति किल्बिषम्॥ २१॥

nirāśīryatacittātmā tyaktasarvaparigrahaḥ śārīraṁ kevalaṁ karma kurvannāpnoti kilbiṣam

Having subdued his mind and body, and given up all objects of enjoyment, and free from craving, he who performs sheer bodily action does not incur sin. (21)

यदृच्छालाभसन्तुष्टो द्वन्द्वातीतो विमत्सरः ।
समः सिद्धावसिद्धौ च कृत्वापि न निबध्यते ॥ २२ ॥

yadṛcchālābhasantuṣṭo dvandvātīto vimatsaraḥ
samaḥ siddhāvasiddhau ca kṛtvāpi na nibadhyate

The Karmayogī, who is contented with whatever is got unsought, is free from jealousy and has transcended all pairs of opposites like joy and grief, and is balanced in success and failure, is not bound by his action. (22)

गतसङ्गस्य मुक्तस्य ज्ञानावस्थितचेतसः ।
यज्ञायाचरतः कर्म समग्रं प्रविलीयते ॥ २३ ॥

gatasaṅgasya muktasya jñānāvasthitacetasaḥ
yajñāyācarataḥ karma samagraṁ pravilīyate

All his actions get dissolved entirely, who is free from attachment and has no identification and no sense of mine with the body; whose mind is established in the knowledge of Self and who works merely for the sake of sacrifice. (23)

ब्रह्मार्पणं ब्रह्म हविर्ब्रह्माग्नौ ब्रह्मणा हुतम् ।
ब्रह्मैव तेन गन्तव्यं ब्रह्मकर्मसमाधिना ॥ २४ ॥

brahmārpaṇaṁ brahma havirbrahmāgnau brahmaṇā hutam
brahmaiva tena gantavyaṁ brahmakarmasamādhinā

In the practice of seeing Brahma everywhere as a

form of sacrifice Brahma is the ladle (with which the oblation is poured into the fire, etc.); Brahma, again, is the oblation; Brahma is the fire, Brahma itself is the sacrificer and so Brahma itself constitutes the act of pouring the oblation into the fire. And finally Brahma is the goal to be reached by him who is absorbed in Brahma as the act of such sacrifice. (24)

दैवमेवापरे यज्ञं योगिनः पर्युपासते।
ब्रह्माग्नावपरे यज्ञं यज्ञेनैवोपजुह्वति॥ २५॥

daivamevāpare yajñaṁ yoginaḥ paryupāsate
brahmāgnāvapare yajñaṁ yajñenaivopajuhvati

Other Yogīs duly offer sacrifice only in the shape of worship to gods. Others pour into the fire of Brahma the very sacrifice in the shape of the Self through the sacrifice known as the perception of identity. (25)

श्रोत्रादीनीन्द्रियाण्यन्ये संयमाग्निषु जुह्वति।
शब्दादीन्विषयानन्य इन्द्रियाग्निषु जुह्वति॥ २६॥

śrotrādīnīndriyāṇyanye saṁyamāgniṣu juhvati
śabdādīnviṣayānanya indriyāgniṣu juhvati

Others offer as sacrifice their senses of hearing etc., into the fires of self-discipline. Other Yogīs, again, offer sound and other objects of perception into the fires of the senses. (26)

सर्वाणीन्द्रियकर्माणि प्राणकर्माणि चापरे।
आत्मसंयमयोगाग्नौ जुह्वति ज्ञानदीपिते॥ २७॥

sarvāṇīndriyakarmāṇi prāṇakarmāṇi cāpare
ātmasaṁyamayogāgnau juhvati jñānadīpite

Others sacrifice all the functions of their senses and the functions of the vital airs into the fire of Yoga in the shape of self-control, kindled by wisdom. (27)

द्रव्ययज्ञास्तपोयज्ञा योगयज्ञास्तथापरे।
स्वाध्यायज्ञानयज्ञाश्च यतयः संशितव्रताः॥ २८॥

dravyayajñāstapoyajñā yogayajñāstathāpare
svādhyāyajñānayajñāśca yatayaḥ saṁśitavratāḥ

Some perform sacrifice with material possessions; some offer sacrifice in the shape of austerities; others sacrifice through the practice of Yoga; while some striving souls, observing austere vows, perform sacrifice in the shape of wisdom through the study of sacred texts. (28)

अपाने जुह्वति प्राणं प्राणेऽपानं तथापरे।
प्राणापानगती रुद्ध्वा प्राणायामपरायणाः॥ २९॥
अपरे नियताहाराः प्राणान्प्राणेषु जुह्वति।
सर्वेऽप्येते यज्ञविदो यज्ञक्षपितकल्मषाः॥ ३०॥

apāne juhvati prāṇaṁ prāṇe'pānaṁ tathāpare
prāṇāpānagatī ruddhvā prāṇāyāmaparāyaṇāḥ
apare niyatāhārāḥ prāṇānprāṇeṣu juhvati
sarve'pyete yajñavido yajñakṣapitakalmaṣāḥ

Other Yogīs offer the act of exhalation into that of inhalation; even so, others the act of inhalation into that of exhalation. There are still others given to the practice of Prāṇāyāma (breath-control), who having regulated their diet and controlled the processes of exhalation and inhalation both pour their vital airs into the vital airs themselves. All these have their sins consumed away by sacrifice and understand the meaning of sacrificial worship. (29-30)

यज्ञशिष्टामृतभुजो यान्ति ब्रह्म सनातनम्।
नायं लोकोऽस्त्ययज्ञस्य कुतोऽन्यः कुरुसत्तम॥ ३१॥

yajñaśiṣṭāmṛtabhujo yānti brahma sanātanam
nāyaṁ loko'styayajñasya kuto'nyaḥ kurusattama

Arjuna, Yogīs who enjoy the nectar that has been left over after the performance of a sacrifice attain the eternal Brahma. To the man who does not offer sacrifice, even this world is not happy; how, then, can the other world be happy? (31)

एवं बहुविधा यज्ञा वितता ब्रह्मणो मुखे।
कर्मजान्विद्धि तान्सर्वानेवं ज्ञात्वा विमोक्ष्यसे॥ ३२॥

evaṁ bahuvidhā yajñā vitatā brahmaṇo mukhe
karmajānviddhi tānsarvānevaṁ jñātvā vimokṣyase

Many such forms of sacrifice have been set forth in detail in the Vedas; know them all as involving the action of mind, senses and body. Thus, knowing the truth about them you shall be freed from the bondage of action (through their performance). (32)

श्रेयान्द्रव्यमयाद्यज्ञाज्ज्ञानयज्ञः परन्तप।
सर्वं कर्माखिलं पार्थ ज्ञाने परिसमाप्यते॥ ३३॥

śreyāndravyamayādyajñājjñānayajñaḥ parantapa
sarvaṁ karmākhilaṁ pārtha jñāne parisamāpyate

Arjuna, sacrifice through Knowledge is superior to sacrifice performed with material things. For all actions without exception culminate in Knowledge, O son of Kuntī. (33)

तद्विद्धि प्रणिपातेन परिप्रश्नेन सेवया।
उपदेक्ष्यन्ति ते ज्ञानं ज्ञानिनस्तत्त्वदर्शिनः॥ ३४॥

tadviddhi praṇipātena paripraśnena sevayā
upadekṣyanti te jñānaṁ jñāninastattvadarśinaḥ

Understand the true nature of that Knowledge by approaching illumined soul. If you prostrate at their feet, render them service, and question them with an open and guileless heart, those wise seers of Truth will instruct you in that Knowledge. (34)

यज्ज्ञात्वा न पुनर्मोहमेवं यास्यसि पाण्डव।
येन भूतान्यशेषेण द्रक्ष्यस्यात्मन्यथो मयि॥ ३५॥

yajjñātvā na punarmohamevaṁ yāsyasi pāṇḍava
yena bhūtānyaśeṣeṇa drakṣyasyātmanyatho mayi

Arjuna, when you have achieved enlightenment, ignorance will delude you no more. In the light of that knowledge you will see the entire creation first within your own Self, and then in Me (the Oversoul). (35)

अपि चेदसि पापेभ्यः सर्वेभ्यः पापकृत्तमः।
सर्वं ज्ञानप्लवेनैव वृजिनं सन्तरिष्यसि ॥ ३६ ॥

api cedasi pāpebhyaḥ sarvebhyaḥ pāpakṛttamaḥ sarvaṁ jñānaplavenaiva vṛjinaṁ santariṣyasi

Even though you were the most sinful of all sinners, this Knowledge alone would carry you, like a raft, across all your sins. (36)

यथैधांसि समिद्धोऽग्निर्भस्मसात्कुरुतेऽर्जुन।
ज्ञानाग्निः सर्वकर्माणि भस्मसात्कुरुते तथा ॥ ३७ ॥

yathaidhāṁsi samiddho'gnirbhasmasātkurute'rjuna jñānāgniḥ sarvakarmāṇi bhasmasātkurute tathā

For, as the blazing fire turns the fuel to ashes, Arjuna, even so the fire of Knowledge turns all actions to ashes. (37)

न हि ज्ञानेन सदृशं पवित्रमिह विद्यते।
तत्स्वयं योगसंसिद्धः कालेनात्मनि विन्दति ॥ ३८ ॥

na hi jñānena sadṛśaṁ pavitramiha vidyate tatsvayaṁ yogasaṁsiddhaḥ kālenātmani vindati

On earth there is no purifier as great as Knowledge; he who has attained purity of heart through prolonged practice of Karmayoga, automatically sees the light of Truth in the self in course of time. (38)

श्रद्धावाँल्लभते ज्ञानं तत्परः संयतेन्द्रियः।
ज्ञानं लब्ध्वा परां शान्तिमचिरेणाधिगच्छति ॥ ३९ ॥

śraddhāvā̐llabhate jñānaṁ tatparaḥ saṁyatendriyaḥ jñānaṁ labdhvā parāṁ śāntimacireṇādhigacchati

He who has mastered his senses, is exclusively devoted to his practice and is full of faith, attains Knowledge; having had the revelation of Truth, he immediately attains supreme peace in the form of God-realization. (39)

अज्ञश्चाश्रद्दधानश्च संशयात्मा विनश्यति।
नायं लोकोऽस्ति न परो न सुखं संशयात्मनः ॥ ४० ॥

ajñaścāśraddadhānaśca saṁśayātmā vinaśyati nāyaṁ loko'sti na paro na sukhaṁ saṁśayātmanaḥ

He who lacks discrimination, is devoid of faith, and is at the same time possessed by doubt, is lost to the spiritual path. For the doubting soul there is neither this world nor the world beyond, nor even happiness. (40)

योगसन्न्यस्तकर्माणं ज्ञानसञ्छिन्नसंशयम्।
आत्मवन्तं न कर्माणि निबध्नन्ति धनञ्जय॥ ४१ ॥

yogasannyastakarmāṇaṁ jñānasañchinnasaṁśayam ātmavantaṁ na karmāṇi nibadhnanti dhanañjaya

Arjuna, actions do not bind him who has dedicated all his actions to God according to the spirit of Karmayoga, whose doubts have been dispelled by wisdom and is self-possessed. (41)

तस्मादज्ञानसम्भूतं हृत्स्थं ज्ञानासिनात्मनः।
छित्त्वैनं संशयं योगमातिष्ठोत्तिष्ठ भारत॥ ४२॥

tasmādajñānasambhūtaṁ hṛtsthaṁ jñānāsinātmanaḥ
chittvainaṁ saṁśayaṁ yogamātiṣṭhottiṣṭha bhārata

Therefore, Arjuna slashing to pieces, with the sword of wisdom, this doubt in your heart, born of ignorance, establish yourself in Karmayoga in the shape of even-mindedness, and stand up for the fight. (42)

ॐ तत्सदिति श्रीमद्भगवद्गीतासूपनिषत्सु ब्रह्मविद्यायां
योगशास्त्रे श्रीकृष्णार्जुनसंवादे ज्ञानकर्मसन्न्यासयोगो
नाम चतुर्थोऽध्यायः॥ ४॥

Thus, in the Upaniṣad sung by the Lord, the Science of Brahma, the scripture of Yoga, the dialogue between Śrī Kṛṣṇa and Arjuna, ends the fourth chapter entitled "The Yoga of Knowledge as well as the disciplines of Action and Knowledge."

ॐ श्रीपरमात्मने नमः

अथ पञ्चमोऽध्यायः

CHAPTER FIVE

अर्जुन उवाच

सन्न्यासं कर्मणां कृष्ण पुनर्योगं च शंससि।
यच्छ्रेय एतयोरेकं तन्मे ब्रूहि सुनिश्चितम्॥ १॥

arjuna uvāca

sannyāsaṁ karmaṇāṁ kṛṣṇa punaryogaṁ ca śaṁsasi
yacchreya etayorekaṁ tanme brūhi suniścitam

Arjuna said : Kṛṣṇa, you extol Sāṅkhyayoga (the Yoga of Knowledge) and then the Yoga of Action. Pray, tell me which of the two is decidedly conducive to my good. (1)

श्रीभगवानुवाच

सन्न्यासः कर्मयोगश्च निःश्रेयसकरावुभौ।
तयोस्तु कर्मसन्न्यासात्कर्मयोगो विशिष्यते॥ २॥

śrībhagavānuvāca

sannyāsaḥ karmayogaśca niḥśreyasakarāvubhau
tayostu karmasannyāsātkarmayogo viśiṣyate

Śrī Bhagavān said : The Yoga of Knowledge and the Yoga of Action both lead to supreme Bliss. Of the two, however, the Yoga of Action being easier of practice is superior to the Yoga of Knowledge. (2)

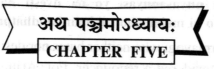

ज्ञेयः स नित्यसन्न्यासी यो न द्वेष्टि न काङ्क्षति।
निर्द्वन्द्वो हि महाबाहो सुखं बन्धात्प्रमुच्यते॥ ३॥

jñeyaḥ sa nityasannyāsī yo na dveṣṭi na kāṅkṣati
nirdvandvo hi mahābāho sukhaṁ bandhātpramucyate

The Karmayogī who neither hates nor desires should ever be considered a renouncer. For, Arjuna, he who is free from the pairs of opposites is easily freed from bondage. (3)

साङ्ख्ययोगौ पृथग्बालाः प्रवदन्ति न पण्डिताः।
एकमप्यास्थितः सम्यगुभयोर्विन्दते फलम्॥ ४॥

sāṅkhyayogau pṛthagbālāḥ pravadanti na paṇḍitāḥ
ekamapyāsthitaḥ samyagubhayorvindate phalam

It is the ignorant, not the wise, who say that Sāṅkhyayoga and Karmayoga lead to divergent results. For, one who is firmly established in either, gets the fruit of both (which is the same, viz., God-realization). (4)

यत्साङ्ख्यैः प्राप्यते स्थानं तद्योगैरपि गम्यते।
एकं साङ्ख्यं च योगं च यः पश्यति स पश्यति॥ ५॥

yatsāṅkhyaiḥ prāpyate sthānaṁ tadyogairapi gamyate
ekaṁ sāṅkhyaṁ ca yogaṁ ca yaḥ paśyati sa paśyati

The (supreme) state which is reached by the Sāṅkhyayogī is attained also by the Karmayogī. Therefore, he alone who sees Sāṅkhyayoga and Karmayoga as identical (so far as their result goes), sees truly. (5)

सन्न्यासस्तु महाबाहो दुःखमाप्तुमयोगतः।
योगयुक्तो मुनिर्ब्रह्म नचिरेणाधिगच्छति॥ ६॥

sannyāsastu mahābāho duḥkhamāptumayogataḥ
yogayukto munirbrahma nacireṇādh'gacchati

Without Karmayoga, however, Sāṅkhyayoga (or renunciation of doership in relation to all activities of the mind, senses and body) is difficult to accomplish; whereas the Karmayogī, who keeps his mind fixed on God, reaches Brahma in no time, Arjuna. (6)

योगयुक्तो विशुद्धात्मा विजितात्मा जितेन्द्रियः।
सर्वभूतात्मभूतात्मा कुर्वन्नपि न लिप्यते॥ ७॥

yogayukto viśuddhātmā vijitātmā jitendriyaḥ
sarvabhūtātmabhūtātmā kurvannapi na lipyate

The Karmayogī, who has fully conquered his mind and mastered his senses, whose heart is pure, and who has identified himself with the Self of all beings (viz., God), remains untainted, even though performing action. (7)

नैव किञ्चित्करोमीति युक्तो मन्येत तत्त्ववित्।
पश्यञ्शृण्वन्स्पृशञ्जिघ्रन्नश्नन्गच्छन्स्वपञ्श्वसन् ॥ ८ ।
प्रलपन्विसृजन्गृह्णन्नुन्मिषन्निमिषन्नपि ।
इन्द्रियाणीन्द्रियार्थेषु वर्तन्त इति धारयन्॥ ९ ।

naiva kiñcitkaromīti yukto manyeta tattvavit
paśyañśṛṇvanspṛśañjighrannaśnangacchansvapañśvasan
pralapanvisṛjangṛhṇannunmiṣannimiṣannapi
indriyāṇīndriyārtheṣu vartanta iti dhārayan

The Sāṅkhyayogī, however, who knows the reality of things, must believe, even though seeing, hearing, touching, smelling, eating or drinking, walking, sleeping, breathing, speaking, answering the calls of nature, grasping, and opening or closing the eyes, that he does nothing, holding that it is the senses that are moving among their objects. (8, 9)

ब्रह्मण्याधाय कर्माणि सङ्गं त्यक्त्वा करोति यः।
लिप्यते न स पापेन पद्मपत्रमिवाम्भसा॥ १०॥

brahmaṇyādhāya karmāṇi saṅgaṁ tyaktvā karoti yaḥ
lipyate na sa pāpena padmapatramivāmbhasā

He who acts offering all actions to God, and shaking off attachment, remains untouched by sin, as the lotus leaf by water. (10)

कायेन मनसा बुद्ध्या केवलैरिन्द्रियैरपि।
योगिनः कर्म कुर्वन्ति सङ्गं त्यक्त्वात्मशुद्धये॥ ११॥

kāyena manasā buddhyā kevalairindriyairapi
yoginaḥ karma kurvanti saṅgaṁ tyaktvātmaśuddhaye

The Karmayogīs perform action only with their senses, mind, intellect and body as well, without the feeling of mine in respect of them and shaking off attachment, simply for the sake of self-purification. (11)

युक्तः कर्मफलं त्यक्त्वा शान्तिमाप्नोति नैष्ठिकीम्।
अयुक्तः कामकारेण फले सक्तो निबध्यते॥ १२॥

yuktaḥ karmaphalaṁ tyaktvā śāntimāpnoti naiṣṭhikīm
ayuktaḥ kāmakāreṇa phale sakto nibadhyate

Offering the fruit of actions to God, the Karmayogī attains everlasting peace in the shape of God-realization, whereas, he who works with a selfish motive, being attached to the fruit of actions through desire, gets tied down. (12)

सर्वकर्माणि मनसा सन्न्यस्यास्ते सुखं वशी।
नवद्वारे पुरे देही नैव कुर्वन्न कारयन्॥ १३॥

sarvakarmāṇi manasā sannyasyāste sukhaṁ vaśī
navadvāre pure dehī naiva kurvanna kārayan

The self-controlled Sāṅkhyayogī, doing nothing himself and getting nothing done by others, rests happily in God—the embodiment of Truth, Knowledge and Bliss, mentally relegating all actions to the mansion of nine gates (the body with nine openings). (13)

न कर्तृत्वं न कर्माणि लोकस्य सृजति प्रभुः।
न कर्मफलसंयोगं स्वभावस्तु प्रवर्तते॥ १४॥

na kartṛtvaṁ na karmāṇi lokasya sṛjati prabhuḥ
na karmaphalasaṁyogaṁ svabhāvastu pravartate

God determines not the doership nor the doings of men, nor even their contact with the fruit of actions; but it is Nature alone that functions. (14)

नादत्ते कस्यचित्पापं न चैव सुकृतं विभुः।
अज्ञानेनावृतं ज्ञानं तेन मुह्यन्ति जन्तवः॥ १५॥

nādatte kasyacitpāpaṁ na caiva sukṛtaṁ vibhuḥ
ajñānenāvṛtaṁ jñānaṁ tena muhyanti jantavaḥ

The omnipresent God does not partake the virtue or sin of anyone. Knowledge is enveloped with ignorance; hence it is that beings are constantly falling a prey to delusion. (15)

ज्ञानेन तु तदज्ञानं येषां नाशितमात्मनः।
तेषामादित्यवज्ज्ञानं प्रकाशयति तत्परम्॥ १६॥

jñānena tu tadajñānaṁ yeṣāṁ nāśitamātmanaḥ
teṣāmādityavajjñānaṁ prakāśayati tatparam

In the case, however, of those whose said ignorance has been destroyed by true knowledge of God, that wisdom shining like the sun reveals the Supreme. (16)

तद्बुद्धयस्तदात्मानस्तन्निष्ठास्तत्परायणाः।
गच्छन्त्यपुनरावृत्तिं ज्ञाननिर्धूतकल्मषाः॥ १७॥

tadbuddhayastadātmānastanniṣṭhāstatparāyaṇāḥ
gacchantyapunarāvṛttiṁ jñānanirdhūtakalmaṣāḥ

Those whose mind and intellect are wholly merged in Him, who remain constantly established in identity with Him, and have finally become one with Him, their sins being wiped out by wisdom, reach the supreme goal whence there is no return. (17)

विद्याविनयसम्पन्ने ब्राह्मणे गवि हस्तिनि।
शुनि चैव श्वपाके च पण्डिताः समदर्शिनः॥ १८॥

vidyāvinayasampanne brāhmaṇe gavi hastini
śuni caiva śvapāke ca paṇḍitāḥ samadarśinaḥ

The wise look with equanimity on all whether it be

a Brāhmaṇa endowed with learning and culture, a cow, an elephant, a dog and a pariah, too. (18)

इहैव तैर्जितः सर्गो येषां साम्ये स्थितं मनः।
निर्दोषं हि समं ब्रह्म तस्माद्ब्रह्मणि ते स्थिताः ॥ १९ ॥

ihaiva tairjitaḥ sargo yeṣāṁ sāmye sthitaṁ manaḥ nirdoṣaṁ hi samaṁ brahma tasmādbrahmaṇi te sthitāḥ

Even here is the mortal plane conquered by those whose mind is established in unity; since the Absolute is untouched by evil and is the same to all, hence they are established in the Eternal. (19)

न प्रहृष्येत्प्रियं प्राप्य नोद्विजेत्प्राप्य चाप्रियम्।
स्थिरबुद्धिरसम्मूढो ब्रह्मविद् ब्रह्मणि स्थितः ॥ २० ॥

na prahṛṣyetpriyaṁ prāpya nodvijetprāpya cāpriyam sthirabuddhirasammūḍho brahmavid brahmaṇi sthitaḥ

He who, with reason firm and free from doubt, rejoices not on obtaining what is pleasant and does not feel perturbed on meeting with the unpleasant, that knower of Brahma lives eternally in identity with Brahma. (20)

बाह्यस्पर्शेष्वसक्तात्मा विन्दत्यात्मनि यत्सुखम्।
स ब्रह्मयोगयुक्तात्मा सुखमक्षयमश्नुते ॥ २१ ॥

bāhyasparśeṣvasaktātmā vindatyātmani yatsukham sa brahmayogayuktātmā sukhamakṣayamaśnute

He whose mind remains unattached to sense-objects, derives through meditation the Sāttvika joy which dwells in the mind; then that Yogī, having completely identified himself through meditation with Brahma, enjoys eternal Bliss. (21)

ये हि संस्पर्शजा भोगा दुःखयोनय एव ते।
आद्यन्तवन्तः कौन्तेय न तेषु रमते बुधः॥ २२॥

ye hi saṁsparśajā bhogā duḥkhayonaya eva te
ādyantavantaḥ kaunteya na teṣu ramate budhaḥ

The pleasures which are born of sense-contacts are verily a source of suffering only (though appearing as enjoyable to worldly-minded people). They have a beginning and an end (they come and go); Arjuna, it is for this reason that a wise man does not indulge in them. (22)

शक्नोतीहैव यः सोढुं प्राक्शरीरविमोक्षणात्।
कामक्रोधोद्भवं वेगं स युक्तः स सुखी नरः॥ २३॥

śaknotīhaiva yaḥ soḍhuṁ prākśarīravimokṣaṇāt
kāmakrodhodbhavaṁ vegaṁ sa yuktaḥ sa sukhī naraḥ

He alone who is able to withstand, in this very life before casting off this body, the urges of lust and anger, is a Yogī; and he alone is a happy man. (23)

योऽन्तःसुखोऽन्तरारामस्तथान्तर्ज्योतिरेव यः।
स योगी ब्रह्मनिर्वाणं ब्रह्मभूतोऽधिगच्छति॥ २४॥

yo'ntaḥsukho'ntarārāmastathāntarjyotireva yaḥ
sa yogī brahmanirvāṇaṁ brahmabhūto'dhigacchati

He who is happy within himself, enjoys within himself the delight of the soul, and even so is illumined by the inner light (light of the soul), such a Yogī

(Sāṅkhyayogī) identified with Brahma attains Brahma, who is all peace. (24)

लभन्ते ब्रह्मनिर्वाणमृषयः क्षीणकल्मषाः ।
छिन्नद्वैधा यतात्मानः सर्वभूतहिते रताः ॥ २५ ॥

labhante brahmanirvāṇamṛṣayaḥ kṣīṇakalmaṣāḥ
chinnadvaidhā yatātmānaḥ sarvabhūtahite ratāḥ

The seers whose sins have been purged, whose doubts have been dispelled by knowledge, whose disciplined mind is firmly established in God and who are devoted to the welfare of all beings, attain Brahma, who is all peace. (25)

कामक्रोधवियुक्तानां यतीनां यतचेतसाम् ।
अभितो ब्रह्मनिर्वाणं वर्तते विदितात्मनाम् ॥ २६ ॥

kāmakrodhaviyuktānāṁ yatīnāṁ yatacetasām
abhito brahmanirvāṇaṁ vartate viditātmanām

To those wise men who are free from lust and anger, who have subdued their mind and have realized God, Brahma, the abode of eternal peace, is present all-round. (26)

स्पर्शान्कृत्वा बहिर्बाह्यांश्चक्षुश्चैवान्तरे भ्रुवोः ।
प्राणापानौ समौ कृत्वा नासाभ्यन्तरचारिणौ ॥ २७ ॥
यतेन्द्रियमनोबुद्धिर्मुनिर्मोक्षपरायणः ।
विगतेच्छाभयक्रोधो यः सदा मुक्त एव सः ॥ २८ ॥

sparśānkṛtvā bahirbāhyāṁścakṣuścaivāntare bhruvoḥ
prāṇāpānau samau kṛtvā nāsābhyantaracāriṇau

yatendriyamanobuddhirmunirmokṣaparāyaṇaḥ
vigatecchābhayakrodho yaḥ sadā mukta eva saḥ

Shutting out all thoughts of external enjoyments, with the gaze fixed on the space between the eye-brows, having regulated the Prāṇa (outgoing) and the Apāna (ingoing) breaths flowing within the nostrils, he who has brought his senses, mind and intellect under control–such a contemplative soul intent on liberation and free from desire, fear and anger, is ever liberated. (27-28)

भोक्तारं यज्ञतपसां सर्वलोकमहेश्वरम्।
सुहृदं सर्वभूतानां ज्ञात्वा मां शान्तिमृच्छति॥ २९॥

bhoktāraṁ yajñatapasāṁ sarvalokamaheśvaram
suhṛdaṁ sarvabhūtānāṁ jñātvā māṁ śāntimṛcchati

Having known Me in reality as the enjoyer of all sacrifices and austerities, the supreme Lord of all the worlds, and the selfless friend of all beings, My devotee attains peace. (29)

ॐ तत्सदिति श्रीमद्भगवद्गीतासूपनिषत्सु ब्रह्मविद्यायां
योगशास्त्रे श्रीकृष्णार्जुनसंवादे कर्मसन्न्यासयोगो
नाम पञ्चमोऽध्यायः॥ ५॥

Thus, in the Upaniṣad sung by the Lord, the Science of Brahma, the scripture of Yoga, the dialogue between Śrī Kṛṣṇa and Arjuna, ends the fifth chapter entitled "The Yoga of Action and Knowledge."

ॐ श्रीपरमात्मने नमः

अथ षष्ठोऽध्यायः

CHAPTER SIX

श्रीभगवानुवाच

अनाश्रितः कर्मफलं कार्यं कर्म करोति यः।
स सन्न्यासी च योगी च न निरग्निर्न चाक्रियः॥ १॥

śrībhagavānuvāca

anāśritaḥ karmaphalaṁ kāryaṁ karma karoti yaḥ
sa sannyāsī ca yogī ca na niragnirna cākriyaḥ

Śrī Bhagavān said : He who does his duty without expecting the fruit of actions is a Sannyāsī (Sāṅkhyayogī) and a Yogī (Karmayogī) both. He is no Sannyāsī (renouncer) who has merely renounced the sacred fire; even so, he is no Yogī who has merely given up all activity. (1)

यं सन्न्यासमिति प्राहुर्योगं तं विद्धि पाण्डव।
न ह्यसन्न्यस्तसङ्कल्पो योगी भवति कश्चन॥ २॥

yaṁ sannyāsamiti prāhuryogaṁ taṁ viddhi pāṇḍava
na hyasannyastasaṅkalpo yogī bhavati kaścana

Arjuna, you must know that what they call Sannyāsa is no other than Yoga; for none becomes a Yogī, who has not abandoned his 'Saṅkalpas' (thoughts of the world). (2)

आरुरुक्षोर्मुनेर्योगं कर्म कारणमुच्यते।
योगारूढस्य तस्यैव शमः कारणमुच्यते॥ ३॥

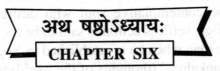

āruruksormuneryogaṁ karma kāraṇamucyate
yogārūḍhasya tasyaiva śamaḥ kāraṇamucyate

To the contemplative soul who desires to attain Karmayoga, selfless action is said to be the means; for the same man when he is established in Yoga, absence of all 'Saṅkalpas' (thoughts of the world) is said to be the way to blessedness. (3)

यदा हि नेन्द्रियार्थेषु न कर्मस्वनुषज्जते।
सर्वसङ्कल्पसन्न्यासी योगारूढस्तदोच्यते॥ ४॥

yadā hi nendriyārtheṣu na karmasvanuṣajjate
sarvasaṅkalpasannyāsī yogārūḍhastadocyate

When a man ceases to have any attachment for the objects of senses and for actions, and has renounced all 'Saṅkalpas' (thoughts of the world), he is said to have attained Yoga. (4)

उद्धरेदात्मनात्मानं नात्मानमवसादयेत्।
आत्मैव ह्यात्मनो बन्धुरात्मैव रिपुरात्मनः॥ ५॥

uddharedātmanātmānaṁ nātmānamavasādayet
ātmaiva hyātmano bandhurātmaiva ripurātmanaḥ

One should lift oneself by one's own efforts and should not degrade oneself; for one's own self is one's friend, and one's own self is one's enemy. (5)

बन्धुरात्मात्मनस्तस्य येनात्मैवात्मना जितः।
अनात्मनस्तु शत्रुत्वे वर्तेतात्मैव शत्रुवत्॥ ६॥

bandhurātmātmanastasya yenātmaivātmanā jitaḥ
anātmanastu śatrutve vartetātmaiva śatruvat

One's own self is the friend of the soul by whom the lower self (consisting of the mind, senses and body) has been conquered; even so, the very self of him, who has not conquered his lower self, behaves antagonistically like an enemy. (6)

जितात्मनः प्रशान्तस्य परमात्मा समाहितः ।
शीतोष्णसुखदुःखेषु तथा मानापमानयोः ॥ ७ ॥

jitātmanaḥ praśāntasya paramātmā samāhitaḥ
śītoṣṇasukhaduḥkheṣu tathā mānāpamānayoḥ

The Supreme Spirit is rooted in the knowledge of the self-controlled man whose mind is perfectly serene in the midst of pairs of opposites, such as cold and heat, joy and sorrow, and honour and ignominy. (7)

ज्ञानविज्ञानतृप्तात्मा कूटस्थो विजितेन्द्रियः ।
युक्त इत्युच्यते योगी समलोष्टाश्मकाञ्चनः ॥ ८ ॥

jñānavijñānatṛptātmā kūṭastho vijitendriyaḥ
yukta ityucyate yogī samaloṣṭāśmakāñcanaḥ

The Yogī whose mind is sated with Jñāna (Knowledge of Nirguṇa Brahma) and Vijñāna (Knowledge of manifest Divinity), who is unmoved under any circumstances, whose senses are completely under control, and to whom earth, stone and gold are all alike, is spoken of as a God-realized soul. (8)

सुहृन्मित्रार्युदासीनमध्यस्थद्वेष्यबन्धुषु ।
साधुष्वपि च पापेषु समबुद्धिर्विशिष्यते ॥ ९ ॥

suhṛnmitrāryudāsīnamadhyasthadveṣyabandhuṣu
sādhuṣvapi ca pāpeṣu samabuddhirviśiṣyate

He who looks upon well-wishers and neutrals as well as mediators, friends and foes, relatives and inimicals, the virtuous and the sinful with equanimity, stands supreme. (9)

योगी युञ्जीत सततमात्मानं रहसि स्थितः।
एकाकी यतचित्तात्मा निराशीरपरिग्रहः॥ १०॥

yogī yuñjīta satatamātmānaṁ rahasi sthitaḥ
ekākī yatacittātmā nirāśīraparigrahaḥ

Living in seclusion all by himself, the Yogī who has controlled his mind and body, and is free from desires and void of possessions, should constantly engage his mind in meditation. (10)

शुचौ देशे प्रतिष्ठाप्य स्थिरमासनमात्मनः।
नात्युच्छ्रितं नातिनीचं चैलाजिनकुशोत्तरम्॥ ११॥

śucau deśe pratiṣṭhāpya sthiramāsanamātmanaḥ
nātyucchritaṁ nātinīcaṁ cailājinakuśottaram

Having set his seat in a spot which is free from dirt and other impurities with the sacred Kuśa grass, a deerskin and a cloth spread thereon, one upon the other, (Kuśa below, deerskin in the middle and cloth uppermost), neither very high nor very low. (11)

तत्रैकाग्रं मनः कृत्वा यतचित्तेन्द्रियक्रियः।
उपविश्यासने युञ्ज्याद्योगमात्मविशुद्धये॥ १२॥

tatraikāgraṁ manaḥ kṛtvā yatacittendriyakriyaḥ
upaviśyāsane yuñjyādyogamātmaviśuddhaye

And occupying that seat, concentrating the mind and controlling the functions of the mind and senses, he should practise Yoga for self-purification. (12)

समं कायशिरोग्रीवं धारयन्नचलं स्थिरः।
सम्प्रेक्ष्य नासिकाग्रं स्वं दिशश्चानवलोकयन्॥ १३॥

samaṁ kāyaśirogrīvaṁ dhārayannacalaṁ sthiraḥ
samprekṣya nāsikāgraṁ svaṁ diśaścānavalokayan

Holding the trunk, head and neck straight and steady, remaining firm and fixing the gaze on the tip of his nose, without looking in other directions. (13)

प्रशान्तात्मा विगतभीर्ब्रह्मचारिव्रते स्थितः।
मनः संयम्य मच्चित्तो युक्त आसीत मत्परः॥ १४॥

praśāntātmā vigatabhīrbrahmacārivrate sthitaḥ
manaḥ saṁyamya maccitto yukta āsīta matparaḥ

Firm in the vow of complete chastity and fearless, keeping himself perfectly calm and with the mind held in restraint and fixed on Me, the vigilant Yogī should sit absorbed in Me. (14)

युञ्जन्नेवं सदात्मानं योगी नियतमानसः।
शान्तिं निर्वाणपरमां मत्संस्थामधिगच्छति॥ १५॥

yuñjannevaṁ sadātmānaṁ yogī niyatamānasaḥ
śāntiṁ nirvāṇaparamāṁ matsaṁsthāmadhigacchati

Thus, constantly applying his mind to Me, the Yogī

of disciplined mind attains everlasting peace, consisting of Supreme Bliss, which abides in Me. (15)

नात्यश्नतस्तु योगोऽस्ति न चैकान्तमनश्नतः।
न चाति स्वप्नशीलस्य जाग्रतो नैव चार्जुन॥ १६॥

nātyaśnatastu yogo'sti na caikāntamanaśnataḥ
na cāti svapnaśīlasya jāgrato naiva cārjuna

Arjuna, this Yoga is neither for him who overeats, nor for him who observes complete fast; it is neither for him who is given to too much sleep, nor even for him who is ceaselessly awake. (16)

युक्ताहारविहारस्य युक्तचेष्टस्य कर्मसु।
युक्तस्वप्नावबोधस्य योगो भवति दुःखहा॥ १७॥

yuktāhāravihārasya yuktaceṣṭasya karmasu
yuktasvapnāvabodhasya yogo bhavati duḥkhahā

Yoga, which rids one of woe, is accomplished only by him who is regulated in diet and recreation, regulated in performing actions, and regulated in sleep and wakefulness. (17)

यदा विनियतं चित्तमात्मन्येवावतिष्ठते।
निःस्पृहः सर्वकामेभ्यो युक्त इत्युच्यते तदा॥ १८॥

yadā viniyataṁ cittamātmanyevāvatiṣṭhate
niḥspṛhaḥ sarvakāmebhyo yukta ityucyate tadā

When the mind which is thoroughly disciplined gets riveted on God alone, then the person who is free from yearning for all enjoyments is said to be established in Yoga. (18)

यथा दीपो निवातस्थो नेङ्गते सोपमा स्मृता।
योगिनो यतचित्तस्य युञ्जतो योगमात्मनः॥ १९॥

yathā dīpo nivātastho neṅgate sopamā smṛtā
yogino yatacittasya yuñjato yogamātmanaḥ

As a flame does not flicker in a windless place, such is stated to be the picture of the disciplined mind of the Yogī practising meditation on God. (19)

यत्रोपरमते चित्तं निरुद्धं योगसेवया।
यत्र चैवात्मनात्मानं पश्यन्नात्मनि तुष्यति॥ २०॥

yatroparamate cittaṁ niruddhaṁ yogasevayā
yatra caivātmanātmānaṁ paśyannātmani tuṣyati

The state in which, curbed through the practice of Yoga, the mind becomes still, and in which, realizing God through subtle reason (purified by meditation on God) the soul rejoices only in God. (20)

सुखमात्यन्तिकं यत्तद्बुद्धिग्राह्यमतीन्द्रियम्।
वेत्ति यत्र न चैवायं स्थितश्चलति तत्त्वतः॥ २१॥

sukhamātyantikaṁ yattadbuddhigrāhyamatīndriyam
vetti yatra na caivāyaṁ sthitaścalati tattvataḥ

Nay, in which the soul experiences the eternal and super-sensuous joy which can be intuited only through the subtle and purified intellect, and wherein established the said Yogī moves not from Truth on any account. (21)

यं लब्ध्वा चापरं लाभं मन्यते नाधिकं ततः।
यस्मिन्स्थितो न दुःखेन गुरुणापि विचाल्यते॥ २२॥

yaṁ labdhvā cāparaṁ lābhaṁ manyate nādhikaṁ tataḥ
yasminsthito na duḥkhena guruṇāpi vicālyate

And having obtained which he does not reckon any other gain as greater than that, and established in which he is not shaken even by the heaviest of sorrows. (22)

तं विद्याद् दुःखसंयोगवियोगं योगसञ्ज्ञितम्।
स निश्चयेन योक्तव्यो योगोऽनिर्विण्णचेतसा॥ २३॥

taṁ vidyād duḥkhasaṁyogaviyogaṁ yogasañjñitam
sa niścayena yoktavyo yogo'nirviṇṇacetasā

That state, called Yoga, which is free from the contact of sorrow (in the form of transmigration), should be known. Nay, this Yoga should be resolutely practised with an unwearied mind. (23)

सङ्कल्पप्रभवान्कामांस्त्यक्त्वा सर्वानशेषतः।
मनसैवेन्द्रियग्रामं विनियम्य समन्ततः॥ २४॥

saṅkalpaprabhavānkāmāṁstyaktvā sarvānaśeṣataḥ
manasaivendriyagrāmaṁ viniyamya samantataḥ

Completely renouncing all desires arising from thoughts of the world, and fully restraining the whole pack of the senses from all sides by the mind. (24)

शनैः शनैरुपरमेद्बुद्ध्या धृतिगृहीतया।
आत्मसंस्थं मनः कृत्वा न किञ्चिदपि चिन्तयेत्॥ २५॥

śanaiḥ śanairuparamedbuddhyā dhṛtigṛhītayā
ātmasaṁsthaṁ manaḥ kṛtvā na kiñcidapi cintayet

He should through gradual practice attain tranquillity; and fixing the mind on God through reason controlled by steadfastness, he should not think of anything else. (25)

यतो यतो निश्चरति मनश्चञ्चलमस्थिरम्।
ततस्ततो नियम्यैतदात्मन्येव वशं नयेत्॥ २६॥

yato yato niścarati manaścañcalamasthiram
tatastato niyamyaitadātmanyeva vaśaṁ nayet

Drawing back the restless and fidgety mind from all those objects after which it runs, he should repeatedly fix it on God. (26)

प्रशान्तमनसं ह्येनं योगिनं सुखमुत्तमम्।
उपैति शान्तरजसं ब्रह्मभूतमकल्मषम्॥ २७॥

praśāntamanasaṁ hyenaṁ yoginaṁ sukhamuttamam
upaiti śāntarajasaṁ brahmabhūtamakalmaṣam

For to the Yogī whose mind is perfectly serene who is sinless, whose passion is subdued, and who is identified with Brahma, the embodiment of Truth, Knowledge and Bliss, supreme happiness comes as a matter of course. (27)

युञ्जन्नेवं सदात्मानं योगीविगतकल्मषः।
सुखेन ब्रह्मसंस्पर्शमत्यन्तं सुखमश्नुते॥ २८॥

yuñjannevaṁ sadātmānaṁ yogī vigatakalmaṣaḥ
sukhena brahmasaṁsparśamatyantaṁ sukhamaśnute

The sinless Yogī, thus uniting his Self constantly

with God, easily enjoys the eternal Bliss of oneness with Brahma. (28)

सर्वभूतस्थमात्मानं सर्वभूतानि चात्मनि।
ईक्षते योगयुक्तात्मा सर्वत्र समदर्शनः॥ २९॥

sarvabhūtasthamātmānaṁ sarvabhūtāni cātmani
īkṣate yogayuktātmā sarvatra samadarśanaḥ

The Yogī who is united in identity with the all-pervading, infinite consciousness, whose vision everywhere is even, beholds the Self existing in all beings and all beings as assumed in the Self. (29)

यो मां पश्यति सर्वत्र सर्वं च मयि पश्यति।
तस्याहं न प्रणश्यामि स च मे न प्रणश्यति॥ ३०॥

yo māṁ paśyati sarvatra sarvaṁ ca mayi paśyati
tasyāhaṁ na praṇaśyāmi sa ca me na praṇaśyati

He who sees Me (the Universal Self) present in all beings, and all beings existing within Me, he is never lost to me, nor am I ever lost to him. (30)

सर्वभूतस्थितं यो मां भजत्येकत्वमास्थितः।
सर्वथा वर्तमानोऽपि स योगी मयि वर्तते॥ ३१॥

sarvabhūtasthitaṁ yo māṁ bhajatyekatvamāsthitaḥ
sarvathā vartamāno'pi sa yogī mayi vartate

The Yogī who is established in union with Me, and worships Me as residing in all beings as their very

Self, does all his activities with Me. (31)

आत्मौपम्येन सर्वत्र समं पश्यति योऽर्जुन।
सुखं वा यदि वा दुःखं स योगी परमो मतः ॥ ३२ ॥

ātmaupamyena sarvatra samaṁ paśyati yo'rjuna
sukhaṁ vā yadi vā duḥkhaṁ sa yogī paramo mataḥ

Arjuna, he who looks on all as one, on the analogy of his own self, and looks upon the joy and sorrow of all equally–such a Yogī is deemed to be the highest of all. (32)

अर्जुन उवाच

योऽयं योगस्त्वया प्रोक्तः साम्येन मधुसूदन।
एतस्याहं न पश्यामि चञ्चलत्वात्स्थितिं स्थिराम् ॥ ३३ ॥

arjuna uvāca

yo'yaṁ yogastvayā proktaḥ sāmyena madhusūdana
etasyāhaṁ na paśyāmi cañcalatvātsthitiṁ sthirām

Arjun said : Kṛṣṇa, owing to restlessness of mind I do not perceive the stability of this Yoga in the form of equanimity, which You have just spoken of. (33)

चञ्चलं हि मनः कृष्ण प्रमाथि बलवद्दृढम्।
तस्याहं निग्रहं मन्ये वायोरिव सुदुष्करम् ॥ ३४ ॥

cañcalaṁ hi manaḥ kṛṣṇa pramāthi balavaddṛḍham
tasyāhaṁ nigrahaṁ manye vāyoriva suduṣkaram

For, Kṛṣṇa, the mind is very unsteady, turbulent, tenacious and powerful; therefore, I consider it as difficult to control as the wind. (34)

श्रीभगवानुवाच

असंशयं महाबाहो मनो दुर्निग्रहं चलम्।
अभ्यासेन तु कौन्तेय वैराग्येण च गृह्यते॥ ३५॥

śrībhagavānuvāca

asaṁśayaṁ mahābāho mano durnigrahaṁ calam
abhyāsena tu kaunteya vairāgyeṇa ca gṛhyate

Śrī Bhagavān said : The mind is restless no doubt, and difficult to curb, Arjuna; but it can be brought under control by repeated practice (of meditation) and by the exercise of dispassion, O son of Kuntī. (35)

असंयतात्मना योगो दुष्प्राप इति मे मतिः।
वश्यात्मना तु यतता शक्योऽवाप्तुमुपायतः॥ ३६॥

asaṁyatātmanā yogo duṣprāpa iti me matiḥ
vaśyātmanā tu yatatā śakyo'vāptumupāyataḥ

Yoga is difficult of achievement for one whose mind is not subdued; by him, however, who has the mind under control, and is ceaselessly striving, it can be easily attained through practice. Such is My conviction. (36)

अर्जुन उवाच

अयतिः श्रद्धयोपेतो योगाच्चलितमानसः।
अप्राप्य योगसंसिद्धिं कां गतिं कृष्ण गच्छति॥ ३७॥

arjuna uvāca

ayatiḥ śraddhayopeto yogāccalitamānasaḥ
aprāpya yogasaṁsiddhiṁ kāṁ gatiṁ kṛṣṇa gacchati

Arjuna said : Kṛṣṇa, what becomes of the soul who, though endowed with faith, has not been able to subdue his passions, and whose mind is therefore diverted from Yoga (at the time of death), and who thus fails to reach perfection in Yoga (God-realization)? (37)

कच्चिन्नोभयविभ्रष्टश्छिन्नाभ्रमिव नश्यति।
अप्रतिष्ठो महाबाहो विमूढो ब्रह्मणः पथि॥ ३८॥

kaccinnobhayavibhraṣṭaśchinnābhramiva naśyati
apratiṣṭho mahābāho vimūḍho brahmaṇaḥ pathi

Kṛṣṇa, swerved from the path leading to God-realization and without anything to stand upon, is he not lost like the scattered cloud, deprived of both God-realization and heavenly enjoyment? (38)

एतन्मे संशयं कृष्ण छेत्तुमर्हस्यशेषतः।
त्वदन्यः संशयस्यास्य छेत्ता न ह्युपपद्यते॥ ३९॥

etanme saṁśayaṁ kṛṣṇa chettumarhasyaśeṣataḥ
tvadanyaḥ saṁśayasyāsya chettā na hyupapadyate

Kṛṣṇa, only You are capable to remove this doubt of mine completely; for none other than you can dispel this doubt. (39)

श्रीभगवानुवाच

पार्थ नैवेह नामुत्र विनाशस्तस्य विद्यते।
न हि कल्याणकृत्कश्चिद्दुर्गतिं तात गच्छति॥ ४०॥

śrībhagavānuvāca

pārtha naiveha nāmutra vināśastasya vidyate
na hi kalyāṇakṛtkaściddurgatiṁ tāta gacchati

Śrī Bhagavān said : Dear Arjuna, there is no fall for him either here or hereafter. For none who strives for self-redemption (i.e., God-realization) ever meets with evil destiny. (40)

प्राप्य पुण्यकृतां लोकानुषित्वा शाश्वतीः समाः ।
शुचीनां श्रीमतां गेहे योगभ्रष्टोऽभिजायते ॥ ४१ ॥

prāpya puṇyakṛtāṁ lokānuṣitvā śāśvatīḥ samāḥ
śucīnāṁ śrīmatāṁ gehe yogabhraṣṭo'bhijāyate

Such a person who has strayed from Yoga, obtains the higher worlds, (heaven etc.) to which men of meritorious deeds alone are entitled, and having resided there for innumerable years, takes birth of pious and prosperous parents. (41)

अथवा योगिनामेव कुले भवति धीमताम् ।
एतद्धि दुर्लभतरं लोके जन्म यदीदृशम् ॥ ४२ ॥

athavā yogināmeva kule bhavati dhīmatām
etaddhi durlabhataraṁ loke janma yadīdṛśam

Or (if he is possessed of dispassion) he is born in the family of enlightened Yogīs; but such a birth in this world is very difficult to obtain. (42)

तत्र तं बुद्धिसंयोगं लभते पौर्वदेहिकम् ।
यतते च ततो भूयः संसिद्धौ कुरुनन्दन ॥ ४३ ॥

tatra taṁ buddhisaṁyogaṁ labhate paurvadehikam
yatate ca tato bhūyaḥ saṁsiddhau kurunandana

Arjuna, he automatically regains in that birth the spiritual insight of his previous birth; and through that he strives, harder than ever, for perfection (in the form of God-realization). (43)

पूर्वाभ्यासेन तेनैव ह्रियते ह्यवशोऽपि सः।
जिज्ञासुरपि योगस्य शब्दब्रह्मातिवर्तते ॥ ४४ ॥

pūrvābhyāsena tenaiva hriyate hyavaśo'pi saḥ
jijñāsurapi yogasya śabdabrahmātivartate

The other one who takes birth in a rich family, though under the sway of his senses, feels drawn towards God by force of the habit acquired in his previous birth; nay, even the seeker of enlightenment on Yoga (in the form of evenmindedness) transcends the fruit of actions performed with some interested motive as laid down in the Vedas. (44)

प्रयत्नाद्यतमानस्तु योगी संशुद्धकिल्बिषः।
अनेकजन्मसंसिद्धस्ततो याति परां गतिम् ॥ ४५ ॥

prayatnādyatamānastu yogī saṁśuddhakilbiṣaḥ
anekajanmasaṁsiddhastato yāti parāṁ gatim

The Yogī, however, who diligently takes up the practice attains perfection in this very life with the help of latencies of many births, and being thoroughly purged of sin, forthwith reaches the supreme state. (45)

तपस्विभ्योऽधिको योगी ज्ञानिभ्योऽपि मतोऽधिकः।
कर्मिभ्यश्चाधिको योगी तस्माद्योगी भवार्जुन॥ ४६॥

tapasvibhyo'dhiko yogī jñānibhyo'pi mato'dhikaḥ
karmibhyaścādhiko yogī tasmādyogī bhavārjuna

The Yogī is superior to the ascetics; he is regarded superior even to those versed in sacred lore. The Yogī is also superior to those who perform action with some interested motive. Therefore, Arjuna, do become a Yogī. (46)

योगिनामपि सर्वेषां मद्गतेनान्तरात्मना।
श्रद्धावान्भजते यो मां स मे युक्ततमो मतः॥ ४७॥

yogināmapi sarveṣāṁ madgatenāntarātmanā
śraddhāvānbhajate yo māṁ sa me yuktatamo mataḥ

Of all Yogīs, again, he who devoutly worships Me with his mind focussed on Me is considered by Me to be the best Yogī. (47)

ॐ तत्सदिति श्रीमद्भगवद्गीतासूपनिषत्सु ब्रह्मविद्यायां
योगशास्त्रे श्रीकृष्णार्जुनसंवादे आत्मसंयमयोगो
नाम षष्ठोऽध्यायः॥ ६॥

Thus, in the Upaniṣad sung by the Lord, the Science of Brahma, the scripture of Yoga, the dialogue between Śrī Kṛṣṇa and Arjuna, ends the sixth chapter entitled "The Yoga of Self-Control."

ॐ श्रीपरमात्मने नमः

अथ सप्तमोऽध्यायः

CHAPTER SEVEN

श्रीभगवानुवाच

मय्यासक्तमनाः पार्थ योगं युञ्जन्मदाश्रयः।
असंशयं समग्रं मां यथा ज्ञास्यसि तच्छृणु॥ १॥

śrībhagavānuvāca

mayyāsaktamanāḥ pārtha yogaṁ yuñjanmadāśrayaḥ
asaṁśayaṁ samagraṁ māṁ yathā jñāsyasi tacchṛṇu

Śrī Bhagavān said : Arjuna, now listen how with the mind attached to Me (through exclusive love) and practising Yoga with absolute dependence on Me, you will know Me (the Repository of all power, strength and glory and other attributes, the Universal soul) in entirety and without any shadow of doubt. (1)

ज्ञानं तेऽहं सविज्ञानमिदं वक्ष्याम्यशेषतः।
यज्ज्ञात्वा नेह भूयोऽन्यज्ज्ञातव्यमवशिष्यते॥ २॥

jñānaṁ te'haṁ savijñānamidaṁ vakṣyāmyaśeṣataḥ
yajjñātvā neha bhūyo'nyajjñātavyamavaśiṣyate

I shall unfold to you in its entirety this wisdom (Knowledge of God in His absolute formless aspect) along with the Knowledge of the qualified aspect of God (both with form and without form), having known which nothing else remains yet to be known in this world. (2)

मनुष्याणां सहस्रेषु कश्चिद्यतति सिद्धये।
यततामपि सिद्धानां कश्चिन्मां वेत्ति तत्त्वतः॥ ३॥

manuṣyāṇāṁ sahasreṣu kaścidyatati siddhaye
yatatāmapi siddhānāṁ kaścinmāṁ vetti tattvataḥ

Hardly one among thousands of men strives to realize Me; of those striving Yogīs, again, some rare one, devoting himself exclusively to Me, knows Me in reality. (3)

भूमिरापोऽनलो वायुः खं मनो बुद्धिरेव च।
अहङ्कार इतीयं मे भिन्ना प्रकृतिरष्टधा॥ ४॥
अपरेयमितस्त्वन्यां प्रकृतिं विद्धि मे पराम्।
जीवभूतां महाबाहो ययेदं धार्यते जगत्॥ ५॥

bhūmirāpo'nalo vāyuḥ khaṁ mano buddhireva ca
ahaṅkāra itīyaṁ me bhinnā prakṛtiraṣṭadhā
apareyamitastvanyāṁ prakṛtiṁ viddhi me parām
jīvabhūtāṁ mahābāho yayedaṁ dhāryate jagat

Earth, water, fire, air, ether, mind, reason and also ego; these constitute My nature divided into eight parts. This indeed is My lower (material) nature; the other than this, by which the whole universe is sustained, know it to be My higher (or spiritual) nature in the form of Jīva (the life-principle), O Arjuna. (4-5)

एतद्योनीनि भूतानि सर्वाणीत्युपधारय।
अहं कृत्स्नस्य जगतः प्रभवः प्रलयस्तथा॥ ६॥

etadyonīni bhūtāni sarvāṇītyupadhāraya
ahaṁ kṛtsnasya jagataḥ prabhavaḥ pralayastathā

Arjuna, know that all beings have evolved from this twofold Prakṛti, and that I am the source of the entire creation, and into Me again it disappears. (6)

मत्तः परतरं नान्यत्किञ्चिदस्ति धनञ्जय।
मयि सर्वमिदं प्रोतं सूत्रे मणिगणा इव॥ ७॥

mattaḥ parataraṁ nānyatkiñcidasti dhanañjaya
mayi sarvamidaṁ protaṁ sūtre maṇigaṇā iva

There is nothing else besides Me, Arjuna. Like clusters of yarn-beads formed by knots on a thread, all this is threaded on Me. (7)

रसोऽहमप्सु कौन्तेय प्रभास्मि शशिसूर्ययोः।
प्रणवः सर्ववेदेषु शब्दः खे पौरुषं नृषु॥ ८॥

raso'hamapsu kaunteya prabhāsmi śaśisūryayoḥ
praṇavaḥ sarvavedeṣu śabdaḥ khe pauruṣaṁ nṛṣu

Arjuna, I am the sap in water and the radiance of the moon and the sun; I am the sacred syllable OṀ in all the Vedas, the sound in ether, and the manliness in men. (8)

पुण्यो गन्धः पृथिव्यां च तेजश्चास्मि विभावसौ।
जीवनं सर्वभूतेषु तपश्चास्मि तपस्विषु॥ ९॥

puṇyo gandhaḥ pṛthivyāṁ ca tejaścāsmi vibhāvasau
jīvanaṁ sarvabhūteṣu tapaścāsmi tapasviṣu

I am the pure odour (the subtle principle of smell) in the earth and the brightness in fire; nay, I am the life in all beings and austerity in men of ascetics. (9)

बीजं मां सर्वभूतानां विद्धि पार्थ सनातनम्।
बुद्धिर्बुद्धिमतामस्मि तेजस्तेजस्विनामहम्॥ १०॥

bījaṁ māṁ sarvabhutānāṁ viddhi pārtha sanātanam
buddhirbuddhimatāmasmi tejastejasvināmaham

Arjuna, know Me the eternal seed of all beings. I am the intelligence of the intelligent; the glory of the glorious am I. (10)

बलं बलवतां चाहं कामरागविवर्जितम्।
धर्माविरुद्धो भूतेषु कामोऽस्मि भरतर्षभ॥ ११॥

balaṁ balavatāṁ cāhaṁ kāmarāgavivarjitam
dharmāviruddho bhūteṣu kāmo'smi bharatarṣabha

Arjuna, of the mighty I am the might, free from passion and desire; in beings I am the sexual desire not conflicting with virtue or scriptural injunctions. (11)

ये चैव सात्त्विका भावा राजसास्तामसाश्च ये।
मत्त एवेति तान्विद्धि न त्वहं तेषु ते मयि॥ १२॥

ye caiva sāttvikā bhāvā rājasāstāmasāśca ye
matta eveti tānviddhi na tvahaṁ teṣu te mayi

Whatever other entities there are, born of Sattva (the quality of goodness), and those that are born of Rājas (the principle of activity) and Tamas (the principle of inertia), know them all as evolved from Me alone. In reality, however, neither do I exist in them, nor do they in Me. (12)

त्रिभिर्गुणमयैर्भावैरेभिः सर्वमिदं जगत्।
मोहितं नाभिजानाति मामेभ्यः परमव्ययम्॥ १३॥

tribhirguṇamayairbhāvairebhiḥ sarvamidaṁ jagat
mohitaṁ nābhijānāti māmebhyaḥ paramavyayam

The whole of this creation is deluded by these objects evolved from the three modes of Prakṛti—Sattva, Rajas and Tamas; that is why the world fails to recognize Me, standing apart from these and imperishable. (13)

दैवी ह्येषा गुणमयी मम माया दुरत्यया।
मामेव ये प्रपद्यन्ते मायामेतां तरन्ति ते॥ १४॥

daivī hyeṣā guṇamayī mama māyā duratyayā
māmeva ye prapadyante māyāmetāṁ taranti te

For this most wonderful Māyā (veil) of Mine, consisting of the three Guṇas (modes of Nature), is extremely difficult to break through; those, however, who constantly adore Me alone are able to cross it. (14)

न मां दुष्कृतिनो मूढाः प्रपद्यन्ते नराधमाः।
माययापहृतज्ञाना आसुरं भावमाश्रिताः॥ १५॥

na māṁ duṣkṛtino mūḍhāḥ prapadyante narādhamāḥ
māyayāpahṛtajñānā āsuraṁ bhāvamāśritāḥ

Those whose wisdom has been carried away by Māyā, and who have embraced the demoniac nature, such foolish and vile men of evil deeds do not adore Me. (15)

चतुर्विधा भजन्ते मां जनाः सुकृतिनोऽर्जुन।
आर्तो जिज्ञासुरर्थार्थी ज्ञानी च भरतर्षभ॥ १६॥

caturvidhā bhajante māṁ janāḥ sukṛtino'rjuna
ārto jijñāsurarthārthī jñānī ca bharatarṣabha

Four types of devotees of noble deeds worship Me, Arjuna, the seeker after worldly possessions, the afflicted, the seeker for knowledge, and the man of wisdom, O best of Bharatas. (16)

तेषां ज्ञानी नित्ययुक्त एकभक्तिर्विशिष्यते।
प्रियो हि ज्ञानिनोऽत्यर्थमहं स च मम प्रियः॥ १७॥

teṣāṁ jñānī nityayukta ekabhaktirviśiṣyate
priyo hi jñānino'tyarthamahaṁ sa ca mama priyaḥ

Of these the best is the man of wisdom, ever established in identity with Me and possessed of exclusive devotion. For, I am extremely dear to the wise man who knows Me in reality, and he is extremely dear to Me. (17)

उदाराः सर्व एवैते ज्ञानी त्वात्मैव मे मतम्।
आस्थितः स हि युक्तात्मा मामेवानुत्तमां गतिम्॥ १८॥

udārāḥ sarva evaite jñānī tvātmaiva me matam
āsthitaḥ sa hi yuktātmā māmevānuttamāṁ gatim

Indeed all these are noble, but the man of wisdom is My very self; such is My view. For such a devotee, who has his mind and intellect merged in Me, is firmly established in Me alone, the highest goal. (18)

बहूनां जन्मनामन्ते ज्ञानवान्मां प्रपद्यते।
वासुदेवः सर्वमिति स महात्मा सुदुर्लभः ॥ १९ ॥

bahūnāṁ janmanāmante jñānavānmāṁ prapadyate
vāsudevaḥ sarvamiti sa mahātmā sudurlabhaḥ

In the very last of all births the enlightened person worships Me by realizing that all this is God. Such a great soul is very rare indeed. (19)

कामैस्तैस्तैर्हृतज्ञानाः प्रपद्यन्तेऽन्यदेवताः।
तं तं नियममास्थाय प्रकृत्या नियताः स्वया ॥ २० ॥

kāmaistaistairhṛtajñānāḥ prapadyante'nyadevatāḥ
taṁ taṁ niyamamāsthāya prakṛtyā niyatāḥ svayā

Those whose wisdom has been carried away by various desires, being prompted by their own nature, worship other deities, adopting rules relating to each. (20)

यो यो यां यां तनुं भक्तः श्रद्धयार्चितुमिच्छति।
तस्य तस्याचलां श्रद्धां तामेव विदधाम्यहम् ॥ २१ ॥

yo yo yāṁ yāṁ tanuṁ bhaktaḥ śraddhayārcitumicchati
tasya tasyācalāṁ śraddhāṁ tāmeva vidadhāmyaham

Whatever celestial form a devotee (craving for some worldly object) chooses to worship with reverence, I stabilize the faith of that particular devotee in that very form. (21)

स तया श्रद्धया युक्तस्तस्याराधनमीहते।
लभते च ततः कामान्मयैव विहितान्हि तान् ॥ २२ ॥

sa tayā śraddhayā yuktastasyārādhanamīhate
labhate ca tataḥ kāmānmayaiva vihitānhi tān

Endowed with such faith he worships that particular deity and obtains through him without doubt his desired enjoyments as ordained by Myself. (22)

अन्तवत्तु फलं तेषां तद्भवत्यल्पमेधसाम्।
देवान्देवयजो यान्ति मद्भक्ता यान्ति मामपि॥ २३॥

antavattu phalaṁ teṣāṁ tadbhavatyalpamedhasām
devāndevayajo yānti madbhaktā yānti māmapi

The fruit gained by these people of small understanding, however, is perishable. The worshippers of gods attain the gods; whereas My devotees, howsoever they worship Me, eventaully come to Me and Me alone. (23)

अव्यक्तं व्यक्तिमापन्नं मन्यन्ते मामबुद्धयः।
परं भावमजानन्तो ममाव्ययमनुत्तमम्॥ २४॥

avyaktaṁ vyaktimāpannaṁ manyante māmabuddhayaḥ
paraṁ bhāvamajānanto mamāvyayamanuttamam

Not knowing My supreme nature, unsurpassable and undecaying, the ignorants believe Me, who am the Supreme Spirit, beyond the reach of mind and senses, and the embodiment of Truth, Knowledge and Bliss, to have assumed a finite form through birth as an ordinary human being. (24)

नाहं प्रकाशः सर्वस्य योगमायासमावृतः।
मूढोऽयं नाभिजानाति लोको मामजमव्ययम्॥ २५॥

nāhaṁ prakāśaḥ sarvasya yogamāyāsamāvṛtaḥ
mūḍho'yaṁ nābhijānāti loko māmajamavyayam

Veiled by My Yogamāyā (divine potency), I am not manifest to all. Hence these ignorant folk fail to recognize

Me, the unborn and imperishable Supreme Deity (i.e., consider Me as subject to birth and death). (25)

वेदाहं समतीतानि वर्तमानानि चार्जुन।
भविष्याणि च भूतानि मां तु वेद न कश्चन॥ २६॥

vedāhaṁ samatītāni vartamānāni cārjuna
bhaviṣyāṇi ca bhūtāni māṁ tu veda na kaścana

Arjuna, I know all beings, past as well as present, nay, even those that are yet to come; but none, devoid of faith and reverence, knows Me. (26)

इच्छाद्वेषसमुत्थेन द्वन्द्वमोहेन भारत।
सर्वभूतानि सम्मोहं सर्गे यान्ति परन्तप॥ २७॥

icchādveṣasamutthena dvandvamohena bhārata
sarvabhūtāni sammohaṁ sarge yānti parantapa

O valiant Arjuna, through delusion in the shape of pairs of opposites (such as pleasure and pain etc.,) born of desire and hatred, all living creatures in this world are falling a prey to infatuation. (27)

येषां त्वन्तगतं पापं जनानां पुण्यकर्मणाम्।
ते द्वन्द्वमोहनिर्मुक्ता भजन्ते मां दृढव्रताः॥ २८॥

yeṣāṁ tvantagataṁ pāpaṁ janānāṁ puṇyakarmaṇām
te dvandvamohanirmuktā bhajante māṁ dṛḍhavratāḥ

But those men of virtuous deeds whose sins have come to an end, being freed from delusion in the shape of pairs of opposites (born of attraction and repulsion), worship Me with a firm resolve in every way. (28)

जरामरणमोक्षाय मामाश्रित्य यतन्ति ये।
ते ब्रह्म तद्विदुः कृत्स्नमध्यात्मं कर्म चाखिलम्॥ २९॥
साधिभूताधिदैवं मां साधियज्ञं च ये विदुः।
प्रयाणकालेऽपि च मां ते विदुर्युक्तचेतसः॥ ३०॥

jarāmaraṇamokṣāya māmāśritya yatanti ye
te brahma tadviduḥ kṛtsnamadhyātmaṁ karma cākhilam
sādhibhūtādhidaivaṁ māṁ sādhiyajñaṁ ca ye viduḥ
prayāṇakāle'pi ca māṁ te viduryuktacetasaḥ

They who, having taken refuge in Me, strive for deliverance from old age and death know Brahma (the Absolute), the whole Adhyātma (the totality of Jīvas or embodied souls), and the entire field of Karma (action) as well as My integral being, comprising Adhibhūta (the field of Matter), Adhidaiva (Brahmā) and Adhiyajña (the unmanifest Divinity dwelling in the heart of all beings as their witness). And they who, possessed of a steadfast mind, know thus even at the hour of death, they too know Me alone. (29-30)

ॐ तत्सदिति श्रीमद्भगवद्गीतासूपनिषत्सु ब्रह्मविद्यायां
योगशास्त्रे श्रीकृष्णार्जुनसंवादे ज्ञानविज्ञानयोगो
नाम सप्तमोऽध्यायः॥ ७॥

Thus, in the Upaniṣad sung by the Lord, the Science of Brahma, the scripture of Yoga, the dialogue between Śrī Kṛṣṇa and Arjuna, ends the seventh chapter entitled "The Yoga of Jñāna (Knowledge of Nirguṇa Brahma) and Vijñāna (Knowledge of Manifest Divinity)."

ॐ श्रीपरमात्मने नमः

अथाष्टमोऽध्यायः

CHAPTER EIGHT

अर्जुन उवाच

किं तद्ब्रह्म किमध्यात्मं किं कर्म पुरुषोत्तम।
अधिभूतं च किं प्रोक्तमधिदैवं किमुच्यते॥ १॥

arjuna uvāca

kiṁ tadbrahma kimadhyātmaṁ kiṁ karma puruṣottama
adhibhūtaṁ ca kiṁ proktamadhidaivaṁ kimucyate

Arjuna said : Kṛṣṇa, what is that Brahma (Absolute), what is Adhyātma (Spirit), and what is Karma (Action)? What is called Adhibhūta (Matter) and what is termed as Adhidaiva (Divine Intelligence)? (1)

अधियज्ञः कथं कोऽत्र देहेऽस्मिन्मधुसूदन।
प्रयाणकाले च कथं ज्ञेयोऽसि नियतात्मभिः॥ २॥

adhiyajñaḥ kathaṁ ko'tra dehe'sminmadhusūdana
prayāṇakāle ca kathaṁ jñeyo'si niyatātmabhiḥ

Kṛṣṇa, who is Adhiyajña here and how does he dwell in the body? And how are You to be realized at the time of death by those of steadfast mind? (2)

श्रीभगवानुवाच

अक्षरं ब्रह्म परमं स्वभावोऽध्यात्ममुच्यते।
भूतभावोद्भवकरो विसर्गः कर्मसञ्ज्ञितः॥ ३॥

śrībhagavānuvāca

akṣaraṁ brahma paramaṁ svabhāvo'dhyātmamucyate
bhūtabhāvodbhavakaro visargaḥ karmasañjñitaḥ

Śrī Bhagavān said:The supreme Indestructible is Brahma, one's own Self (the individual soul) is called Adhyātma; and the discharge of spirits, (Visarga), which brings forth the existence of beings, is called Karma (Action). (3)

अधिभूतं क्षरो भावः पुरुषश्चाधिदैवतम्।
अधियज्ञोऽहमेवात्र देहे देहभृतां वर॥ ४॥

adhibhūtaṁ kṣaro bhāvaḥ puruṣaścādhidaivatam
adhiyajño'hamevātra dehe dehabhṛtāṁ vara

All perishable objects are Adhibhūta; the shining Puruṣa (Brahmā) is Adhidaiva; and in this body I Myself, dwelling as the inner witness, am Adhiyajña, O Arjuna! (4)

अन्तकाले च मामेव स्मरन्मुक्त्वा कलेवरम्।
यः प्रयाति स मद्भावं याति नास्त्यत्र संशयः॥ ५॥

antakāle ca māmeva smaranmuktvā kalevaram
yaḥ prayāti sa madbhāvaṁ yāti nāstyatra saṁśayaḥ

He who departs from the body, thinking of Me alone even at the time of death, attains My state; there is no doubt about it. (5)

यं यं वापि स्मरन्भावं त्यजत्यन्ते कलेवरम्।
तं तमेवैति कौन्तेय सदा तद्भावभावितः॥ ६॥

yaṁ yaṁ vāpi smaranbhāvaṁ tyajatyante kalevaram
taṁ tamevaiti kaunteya sadā tadbhāvabhāvitaḥ

Arjuna, thinking of whatever entity one leaves the body at the time of death, that and that alone one attains, being ever absorbed in its thought. (6)

तस्मात्सर्वेषु कालेषु मामनुस्मर युध्य च।
मय्यर्पितमनोबुद्धिर्मामेवैष्यस्यसंशयम् ॥ ७ ॥

tasmātsarveṣu kāleṣu māmanusmara yudhya ca
mayyarpitamanobuddhirmāmevaiṣyasyasaṁśayam

Therefore, Arjuna, think of Me at all times and fight. With mind and reason thus set on Me, you will doubtless come to Me. (7)

अभ्यासयोगयुक्तेन चेतसा नान्यगामिना।
परमं पुरुषं दिव्यं याति पार्थानुचिन्तयन्॥ ८ ॥

abhyāsayogayuktena cetasā nānyagāminā
paramaṁ puruṣaṁ divyaṁ yāti pārthānucintayan

Arjuna, he who with his mind disciplined through Yoga in the form of practice of meditation and thinking of nothing else, is constantly engaged in contemplation of God attains the supremely effulgent Divine Puruṣa (God). (8)

कविं पुराणमनुशासितार-
मणोरणीयांसमनुस्मरेद्यः ।
सर्वस्य धातारमचिन्त्यरूप-
मादित्यवर्णं तमसः परस्तात्॥ ९ ॥

kavim purāṇamanuśāsitāra-
maṇoraṇīyāṁsamanusmaredyaḥ
sarvasya dhātāramacintyarūpa-
mādityavarṇaṁ tamasaḥ parastāt

He who contemplates on the all-wise, ageless Being, the Ruler of all, subtler than the subtle, the universal sustainer, possessing a form beyond human conception, effulgent like the sun and far beyond the darkness of ignorance. (9)

प्रयाणकाले मनसाचलेन
भक्त्या युक्तो योगबलेन चैव।
भ्रुवोर्मध्ये प्राणमावेश्य सम्यक्-
स तं परं पुरुषमुपैति दिव्यम्॥ १०॥

prayāṇakāle manasācalena
bhaktyā yukto yogabalena caiva
bhruvormadhye prāṇamāveśya samyak-
sa taṁ paraṁ puruṣamupaiti divyam

Having by the power of Yoga firmly held the life-breath in the space between the two eyebrows even at the time of death, and then contemplating on God with a steadfast mind, full of devotion, he reaches verily that supreme divine Puruṣa (God). (10)

यदक्षरं वेदविदो वदन्ति
विशन्ति यद्यतयो वीतरागाः।
यदिच्छन्तो ब्रह्मचर्यं चरन्ति
तत्ते पदं सङ्ग्रहेण प्रवक्ष्ये॥ ११॥

yadakṣaraṁ vedavido vadanti
viśanti yadyatayo vītarāgāḥ
yadicchanto brahmacaryaṁ caranti
tatte padaṁ saṅgraheṇa pravakṣye

I shall tell you briefly about that Supreme goal (viz., God, who is an embodiment of Truth, Knowledge and Bliss), which the knowers of the Veda term as the Indestructible; which striving recluses free from passion enter, and desiring which the celibates practise Brahmacarya. (11)

सर्वद्वाराणि संयम्य मनो हृदि निरुध्य च।
मूर्ध्न्याधायात्मनः प्राणमास्थितो योगधारणाम्॥ १२॥
ओमित्येकाक्षरं ब्रह्म व्याहरन्मामनुस्मरन्।
यः प्रयाति त्यजन्देहं स याति परमां गतिम्॥ १३॥

sarvadvārāṇi saṁyamya mano hṛdi nirudhya ca
mūrdhnyādhāyātmanaḥ prāṇamāsthito yogadhāraṇām
omityekākṣaraṁ brahma vyāharanmāmanusmaran
yaḥ prayāti tyajandehaṁ sa yāti paramāṁ gatim

Having closed all the doors of the senses, and firmly holding the mind in the cavity of the heart, and then fixing the life-breath in the head, and thus remaining steadfast in Yogic concentration on God, he who leaves the body and departs uttering the one Indestructible Brahma, OM, and dwelling on Me in My absolute aspect, reaches the supreme goal. (12-13)

अनन्यचेताः सततं यो मां स्मरति नित्यशः।
तस्याहं सुलभः पार्थ नित्ययुक्तस्य योगिनः॥ १४॥

ananyacetāḥ satataṁ yo māṁ smarati nityaśaḥ
tasyāhaṁ sulabhaḥ pārtha nityayuktasya yoginaḥ

Arjuna, whosoever always and constantly thinks of Me with undivided mind, to that Yogī ever absorbed in Me I am easily attainable. (14)

मामुपेत्य पुनर्जन्म दुःखालयमशाश्वतम्।
नाप्नुवन्ति महात्मानः संसिद्धिं परमां गताः॥ १५॥

māmupetya punarjanma duḥkhālayamaśāśvatam
nāpnuvanti mahātmānaḥ saṁsiddhiṁ paramāṁ gatāḥ

Great souls, who have attained the highest perfection, having come to Me, are no more subjected to rebirth, which is the abode of sorrow, and transient by nature. (15)

आब्रह्मभुवनाल्लोकाः पुनरावर्तिनोऽर्जुन।
मामुपेत्य तु कौन्तेय पुनर्जन्म न विद्यते॥ १६॥

ābrahmabhuvanāllokāḥ punarāvartino'rjuna
māmupetya tu kaunteya punarjanma na vidyate

Arjuna, all the worlds from Brahmaloka (the heavenly realm of the Creator, Brahmā) downwards are liable to appear and reappear. But, O son of Kuntī, on attaining Me there is no rebirth (For, while I am beyond Time, regions like Brahmaloka, being conditioned by time, are transitory). (16)

सहस्रयुगपर्यन्तमहर्यद्ब्रह्मणो विदुः।
रात्रिं युगसहस्रान्तां तेऽहोरात्रविदो जनाः॥ १७॥

sahasrayugaparyantamaharyadbrahmaṇo viduḥ
rātriṁ yugasahasrāntāṁ te'horātravido janāḥ

Those Yogīs who know from realization Brahmā's day as covering a thousand Mahāyugas, and so his night as extending to another thousand Mahāyugas know the reality about Time. (17)

अव्यक्ताद्व्यक्तयः सर्वाः प्रभवन्त्यहरागमे।
रात्र्यागमे प्रलीयन्ते तत्रैवाव्यक्तसञ्ज्ञके॥ १८॥

avyaktādvyaktayaḥ sarvāḥ prabhavantyaharāgame
rātryāgame pralīyante tatraivāvyaktasañjñake

All embodied beings emanate from the Unmanifest (i.e., Brahmā's subtle body) at the coming of the cosmic day; at the cosmic nightfall they merge into the same subtle body of Brahmā, known as the Unmanifest. (18)

भूतग्रामः स एवायं भूत्वा भूत्वा प्रलीयते।
रात्र्यागमेऽवशः पार्थ प्रभवत्यहरागमे॥ १९॥

bhūtagrāmaḥ sa evāyaṁ bhūtvā bhūtvā pralīyate
rātryāgame'vaśaḥ pārtha prabhavatyaharāgame

Arjuna, this multitude of beings, being born again and again, is dissolved under compulsion of its nature at the coming of the cosmic night, and rises again at the commencement of the cosmic day. (19)

परस्तस्मात्तु भावोऽन्योऽव्यक्तोऽव्यक्तात्सनातनः।
यः स सर्वेषु भूतेषु नश्यत्सु न विनश्यति॥ २०॥

parastasmāttu bhāvo'nyo'vyakto'vyaktātsanātanaḥ
yaḥ sa sarveṣu bhūteṣu naśyatsu na vinaśyati

Far beyond even this unmanifest, there is yet another unmanifest Existence, that Supreme Divine Person, who does not perish even though all beings perish. (20)

अव्यक्तोऽक्षर इत्युक्तस्तमाहुः परमां गतिम्।
यं प्राप्य न निवर्तन्ते तद्धाम परमं मम॥ २१॥

avyakto'kṣara ityuktastamāhuḥ paramāṁ gatim
yaṁ prāpya na nivartante taddhāma paramaṁ mama

The same unmanifest which has been spoken of as the Indestructible is also called the supreme Goal; that again is My supreme Abode, attaining which they return not to this mortal world. (21)

पुरुषः स परः पार्थ भक्त्या लभ्यस्त्वनन्यया।
यस्यान्तःस्थानि भूतानि येन सर्वमिदं ततम्॥ २२॥

puruṣaḥ sa paraḥ pārtha bhaktyā labhyastvananyayā
yasyāntaḥsthāni bhūtāni yena sarvamidaṁ tatam

Arjuna, that eternal unmanifest supreme Puruṣa in whom all beings reside and by whom all this is pervaded, is attainable only through exclusive Devotion. (22)

यत्र काले त्वनावृत्तिमावृत्तिं चैव योगिनः।
प्रयाता यान्ति तं कालं वक्ष्यामि भरतर्षभ॥ २३॥

yatra kāle tvanāvṛttimāvṛttiṁ caiva yoginaḥ
prayātā yānti taṁ kālaṁ vakṣyāmi bharatarṣabha

Arjuna, I shall now tell you the time (path) departing when Yogīs do not return, and also the time (path) departing when they do return. (23)

अग्निर्ज्योतिरहः शुक्लः षण्मासा उत्तरायणम्।
तत्र प्रयाता गच्छन्ति ब्रह्म ब्रह्मविदो जनाः॥ २४॥

agnirjyotirahaḥ śuklaḥ ṣaṇmāsā uttarāyaṇam
tatra prayātā gacchanti brahma brahmavido janāḥ

(Of the two paths) the one is that in which are stationed the all-effulgent fire-god and the deities presiding over daylight, the bright fortnight, and the six months of the northward course of the sun respectively; proceeding along it after death Yogīs, who have known Brahma, being successively led by the above gods, finally reach Brahma. (24)

धूमो रात्रिस्तथा कृष्णः षण्मासा दक्षिणायनम्।
तत्र चान्द्रमसं ज्योतिर्योगी प्राप्य निवर्तते॥ २५॥

dhūmo rātristathā kṛṣṇaḥ ṣaṇmāsā dakṣiṇāyanam
tatra cāndramasaṁ jyotiryogī prāpya nivartate

The other path is that wherein are stationed the gods presiding over smoke, night, the dark fortnight, and the six months of the southward course of the sun; the Yogī (devoted to action with an interested motive) taking to this path after death is led by the above gods, one after another, and attaining the lustre of the moon (and enjoying the fruit of his meritorious deeds in heaven) returns to this mortal world. (25)

शुक्लकृष्णे गती ह्येते जगतः शाश्वते मते।
एकया यात्यनावृत्तिमन्ययावर्तते पुनः॥ २६॥

śuklakṛṣṇe gatī hyete jagataḥ śāśvate mate
ekayā yātyanāvṛttimanyayāvartate punaḥ

For these two paths of the world, the bright and the dark, are considered to be eternal. Proceeding by one of them, one reaches the supreme state from which there is no return; and proceeding by the other, one returns to the mortal world, i.e., becomes subject to birth and death once more. (26)

नैते सृती पार्थ जानन्योगी मुह्यति कश्चन।
तस्मात्सर्वेषु कालेषु योगयुक्तो भवार्जुन॥ २७॥

naite sṛtī pārtha jānanyogī muhyati kaścana
tasmātsarveṣu kāleṣu yogayukto bhavārjuna

Knowing thus the secret of these two paths, O son of Kuntī no Yogī gets deluded. Therefore, Arjuna, at all times be steadfast in Yoga in the form of equanimity (i.e., strive constantly for My realization). (27)

वेदेषु यज्ञेषु तपःसु चैव
दानेषु यत्पुण्यफलं प्रदिष्टम्।
अत्येति तत्सर्वमिदं विदित्वा
योगी परं स्थानमुपैति चाद्यम्॥ २८॥

vedeṣu yajñeṣu tapaḥsu caiva
dāneṣu yatpuṇyaphalaṁ pradiṣṭam
atyeti tatsarvamidaṁ viditvā
yogī paraṁ sthānamupaiti cādyam

The Yogī, realizing this profound truth, doubtless transcends all the rewards enumerated for the study of the Vedas as well as for the performance of sacrifices, austerities and charities, and attains the supreme and primal state. (28)

ॐ तत्सदिति श्रीमद्भगवद्गीतासूपनिषत्सु ब्रह्मविद्यायां
योगशास्त्रे श्रीकृष्णार्जुनसंवादे अक्षरब्रह्मयोगो
नामाष्टमोऽध्यायः ॥ ८ ॥

Thus, in the Upaniṣad sung by the Lord, the Science of Brahma, the scripture of Yoga, the dialogue between Śrī Kṛṣṇa and Arjuna, ends the eighth chapter entitled "The Yoga of the Indestructible Brahma."

ॐ श्रीपरमात्मने नमः

अथ नवमोऽध्यायः

CHAPTER NINE

श्रीभगवानुवाच

इदं तु ते गुह्यतमं प्रवक्ष्याम्यनसूयवे।
ज्ञानं विज्ञानसहितं यज्ज्ञात्वा मोक्ष्यसेऽशुभात्॥ १॥

śrībhagavānuvāca

idaṁ tu te guhyatamaṁ pravakṣyāmyanasūyave
jñānaṁ vijñānasahitaṁ yajjñātvā mokṣyase'śubhāt

Śrī Bhagavān said : To you, who are devoid of the carping spirit, I shall now unfold the most secret knowledge of Nirguṇa Brahma along with the knowledge of manifest Divinity, knowing which you shall be free from the evil of worldly existence. (1)

राजविद्या राजगुह्यं पवित्रमिदमुत्तमम्।
प्रत्यक्षावगमं धर्म्यं सुसुखं कर्तुमव्ययम्॥ २॥

rājavidyā rājaguhyaṁ pavitramidamuttamam
pratyakṣāvagamaṁ dharmyaṁ susukhaṁ kartumavyayam

This knowledge (of both the Nirguṇa and Saguṇa aspects of Divinity) is a sovereign science, a sovereign secret, supremely holy, most excellent, directly enjoyable, attended with virtue, very easy to practise and imperishable. (2)

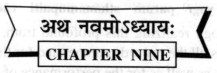

अश्रद्दधानाः पुरुषा धर्मस्यास्य परन्तप।
अप्राप्य मां निवर्तन्ते मृत्युसंसारवर्त्मनि॥ ३॥

aśraddadhānāḥ puruṣā dharmasyāsya parantapa
aprāpya māṁ nivartante mṛtyusaṁsāravartmani

Arjuna, people having no faith in this Dharma, failing to reach Me, continue to revolve in the path of the world of birth and death. (3)

मया ततमिदं सर्वं जगदव्यक्तमूर्तिना।
मत्स्थानि सर्वभूतानि न चाहं तेष्ववस्थितः॥ ४॥

mayā tatamidaṁ sarvaṁ jagadavyaktamūrtinā
matsthāni sarvabhūtāni na cāhaṁ teṣvavasthitaḥ

The whole of this universe is permeated by Me as unmanifest Divinity, and all beings rest on the idea within Me. Therefore, really speaking, I am not present in them. (4)

न च मत्स्थानि भूतानि पश्य मे योगमैश्वरम्।
भूतभृन्न च भूतस्थो ममात्मा भूतभावनः॥ ५॥

na ca matsthāni bhūtāni paśya me yogamaiśvaram
bhūtabhṛnna ca bhūtastho mamātmā bhūtabhāvanaḥ

Nay, all those beings abide not in Me; but behold the wonderful power of My divine Yoga; though the Sustainer and Creator of beings, Myself in reality dwells not in those beings. (5)

यथाकाशस्थितो नित्यं वायुः सर्वत्रगो महान्।
तथा सर्वाणि भूतानि मत्स्थानीत्युपधारय॥ ६॥

**yathākāśasthito nityaṁ vāyuḥ sarvatrago mahān
tathā sarvāṇi bhūtāni matsthānītyupadhāraya**

Just as the extensive air, which is moving everywhere, (being born of ether) ever remains in ether, likewise know that all beings (who have originated from My thought) abide in Me. (6)

सर्वभूतानि कौन्तेय प्रकृतिं यान्ति मामिकाम्।
कल्पक्षये पुनस्तानि कल्पादौ विसृजाम्यहम्॥ ७॥

**sarvabhūtāni kaunteya prakṛtiṁ yānti māmikām
kalpakṣaye punastāni kalpādau visṛjāmyaham**

Arjuna, during the Final Dissolution all beings enter My Prakṛti (the prime cause), and at the beginning of creation, I send them forth again. (7)

प्रकृतिं स्वामवष्टभ्य विसृजामि पुनः पुनः।
भूतग्राममिमं कृत्स्नमवशं प्रकृतेर्वशात्॥ ८॥

**prakṛtiṁ svāmavaṣṭabhya visṛjāmi punaḥ punaḥ
bhūtagrāmamimaṁ kṛtsnamavaśaṁ prakṛtervaśāt**

Wielding My Nature I release, again and again (according to their respective Karmas) all this multitude of beings subject to the influence of their own nature. (8)

न च मां तानि कर्माणि निबध्नन्ति धनञ्जय।
उदासीनवदासीनमसक्तं तेषु कर्मसु॥ ९॥

**na ca māṁ tāni karmāṇi nibadhnanti dhanañjaya
udāsīnavadāsīnamasaktaṁ teṣu karmasu**

Arjuna, those actions, however, do not bind Me, unattached as I am to such actions and standing apart as it were. (9)

मयाध्यक्षेण प्रकृतिः सूयते सचराचरम्।
हेतुनानेन कौन्तेय जगद्विपरिवर्तते॥ १०॥

mayādhyakṣeṇa prakṛtiḥ sūyate sacarācaram
hetunānena kaunteya jagadviparivartate

Arjuna, with Me as the supervisor, Nature brings forth the whole creation, consisting of both sentient and insentient beings; it is due to this cause that the wheel of Saṁsāra is going round. (10)

अवजानन्ति मां मूढा मानुषीं तनुमाश्रितम्।
परं भावमजानन्तो मम भूतमहेश्वरम्॥ ११॥

avajānanti māṁ mūḍhā mānuṣīṁ tanumāśritam
paraṁ bhāvamajānanto mama bhūtamaheśvaram

Not Knowing My supreme nature, fools disregard Me, the Overlord of the entire creation, who have assumed the human form. (That is to say, they take Me, who have appeared in human form through My 'Yogamāyā' for deliverance of the world, as an ordinary mortal.) (11)

मोघाशा मोघकर्माणो मोघज्ञाना विचेतसः।
राक्षसीमासुरीं चैव प्रकृतिं मोहिनीं श्रिताः॥ १२॥

moghāśā moghakarmāṇo moghajñānā vicetasaḥ
rākṣasīmāsurīṁ caiva prakṛtiṁ mohinīṁ śritāḥ

Those bewildered persons with vain hopes, futile actions and fruitless knowledge have embraced a fiendish, demoniacal and delusive nature. (12)

महात्मानस्तु मां पार्थ दैवीं प्रकृतिमाश्रिताः।
भजन्त्यनन्यमनसो ज्ञात्वा भूतादिमव्ययम्॥ १३॥

mahātmānastu māṁ pārtha daivīṁ prakṛtimāśritāḥ
bhajantyananyamanaso jñātvā bhūtādimavyayam

On the other hand, Arjuna, great souls who have adopted the divine nature, knowing Me as the prime source of all beings and the imperishable, eternal, worship Me constantly with one pointedness of mind. (13)

सततं कीर्तयन्तो मां यतन्तश्च दृढव्रताः।
नमस्यन्तश्च मां भक्त्या नित्ययुक्ता उपासते॥ १४॥

satataṁ kīrtayanto māṁ yatantaśca dṛḍhavratāḥ
namasyantaśca māṁ bhaktyā nityayuktā upāsate

Constantly chanting My names and glories and striving for My realization, and bowing again and again to Me, those devotees of firm resolve, ever united with me through meditation, worship Me with single-minded devotion. (14)

ज्ञानयज्ञेन चाप्यन्ये यजन्तो मामुपासते।
एकत्वेन पृथक्त्वेन बहुधा विश्वतोमुखम्॥ १५॥

jñānayajñena cāpyanye yajanto māmupāsate
ekatvena pṛthaktvena bahudhā viśvatomukham

Others (who follow the path of Knowledge) betake

themselves to Me through their offering of Knowledge, worshipping Me (in My absolute, formless aspect) as one with themselves; while still others worship Me in My Universal Form in many ways, taking Me to be diverse in diverse celestial forms. (15)

अहं क्रतुरहं यज्ञः स्वधाहमहमौषधम्।
मन्त्रोऽहमहमेवाज्यमहमग्निरहं हुतम्॥ १६॥

ahaṁ kraturahaṁ yajñaḥ svadhāhamahamauṣadham
mantro'hamahamevājyamahamagniraham hutam

I am the Vedic ritual, I am the sacrifice, I am the offering to the departed; I am the herbage and foodgrains; I am the sacred mantra, I am the clarified butter, I am the sacred fire, and I am verily the act of offering oblations into the fire. (16)

पिताहमस्य जगतो माता धाता पितामहः।
वेद्यं पवित्रमोङ्कार ऋक्साम यजुरेव च॥ १७॥

pitāhamasya jagato mātā dhātā pitāmahaḥ
vedyaṁ pavitramoṅkāra ṛksāma yajureva ca

I am the sustainer and ruler of this universe, its father, mother and grandfather, the one worth knowing, the purifier, the sacred syllable OṀ, and the three Vedas—Ṛk, Yajuṣ and Sāma. (17)

गतिर्भर्ता प्रभुः साक्षी निवासः शरणं सुहृत्।
प्रभवः प्रलयः स्थानं निधानं बीजमव्ययम्॥ १८॥

gatirbhartā prabhuḥ sākṣī nivāsaḥ śaraṇaṁ suhṛt
prabhavaḥ pralayaḥ sthānaṁ nidhānaṁ bījamavyayam

I am the supreme goal, sustainer, lord, witness, abode, refuge, well-wisher seeking no return, origin and end, resting-place, store-house to which all beings return at the time of universal destruction, and the imperishable seed. (18)

तपाम्यहमहं वर्षं निगृह्णाम्युत्सृजामि च।
अमृतं चैव मृत्युश्च सदसच्चाहमर्जुन॥ १९॥

tapāmyahamahaṁ varṣaṁ nigṛhṇāmyutsṛjāmi ca
amṛtaṁ caiva mṛtyuśca sadasaccāhamarjuna

I radiate heat as the sun, and hold back as well as send forth showers, Arjuna. I am immortality as well as death; even so, I am being and non-being both. (19)

त्रैविद्या मां सोमपाः पूतपापा-
यज्ञैरिष्ट्वा स्वर्गतिं प्रार्थयन्ते।
ते पुण्यमासाद्य सुरेन्द्रलोक-
मश्नन्ति दिव्यान्दिवि देवभोगान्॥ २०॥

traividyā māṁ somapāḥ pūtapāpā-
yajñairiṣṭvā svargatiṁ prārthayante
te puṇyamāsādya surendraloka-
maśnanti divyāndivi devabhogān

Those who perform action with some interested motive as laid down in these three Vedas and drink the sap of the Soma plant, and have thus been purged of sin, worshipping Me through sacrifices, seek access to heaven; attaining Indra's paradise as the result of their virtuous deeds, they enjoy the celestial pleasures of gods in heaven. (20)

ते तं भुक्त्वा स्वर्गलोकं विशालं-
क्षीणे पुण्ये मर्त्यलोकं विशन्ति।
एवं त्रयीधर्ममनुप्रपन्ना-
गतागतं कामकामा लभन्ते॥ २१॥

te taṁ bhuktvā svargalokaṁ viśālaṁ-
kṣīṇe puṇye martyalokaṁ viśanti
evaṁ trayīdharmamanuprapannā-
gatāgataṁ kāmakāmā labhante

Having enjoyed the extensive heaven-world, they return to this world of mortals on the stock of their merits being exhausted. Thus devoted to the ritual with interested motive recommended by the three Vedas (as the means of attaining heavenly bliss), and seeking worldly enjoyments, they repeatedly come and go (i.e., ascend to heaven by virtue of their merits and return to earth when their fruit has been enjoyed). (21)

अनन्याश्चिन्तयन्तो मां ये जनाः पर्युपासते।
तेषां नित्याभियुक्तानां योगक्षेमं वहाम्यहम्॥ २२॥

ananyāścintayanto māṁ ye janāḥ paryupāsate
teṣāṁ nityābhiyuktānāṁ yogakṣemaṁ vahāmyaham

The devotees, however, who loving no one else constantly think of Me, and worship Me in a disinterested spirit, to those ever united in thought with Me, I bring full security and personally attend to their needs. (22)

येऽप्यन्यदेवता भक्ता यजन्ते श्रद्धयान्विताः।
तेऽपि मामेव कौन्तेय यजन्त्यविधिपूर्वकम्॥ २३॥

ye'pyanyadevatā bhaktā yajante śraddhayānvitāḥ
te'pi māmeva kaunteya yajantyavidhipūrvakam

Arjuna, even those devotees who, endowed with faith, worship other gods (with some interested motive) worship Me alone, though with a mistaken approach. (23)

अहं हि सर्वयज्ञानां भोक्ता च प्रभुरेव च।
न तु मामभिजानन्ति तत्त्वेनातश्च्यवन्ति ते॥ २४॥

ahaṁ hi sarvayajñānāṁ bhoktā ca prabhureva ca
na tu māmabhijānanti tattvenātaścyavanti te

For, I am the enjoyer and also the lord of all sacrifices; but they who do not know Me in reality as the Supreme Deity, they fall (i.e., return to life on earth). (24)

यान्ति देवव्रता देवान्पितॄन्यान्ति पितृव्रताः।
भूतानि यान्ति भूतेज्या यान्ति मद्याजिनोऽपि माम्॥ २५॥

yānti devavratā devānpitṝnyānti pitṛvratāḥ
bhūtāni yānti bhūtejyā yānti madyājino'pi mām

Those who are votaries of gods, go to gods, those who are votaries of manes reach the manes; those who adore the spirits, reach the spirits and those who worship Me, come to Me alone. (That is why My devotees are no longer subject to birth and death.) (25)

पत्रं पुष्पं फलं तोयं यो मे भक्त्या प्रयच्छति।
तदहं भक्त्युपहृतमश्नामि प्रयतात्मनः॥ २६॥

patraṁ puṣpaṁ phalaṁ toyaṁ yo me bhaktyā prayacchati tadahaṁ bhaktyupahṛtamaśnāmi prayatātmanaḥ

Whosoever offers Me with love a leaf, a flower, a fruit or even water, I appear in person before that selfless devotee of sinless mind, and delightfully partake of that article offered by him with love. (26)

यत्करोषि यदश्नासि यज्जुहोषि ददासि यत्।
यत्तपस्यसि कौन्तेय तत्कुरुष्व मदर्पणम्॥ २७॥

yatkaroṣi yadaśnāsi yajjuhoṣi dadāsi yat yattapasyasi kaunteya tatkuruṣva madarpaṇam

Arjuna, whatever you do, whatever you eat, whatever you offer as oblation to the sacred fire, whatever you bestow as a gift, whatever you do by way of penance, offer it all to Me. (27)

शुभाशुभफलैरेवं मोक्ष्यसे कर्मबन्धनैः।
सन्न्यासयोगयुक्तात्मा विमुक्तो मामुपैष्यसि॥ २८॥

śubhāśubhaphalairevaṁ mokṣyase karmabandhanaiḥ sannyāsayogayuktātmā vimukto māmupaiṣyasi

With your mind thus established in the Yoga of renunciation (offering of all actions to Me), you will be freed from the bondage of action in the shape of good and evil results; thus freed from them, you will attain Me. (28)

समोऽहं सर्वभूतेषु न मे द्वेष्योऽस्ति न प्रियः।
ये भजन्ति तु मां भक्त्या मयि ते तेषु चाप्यहम्॥ २९॥

samo'ham sarvabhūteṣu na me dveṣyo'sti na priyaḥ
ye bhajanti tu māṁ bhaktyā mayi te teṣu cāpyaham

I am equally present in all beings; there is none hateful or dear to Me. They, however, who devoutly worship Me abide in Me; and I too stand revealed in them. (29)

अपि चेत्सुदुराचारो भजते मामनन्यभाक्।
साधुरेव स मन्तव्यः सम्यग्व्यवसितो हि सः॥ ३०॥

api cetsudurācāro bhajate māmananyabhāk
sādhureva sa mantavyaḥ samyagvyavasito hi saḥ

Even if the vilest sinner worships Me with exclusive devotion, he should be accounted a saint; for he has rightly resolved (He is positive in his belief that there is nothing like devoted worship of God). (30)

क्षिप्रं भवति धर्मात्मा शश्वच्छान्तिं निगच्छति।
कौन्तेय प्रतिजानीहि न मे भक्तः प्रणश्यति॥ ३१॥

kṣipraṁ bhavati dharmātmā śaśvacchāntiṁ nigacchati
kaunteya pratijānīhi na me bhaktaḥ praṇaśyati

Speedily he becomes virtuous and attains abiding peace. Know it for certain, Arjuna, that My devotee never suffers degradation. (31)

मां हि पार्थ व्यपाश्रित्य येऽपि स्युः पापयोनयः।
स्त्रियो वैश्यास्तथा शूद्रास्तेऽपि यान्ति परां गतिम्॥ ३२॥

māṁ hi pārtha vyapāśritya ye'pi syuḥ pāpayonayaḥ
striyo vaiśyāstathā śūdrāste'pi yānti parāṁ gatim

Arjuna, women, Vaiśyas (members of the trading

and agriculturist classes), Śūdras (those belonging to the labour and artisan classes), as well as those of impious birth (such as the pariah), whoever they may be, taking refuge in Me, they too attain the supreme goal. (32)

किं पुनर्ब्राह्मणाः पुण्या भक्ता राजर्षयस्तथा।
अनित्यमसुखं लोकमिमं प्राप्य भजस्व माम्॥ ३३॥

kiṁ punarbrāhmaṇāḥ puṇyā bhaktā rājarṣayastathā
anityamasukhaṁ lokamimaṁ prāpya bhajasva mām

How much more, then, if they be holy Brāhmaṇas and royal sages devoted to Me! Therefore, having obtained this joyless and transient human life, constantly worship Me. (33)

मन्मना भव मद्भक्तो मद्याजी मां नमस्कुरु।
मामेवैष्यसि युक्त्वैवमात्मानं मत्परायणः॥ ३४॥

manmanā bhava madbhakto madyājī māṁ namaskuru
māmevaiṣyasi yuktvaivamātmānaṁ matparāyaṇaḥ

Fix your mind on Me, be devoted to Me, worship Me and make obeisance to Me; thus linking yourself with Me and entirely depending on Me, you shall come to Me. (34)

ॐ तत्सदिति श्रीमद्भगवद्गीतासूपनिषत्सु ब्रह्मविद्यायां
योगशास्त्रे श्रीकृष्णार्जुनसंवादे राजविद्याराजगुह्ययोगो
नाम नवमोऽध्यायः॥ ९॥

Thus, in the Upaniṣad sung by the Lord, the Science of Brahma, the scripture of Yoga, the dialogue between Śrī Kṛṣṇa and Arjuna, ends the ninth chapter entitled "The Yoga of Sovereign Science and the Sovereign Secret."

ॐ श्रीपरमात्मने नमः

अथ दशमोऽध्यायः

CHAPTER TEN

श्रीभगवानुवाच

भूय एव महाबाहो शृणु मे परमं वचः।
यत्तेऽहं प्रीयमाणाय वक्ष्यामि हितकाम्यया॥ १॥

śrībhagavānuvāca

bhūya eva mahābāho śṛṇu me paramaṁ vacaḥ
yatte'haṁ prīyamāṇāya vakṣyāmi hitakāmyayā

Śrī Bhagavān said : Arjuna, hear once again My supreme word, which I shall speak to you, who are so loving, out of solicitude for your welfare. (1)

न मे विदुः सुरगणाः प्रभवं न महर्षयः।
अहमादिर्हि देवानां महर्षीणां च सर्वशः॥ २॥

na me viduḥ suragaṇāḥ prabhavaṁ na maharṣayaḥ
ahamādirhi devānāṁ maharṣīṇāṁ ca sarvaśaḥ

Neither gods nor the great sages know the secret of My birth (i.e., My appearance in human or other garb out of mere sport); for I am the prime cause in all respects of gods as well as of the great seers. (2)

यो मामजमनादिं च वेत्ति लोकमहेश्वरम्।
असम्मूढः स मर्त्येषु सर्वपापैः प्रमुच्यते॥ ३॥

yo māmajamanādiṁ ca vetti lokamaheśvaram
asammūḍhaḥ sa martyeṣu sarvapāpaiḥ pramucyate

He who knows Me in reality as unborn and without beginning, and as the supreme Lord of the Universe, he, undeluded among men, is purged of all sins. (3)

बुद्धिर्ज्ञानमसम्मोहः क्षमा सत्यं दमः शमः।
सुखं दुःखं भवोऽभावो भयं चाभयमेव च॥ ४॥
अहिंसा समता तुष्टिस्तपो दानं यशोऽयशः।
भवन्ति भावा भूतानां मत्त एव पृथग्विधाः॥ ५॥

buddhirjñānamasammohaḥ kṣamā satyaṁ damaḥ śamaḥ
sukhaṁ duḥkhaṁ bhavo'bhāvo bhayaṁ cābhayameva ca
ahiṁsā samatā tuṣṭistapo dānaṁ yaśo'yaśaḥ
bhavanti bhāvā bhūtānāṁ matta eva pṛthagvidhāḥ

Reason, right knowledge, unclouded understanding, forbearance, veracity, control over the senses and mind, joy and sorrow, evolution and dissolution, fear and fearlessness, non-violence, equanimity, contentment, austerity, charity, fame and obloquy—these diverse traits of creatures emanate from Me alone. (4-5)

महर्षयः सप्त पूर्वे चत्वारो मनवस्तथा।
मद्भावा मानसा जाता येषां लोक इमाः प्रजाः॥ ६॥

maharṣayaḥ sapta pūrve catvāro manavastathā
madbhāvā mānasā jātā yeṣāṁ loka imāḥ prajāḥ

The seven great seers, their four elders (Sanaka and others), and the fourteen Manus or progenitors of mankind (such as Svāyambhuva and his successors), who are all devoted to Me, were born of My will; from them all these creatures in the world have descended. (6)

एतां विभूतिं योगं च मम यो वेत्ति तत्त्वतः।
सोऽविकम्पेन योगेन युज्यते नात्र संशयः॥ ७॥

etāṁ vibhūtiṁ yogaṁ ca mama yo vetti tattvataḥ
so'vikampena yogena yujyate nātra saṁśayaḥ

He who knows in reality this supreme divine glory and supernatural power of Mine gets established in Me through unfaltering devotion; of this there is no doubt. (7)

अहं सर्वस्य प्रभवो मत्तः सर्वं प्रवर्तते।
इति मत्वा भजन्ते मां बुधा भावसमन्विताः॥ ८॥

ahaṁ sarvasya prabhavo mattaḥ sarvaṁ pravartate
iti matvā bhajante māṁ budhā bhāvasamanvitāḥ

In am the source of all creation and everything in the world moves because of Me; knowing thus the wise, full of devotion, constantly worship Me. (8)

मच्चित्ता मद्गतप्राणा बोधयन्तः परस्परम्।
कथयन्तश्च मां नित्यं तुष्यन्ति च रमन्ति च॥ ९॥

maccittā madgataprāṇā bodhayantaḥ parasparam
kathayantaśca māṁ nityaṁ tuṣyanti ca ramanti ca

With their mind fixed on Me, and their lives surrendered to Me, enlightening one another about My greatness and speaking of Me, My devotees ever remain contented and take delight in Me. (9)

तेषां सततयुक्तानां भजतां प्रीतिपूर्वकम्।
ददामि बुद्धियोगं तं येन मामुपयान्ति ते॥ १०॥

teṣāṁ satatayuktānāṁ bhajatāṁ prītipūrvakam
dadāmi buddhiyogaṁ taṁ yena māmupayānti te

On those ever united through meditation with Me and worshipping Me with love, I confer that Yoga of wisdom through which they come to Me. (10)

तेषामेवानुकम्पार्थमहमज्ञानजं तमः।
नाशयाम्यात्मभावस्थो ज्ञानदीपेन भास्वता॥ ११॥

teṣāmevānukampārthamahamajñānajaṁ tamaḥ
nāśayāmyātmabhāvastho jñānadīpena bhāsvatā

In order to bestow My compassion on them, I, dwelling in their heart, dispel their darkness born of ignorance by the illuminating lamp of knowledge. (11)

अर्जुन उवाच

परं ब्रह्म परं धाम पवित्रं परमं भवान्।
पुरुषं शाश्वतं दिव्यमादिदेवमजं विभुम्॥ १२॥
आहुस्त्वामृषयः सर्वे देवर्षिर्नारदस्तथा।
असितो देवलो व्यासः स्वयं चैव ब्रवीषि मे॥ १३॥

arjuna uvāca

paraṁ brahma paraṁ dhāma pavitraṁ paramaṁ bhavān
puruṣaṁ śāśvataṁ divyamādidevamajaṁ vibhum
āhustvāmṛṣayaḥ sarve devarṣirnāradastathā
asito devalo vyāsaḥ svayaṁ caiva bravīṣi me

Arjuna, said : You are the transcendent Eternal, the supreme Abode and the greatest purifier; all the seers speak of You as the eternal divine Puruṣa, the primal Deity, unborn and all-pervading. Likewise speak the celestial sage Nārada, the sages Asita and Devala and the great sage Vyāsa; and Yourself too proclaim this to me. (12-13)

सर्वमेतदृतं मन्ये यन्मां वदसि केशव।
न हि ते भगवन्व्यक्तिं विदुर्देवा न दानवाः ॥ १४ ॥

sarvametadṛtaṁ manye yanmāṁ vadasi keśava
na hi te bhagavanvyaktiṁ vidurdevā na dānavāḥ

Krsna, I believe as true all that You tell me. Lord, neither demons nor gods are aware of Your manifestations. (14)

स्वयमेवात्मनात्मानं वेत्थ त्वं पुरुषोत्तम।
भूतभावन भूतेश देवदेव जगत्पते ॥ १५ ॥

svayamevātmanātmānaṁ vettha tvaṁ puruṣottama
bhūtabhāvana bhūteśa devadeva jagatpate

O Creator of beings, O Ruler of creatures, god of gods, the Lord of the universe, O supreme Puruṣa, You alone know what You are by Yourself. (15)

वक्तुमर्हस्यशेषेण दिव्या ह्यात्मविभूतयः।
याभिर्विभूतिभिर्लोकानिमांस्त्वं व्याप्य तिष्ठसि ॥ १६ ॥

vaktumarhasyaśeṣeṇa divyā hyātmavibhūtayaḥ
yābhirvibhūtibhirlokānimāṁstvaṁ vyāpya tiṣṭhasi

Therefore, You alone can describe in full Your divine glories, whereby You pervade all these worlds. (16)

कथं विद्यामहं योगिंस्त्वां सदा परिचिन्तयन्।
केषु केषु च भावेषु चिन्त्योऽसि भगवन्मया॥ १७॥

katham̐ vidyāmaham̐ yogim̐stvām̐ sadā paricintayan
keṣu keṣu ca bhāveṣu cintyo'si bhagavanmayā

O Master of Yoga, through what process of continuous meditation shall I know You? And in what particular forms, O Lord, are You to be meditated upon by me? (17)

विस्तरेणात्मनो योगं विभूतिं च जनार्दन।
भूयः कथय तृप्तिर्हि शृण्वतो नास्ति मेऽमृतम्॥ १८॥

vistareṇātmano yogam̐ vibhūtim̐ ca janārdana
bhūyaḥ kathaya tṛptirhi śṛṇvato nāsti me'mṛtam

Kṛṣṇa, tell me once more in detail Your power of Yoga and Your glory; for I know no satiety in hearing Your nectar-like words. (18)

श्रीभगवानुवाच

हन्त ते कथयिष्यामि दिव्या ह्यात्मविभूतयः।
प्राधान्यतः कुरुश्रेष्ठ नास्त्यन्तो विस्तरस्य मे॥ १९॥

śrībhagavānuvāca

hanta te kathayiṣyāmi divyā hyātmavibhūtayaḥ
prādhānyataḥ kuruśreṣṭha nāstyanto vistarasya me

Śrī Bhagavān said : Arjuna, now I shall tell you My prominent divine glories; for there is no limit to My manifestations. (19)

अहमात्मा गुडाकेश सर्वभूताशयस्थितः।
अहमादिश्च मध्यं च भूतानामन्त एव च॥ २०॥

ahamātmā guḍākeśa sarvabhūtāśayasthitaḥ
ahamādiśca madhyaṁ ca bhūtānāmanta eva ca

Arjuna, I am the universal Self seated in the heart of all beings; so, I alone am the beginning, the middle and also the end of all beings. (20)

आदित्यानामहं विष्णुर्ज्योतिषां रविरंशुमान्।
मरीचिर्मरुतामस्मि नक्षत्राणामहं शशी॥ २१॥

ādityānāmahaṁ viṣṇurjyotiṣāṁ raviraṁśumān
marīcirmarutāmasmi nakṣatrāṇāmahaṁ śaśī

I am Viṣṇu among the twelve sons of Aditi, and the radiant sun among the luminaries; I am the glow of the Maruts (the forty-nine wind-gods), and the moon among the stars. (21)

वेदानां सामवेदोऽस्मि देवानामस्मि वासवः।
इन्द्रियाणां मनश्चास्मि भूतानामस्मि चेतना॥ २२॥

vedānāṁ sāmavedo'smi devānāmasmi vāsavaḥ
indriyāṇāṁ manaścāsmi bhūtānāmasmi cetanā

Among the Vedas, I am the Sāmaveda; among the gods, I am Indra. Among the organs of perception i.e., senses, I am the mind; and I am the consciousness (life-energy) in living beings. (22)

रुद्राणां शङ्करश्चास्मि वित्तेशो यक्षरक्षसाम्।
वसूनां पावकश्चास्मि मेरुः शिखरिणामहम्॥ २३॥

rudrāṇāṁ śaṅkaraścāsmi vitteśo yakṣarakṣasām
vasūnāṁ pāvakaścāsmi meruḥ śikhariṇāmaham

Among the eleven Rudras (gods of destruction), I am Śiva; and among the Yakṣas and Rākṣasas, I am the lord of riches (Kubera). Among the eight Vasus, I am the god of fire; and among the mountains, I am the Meru. (23)

पुरोधसां च मुख्यं मां विद्धि पार्थ बृहस्पतिम्।
सेनानीनामहं स्कन्दः सरसामस्मि सागरः॥ २४॥

purodhasāṁ ca mukhyaṁ māṁ viddhi pārtha bṛhaspatim
senānīnāmahaṁ skandaḥ sarasāmasmi sāgaraḥ

Among the priests, Arjuna, know Me to be their chief, Bṛhaspati. Among warrior-chiefs, I am Skanda (the generalissimo of the gods); and among reservoirs of water, I am the ocean. (24)

महर्षीणां भृगुरहं गिरामस्म्येकमक्षरम्।
यज्ञानां जपयज्ञोऽस्मि स्थावराणां हिमालयः॥ २५॥

maharṣīṇāṁ bhṛgurahaṁ girāmasmyekamakṣaram
yajñānāṁ japayajño'smi sthāvarāṇāṁ himālayaḥ

Among the great seers, I am Bhṛgu; among words, I am the sacred syllable OṀ, among sacrifices, I am the sacrifice of Japa (muttering of sacred formulas); and among the immovables, the Himālaya. (25)

अश्वत्थः सर्ववृक्षाणां देवर्षीणां च नारदः।
गन्धर्वाणां चित्ररथः सिद्धानां कपिलो मुनिः ॥ २६ ॥

aśvatthaḥ sarvavṛkṣāṇāṁ devarṣīṇāṁ ca nāradaḥ gandharvāṇāṁ citrarathaḥ siddhānāṁ kapilo muniḥ

Among all trees, I am the Aśvattha (the holy fig tree); among the celestial sages, Nārada; among the Gandharvas (celestial musicians), Citraratha, and among the Siddhas, I am the sage Kapila. (26)

उच्चैःश्रवसमश्वानां विद्धि माममृतोद्भवम्।
ऐरावतं गजेन्द्राणां नराणां च नराधिपम् ॥ २७ ॥

uccaiḥśravasamaśvānāṁ viddhi māmamṛtodbhavam airāvataṁ gajendrāṇāṁ narāṇāṁ ca narādhipam

Among horses, know me to be the celestial horse Uccaiḥśravā, begotten of the churning of the ocean along with nectar; among mighty elephants, Airāvata (Indra's elephant); and among men, the king. (27)

आयुधानामहं वज्रं धेनूनामस्मि कामधुक्।
प्रजनश्चास्मि कन्दर्पः सर्पाणामस्मि वासुकिः ॥ २८ ॥

āyudhānāmahaṁ vajraṁ dhenūnāmasmi kāmadhuk prajanaścāsmi kandarpaḥ sarpāṇāmasmi vāsukiḥ

Among weapons, I am the thunderbolt; among cows, I am the celestial cow Kāmadhenu (the cow of plenty). I am the sexual desire which leads to procreation (as enjoined by the scriptures); among serpents I am Vāsuki. (28)

अनन्तश्चास्मि नागानां वरुणो यादसामहम्।
पितॄणामर्यमा चास्मि यमः संयमतामहम्॥ २९॥

anantaścāsmi nāgānāṁ varuṇo yādasāmaham
pitṝṇāmaryamā cāsmi yamaḥ saṁyamatāmaham

Among Nāgas (a special class of serpents), I am the serpent-god Ananta; and I am Varuṇa, the lord of aquatic creatures. Among the manes, I am Aryamā (the head of the Pitṛs); and among rulers, I am Yama (the god of death). (29)

प्रह्लादश्चास्मि दैत्यानां कालः कलयतामहम्।
मृगाणां च मृगेन्द्रोऽहं वैनतेयश्च पक्षिणाम्॥ ३०॥

prahlādaścāsmi daityānāṁ kālaḥ kalayatāmaham
mṛgāṇāṁ ca mṛgendro'haṁ vainateyaśca pakṣiṇām

Among the Daityas, I am the great devotee Prahlāda; and of calculators, I am Time; among quadrupeds, I am the lion; and among birds, Garuḍa. (30)

पवनः पवतामस्मि रामः शस्त्रभृतामहम्।
झषाणां मकरश्चास्मि स्रोतसामस्मि जाह्नवी॥ ३१॥

pavanaḥ pavatāmasmi rāmaḥ śastrabhṛtāmaham
jhaṣāṇāṁ makaraścāsmi srotasāmasmi jāhnavī

Among purifiers, I am the wind; among warriors, I am Śrī Rāma. Among fishes, I am the shark; and among streams, I am the Ganges. (31)

सर्गाणामादिरन्तश्च मध्यं चैवाहमर्जुन।
अध्यात्मविद्या विद्यानां वादः प्रवदतामहम्॥ ३२॥

sargāṇāmādirantaśca madhyaṁ caivāhamarjuna
adhyātmavidyā vidyānāṁ vādaḥ pravadatāmaham

Arjuna, I am the beginning and the middle and the end of all creations. Of all knowledge, I am the knowledge of the soul, (metaphysics); among disputants, I am the right type of reasoning. (32)

अक्षराणामकारोऽस्मि द्वन्द्वः सामासिकस्य च।
अहमेवाक्षयः कालो धाताहं विश्वतोमुखः॥ ३३॥

akṣarāṇāmakāro'smi dvandvaḥ sāmāsikasya ca
ahamevākṣayaḥ kālo dhātāhaṁ viśvatomukhaḥ

Among the sounds represented by the various letters, I am 'A' (the sound represented by the first letter of the alphabet); of the different kinds of compounds in grammar, I am the copulative compound. I am verily the endless Time (the devourer of Time, God); I am the sustainer of all, having My face on all sides. (33)

मृत्युः सर्वहरश्चाहमुद्भवश्च भविष्यताम्।
कीर्तिः श्रीर्वाक्च नारीणां स्मृतिर्मेधा धृतिः क्षमा॥ ३४॥

mṛtyuḥ sarvaharaścāhamudbhavaśca bhaviṣyatām
kīrtiḥ śrīrvākca nārīṇāṁ smṛtirmedhā dhṛtiḥ kṣamā

I am the all-destroying Death that annihilates all, and the origin of all that are to be born. Of feminities, I am Kīrti, Śrī, Vāk, Smṛti, Medhā, Dhṛti and Kṣamā (the goddesses presiding over glory, prosperity, speech, memory, intelligence, endurance and forbearance, respectively). (34)

बृहत्साम तथा साम्नां गायत्री छन्दसामहम्।
मासानां मार्गशीर्षोऽहमृतूनां कुसुमाकरः॥ ३५॥

bṛhatsāma tathā sāmnāṁ gāyatrī chandasāmaham
māsānāṁ mārgaśīrṣo'hamṛtūnāṁ kusumākaraḥ

Likewise, among the Śrutis that can be sung, I am the variety known as Bṛhatsāma; while among the Vedic hymns, I am the hymn known as Gāyatrī. Again, among, the twelve months of the Hindu calendar, I am the month known as 'Mārgaśīrṣa' (corresponding approximately to November); and among the six seasons (successively appearing in India in the course of a year) I am the spring season. (35)

द्यूतं छलयतामस्मि तेजस्तेजस्विनामहम्।
जयोऽस्मि व्यवसायोऽस्मि सत्त्वं सत्त्ववतामहम्॥ ३६॥

dyūtaṁ chalayatāmasmi tejastejasvināmaham
jayo'smi vyavasāyo'smi sattvaṁ sattvavatāmaham

I am gambling among deceitful practices, and the glory of the glorious. I am the victory of the victorious, the resolve of the resolute, the goodness of the good. (36)

वृष्णीनां वासुदेवोऽस्मि पाण्डवानां धनञ्जयः।
मुनीनामप्यहं व्यासः कवीनामुशना कविः॥ ३७॥

vṛṣṇīnāṁ vāsudevo'smi pāṇḍavānāṁ dhanañjayaḥ
munīnāmapyahaṁ vyāsaḥ kavīnāmuśanā kaviḥ

I am Kṛṣṇa among the Vṛṣṇis, Arjuna among the sons of Pāṇḍu, Vyāsa among the sages, and the sage Śukrācārya among the wise. (37)

दण्डो दमयतामस्मि नीतिरस्मि जिगीषताम्।
मौनं चैवास्मि गुह्यानां ज्ञानं ज्ञानवतामहम्॥ ३८॥

daṇḍo damayatāmasmi nītirasmi jigīṣatām
maunaṁ caivāsmi guhyānāṁ jñānaṁ jñānavatāmaham

I am the subduing power of rulers; I am righteousness in those who seek to conquer. Of things to be kept secret, I am the custodian in the shape of reticence; and I am the wisdom of the wise. (38)

यच्चापि सर्वभूतानां बीजं तदहमर्जुन।
न तदस्ति विना यत्स्यान्मया भूतं चराचरम्॥ ३९॥

yaccāpi sarvabhūtānāṁ bījaṁ tadahamarjuna
na tadasti vinā yatsyānmayā bhūtaṁ carācaram

Arjuna, I am even that which is the seed of all life. For there is no creature, moving or inert, which exists without Me. (39)

नान्तोऽस्ति मम दिव्यानां विभूतीनां परन्तप।
एष तूद्देशतः प्रोक्तो विभूतेर्विस्तरो मया॥ ४०॥

nānto'sti mama divyānāṁ vibhūtīnāṁ parantapa
eṣa tūddeśataḥ prokto vibhūtervistaro mayā

Arjuna, there is no limit to My divine manifestations. This is only a brief description by Me of the extent of My glory. (40)

यद्यद्विभूतिमत्सत्त्वं श्रीमदूर्जितमेव वा।
तत्तदेवावगच्छ त्वं मम तेजोंऽशसम्भवम्॥ ४१॥

yadyadvibhūtimatsattvaṁ śrīmadūrjitameva vā tattadevāvagaccha tvaṁ mama tejoṁ'śasambhavam

Every such being as is glorious, brilliant and powerful, know that to be a part manifestation of My glory. (41)

अथवा बहुनैतेन किं ज्ञातेन तवार्जुन।
विष्टभ्याहमिदं कृत्स्नमेकांशेन स्थितो जगत्॥ ४२॥

athavā bahunaitena kiṁ jñātena tavārjuna viṣṭabhyāhamidaṁ kṛtsnamekāṁśena sthito jagat

Or, what will you gain by knowing all this in detail, Arjuna? Suffice it to say that I stand holding this entire universe by a fraction of My Yogic Power. (42)

ॐ तत्सदिति श्रीमद्भगवद्गीतासूपनिषत्सु ब्रह्मविद्यायां
योगशास्त्रे श्रीकृष्णार्जुनसंवादे विभूतियोगो
नाम दशमोऽध्यायः॥ १०॥

Thus, in the Upaniṣad sung by the Lord, the Science of Brahma, the scripture of Yoga, the dialogue between Śrī Kṛṣṇa and Arjuna, ends the tenth chapter entitled "The Yoga of Divine Glories."

ॐ श्रीपरमात्मने नमः

अथैकादशोऽध्यायः

CHAPTER ELEVEN

अर्जुन उवाच

मदनुग्रहाय परमं गुह्यमध्यात्मसञ्ज्ञितम्।
यत्त्वयोक्तं वचस्तेन मोहोऽयं विगतो मम॥ १॥

arjuna uvāca

madanugrahāya paramaṁ guhyamadhyātmasañjñitam
yattvayoktaṁ vacastena moho'yaṁ vigato mama

Arjuna said : Thanks to the most profound words of spiritual wisdom that You have spoken out of kindness to me, this delusion of mine has entirely disappeared. (1)

भवाप्ययौ हि भूतानां श्रुतौ विस्तरशो मया।
त्वत्तः कमलपत्राक्ष माहात्म्यमपि चाव्ययम्॥ २॥

bhavāpyayau hi bhūtānāṁ śrutau vistaraśo mayā
tvattaḥ kamalapatrākṣa māhātmyamapi cāvyayam

For, Kṛṣṇa, I have heard from You in detail an account of the evolution and dissolution of beings, and also Your immortal glory. (2)

एवमेतद्यथात्थ त्वमात्मानं परमेश्वर।
द्रष्टुमिच्छामि ते रूपमैश्वरं पुरुषोत्तम॥ ३॥

evametadyathāttha tvamātmānaṁ parameśvara
draṣṭumicchāmi te rūpamaiśvaraṁ puruṣottama

Lord, You are precisely what You declare Yourself

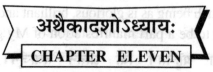

to be. But I long to see Your divine form (possessed of wisdom, glory, energy, strength, valour and effulgence), O Best of persons! (3)

मन्यसे यदि तच्छक्यं मया द्रष्टुमिति प्रभो।
योगेश्वर ततो मे त्वं दर्शयात्मानमव्ययम्॥ ४॥

manyase yadi tacchakyaṁ mayā draṣṭumiti prabho
yogeśvara tato me tvaṁ darśayātmānamavyayam

Kṛṣṇa, if You think that it can be seen by me, then, O Lord of Yoga, reveal to me Your imperishable form. (4)

श्रीभगवानुवाच

पश्य मे पार्थ रूपाणि शतशोऽथ सहस्रशः।
नानाविधानि दिव्यानि नानावर्णाकृतीनि च॥ ५॥

śrībhagavānuvāca

paśya me pārtha rūpāṇi śataśo'tha sahasraśaḥ
nānāvidhāni divyāni nānāvarṇākṛtīni ca

Śrī Bhagavān said: Arjuna, behold My manifold, multifarious divine forms of various colours and shapes, in hundreds and thousands. (5)

पश्यादित्यान्वसून्रुद्रानश्विनौ मरुतस्तथा।
बहून्यदृष्टपूर्वाणि पश्याश्चर्याणि भारत॥ ६॥

paśyādityānvasūnrudrānaśvinau marutastathā
bahūnyadṛṣṭapūrvāṇi paśyāścaryāṇi bhārata

Behold in Me, Arjuna, the twelve sons of Aditi, the eight Vasus, the eleven Rudras (gods of destruction), the two Aśvinīkumāras (the twin-born physicians of gods) and the forty-nine Maruts (wind-gods), and witness many more wonderful forms never seen before. (6)

इहैकस्थं जगत्कृत्स्नं पश्याद्य सचराचरम्।
मम देहे गुडाकेश यच्चान्यद्द्रष्टुमिच्छसि॥ ७॥

ihaikastham̐ jagatkṛtsnam̐ paśyādya sacarācaram
mama dehe guḍākeśa yaccānyaddraṣṭumicchasi

Arjuna, behold as concentrated within this body of Mine the entire creation consisting of both animate and inanimate beings, and whatever else you desire to see. (7)

न तु मां शक्यसे द्रष्टुमनेनैव स्वचक्षुषा।
दिव्यं ददामि ते चक्षुः पश्य मे योगमैश्वरम्॥ ८॥

na tu mām̐ śakyase draṣṭumanenaiva svacakṣuṣā
divyam̐ dadāmi te cakṣuḥ paśya me yogamaiśvaram

But surely you cannot see Me with these human eyes of yours; therefore, I vouchsafe to you the divine eye. With this you behold My divine power of Yoga. (8)

सञ्जय उवाच

एवमुक्त्वा ततो राजन्महायोगेश्वरो हरिः।
दर्शयामास पार्थाय परमं रूपमैश्वरम्॥ ९॥

sañjaya uvāca

evamuktvā tato rājanmahāyogeśvaro hariḥ
darśayāmāsa pārthāya paramam̐ rūpamaiśvaram

Sañjaya said : My lord! having spoken thus, Śrī

Kṛṣṇa, the supreme Master of Yoga, forthwith revealed to Arjuna His supremely glorious divine Form. (9)

अनेकवक्त्रनयनमनेकाद्भुतदर्शनम् ।
अनेकदिव्याभरणं दिव्यानेकोद्यतायुधम् ॥ १० ॥
दिव्यमाल्याम्बरधरं दिव्यगन्धानुलेपनम् ।
सर्वाश्चर्यमयं देवमनन्तं विश्वतोमुखम् ॥ ११ ॥

anekavaktranayanamanekādbhutadarśanam
anekadivyābharaṇaṁ divyānekodyatāyudham
divyamālyāmbaradharaṁ divyagandhānulepanam
sarvāścaryamayaṁ devamanantaṁ viśvatomukham

Arjuna saw the supreme Deity possessing many mouths and eyes, presenting many a wonderful sight, decked with many divine ornaments, wielding many uplifted divine weapons, wearing divine garlands and vestments, anointed all over with divine sandal-pastes, full of all wonders, infinite and having faces on all sides.(10-11)

दिवि सूर्यसहस्रस्य भवेद्युगपदुत्थिता ।
यदि भाः सदृशी सा स्याद्भासस्तस्य महात्मनः ॥ १२ ॥

divi sūryasahasrasya bhavedyugapadutthitā
yadi bhāḥ sadṛśī sā syādbhāsastasya mahātmanaḥ

If there be the effulgence of a thousand suns bursting forth all at once in the heavens, even that would hardly approach the splendour of the mighty Lord. (12)

तत्रैकस्थं जगत्कृत्स्नं प्रविभक्तमनेकधा ।
अपश्यद्देवदेवस्य शरीरे पाण्डवस्तदा ॥ १३ ॥

tatraikasthaṁ jagatkṛtsnaṁ pravibhaktamanekadhā
apaśyaddevadevasya śarīre pāṇḍavastadā

Concentrated at one place in the person of that supreme Deity, Arjuna then beheld the whole universe with its manifold divisions. (13)

ततः स विस्मयाविष्टो हृष्टरोमा धनञ्जयः।
प्रणम्य शिरसा देवं कृताञ्जलिरभाषत॥ १४॥

tataḥ sa vismayāviṣṭo hṛṣṭaromā dhanañjayaḥ
praṇamya śirasā devaṁ kṛtāñjalirabhāṣata

Then Arjuna, full of wonder and with the hair standing on end, reverentially bowed his head to the divine Lord, and with joined palms addressed Him thus. (14)

अर्जुन उवाच

पश्यामि देवांस्तव देव देहे
सर्वांस्तथा भूतविशेषसङ्घान्।
ब्रह्माणमीशं कमलासनस्थ-
मृषींश्च सर्वानुरगांश्च दिव्यान्॥ १५॥

arjuna uvāca

paśyāmi devāṁstava deva dehe
sarvāṁstathā bhūtaviśeṣasaṅghān
brahmāṇamīśaṁ kamalāsanastha-
mṛṣīṁśca sarvānuragāṁśca divyān

Arjuna said : Lord, I behold within your body all gods and hosts of different beings, Brahmā throned on his lotus-seat, Śiva and all Ṛṣis and celestial serpents. (15)

अनेकबाहूदरवक्त्रनेत्रं-
पश्यामि त्वां सर्वतोऽनन्तरूपम्।
नान्तं न मध्यं न पुनस्तवादिं-
पश्यामि विश्वेश्वर विश्वरूप॥ १६॥

anekabāhūdaravaktranetraṁ-
paśyāmi tvāṁ sarvato'nantarūpam
nāntaṁ na madhyaṁ na punastavādiṁ-
paśyāmi viśveśvara viśvarūpa

O Lord of the universe, I see you endowed with numerous arms, bellies, mouths, and eyes and having innumerable forms extended on all sides. I see neither your beginning nor middle, nor even your end, manifested as you are in the form of the universe. (16)

किरीटिनं गदिनं चक्रिणं च
तेजोराशिं सर्वतो दीप्तिमन्तम्।
पश्यामि त्वां दुर्निरीक्ष्यं समन्ता-
द्दीप्तानलार्कद्युतिमप्रमेयम् ॥ १७॥

kirīṭinaṁ gadinaṁ cakriṇaṁ ca
tejorāśiṁ sarvato dīptimantam
paśyāmi tvāṁ durnirīkṣyaṁ samantā-
ddīptānalārkadyutimaprameyam

I see you endowed with diadems, clubs and discuses, a mass of splendour glowing all round, having the brilliance of a blazing fire and the sun, hard to gaze at and immeasurable on all sides. (17)

त्वमक्षरं परमं वेदितव्यं-
त्वमस्य विश्वस्य परं निधानम्।
त्वमव्ययः शाश्वतधर्मगोप्ता
सनातनस्त्वं पुरुषो मतो मे॥ १८॥

tvamakṣaraṁ paramaṁ veditavyaṁ-
tvamasya viśvasya paraṁ nidhānam
tvamavyayaḥ śāśvatadharmagoptā
sanātanastvaṁ puruṣo mato me

You are the supreme indestructible worthy of being known; you are the ultimate refuge of this universe. You are, again, the protector of the ageless Dharma; I consider You to be the eternal imperishable Being. (18)

अनादिमध्यान्तमनन्तवीर्य-
मनन्तबाहुं शशिसूर्यनेत्रम्।
पश्यामि त्वां दीप्तहुताशवक्त्रं-
स्वतेजसा विश्वमिदं तपन्तम्॥ १९॥

anādimadhyāntamanantavīrya-
manantabāhuṁ śaśisūryanetram
paśyāmi tvāṁ dīptahutāśavaktraṁ-
svatejasā viśvamidaṁ tapantam

I see You without beginning, middle or end, possessing unlimited prowess and endowed with numberless arms, having the moon and the sun for Your eyes, and blazing fire for Your mouth, and scorching this universe by Your radiance. (19)

द्यावापृथिव्योरिदमन्तरं हि
व्याप्तं त्वयैकेन दिशश्च सर्वाः।
दृष्ट्वाद्भुतं रूपमुग्रं तवेदं-
लोकत्रयं प्रव्यथितं महात्मन्॥ २०॥

dyāvāpṛthivyoridamantaraṁ hi
vyāptaṁ tvayaikena diśaśca sarvāḥ
dṛṣṭvādbhutaṁ rūpamugraṁ tavedaṁ-
lokatrayaṁ pravyathitaṁ mahātman

Yonder space between heaven and earth and all the quarters are entirely filled by You alone. Seeing this transcendent, dreadful Form of Yours, O Soul of the universe, all the three worlds feel greatly alarmed. (20)

अमी हि त्वां सुरसङ्घा विशन्ति
केचिद्भीताः प्राञ्जलयो गृणन्ति।
स्वस्तीत्युक्त्वा महर्षिसिद्धसङ्घाः
स्तुवन्ति त्वां स्तुतिभिः पुष्कलाभिः॥ २१॥

amī hi tvāṁ surasaṅghā viśanti
kecidbhītāḥ prāñjalayo gṛṇanti
svastītyuktvā maharṣisiddhasaṅghāḥ
stuvanti tvāṁ stutibhiḥ puṣkalābhiḥ

Yonder hosts of gods are entering You; some with palms joined out of fear are uttering Your names and glories. Multitudes of Maharṣis and Siddhas, saying 'Let there be peace', are extolling You by means of excellent hymns. (21)

रुद्रादित्या वसवो ये च साध्या-
विश्वेऽश्विनौ मरुतश्चोष्मपाश्च।
गन्धर्वयक्षासुरसिद्धसङ्घा-
वीक्षन्ते त्वां विस्मिताश्चैव सर्वे॥ २२॥

rudrādityā vasavo ye ca sādhyā-
viśve'śvinau marutaścoṣmapāśca
gandharvayakṣāsurasiddhasaṅghā-
vīkṣante tvāṁ vismitāścaiva sarve

The eleven Rudras, twelve Ādityas and eight Vasus, the Sādhyas and Viśvedevas, the two Aśvinīkumāras and forty-nine Maruts, as well as the manes and multitudes of Gandharvas, Yakṣas, Asuras and Siddhas, all these gaze upon You in amazement. (22)

रूपं महत्ते बहुवक्त्रनेत्रं-
महाबाहो बहुबाहूरुपादम्।
बहूदरं बहुदंष्ट्राकरालं-
दृष्ट्वा लोकाः प्रव्यथितास्तथाहम्॥ २३॥

rūpaṁ mahatte bahuvaktranetraṁ-
mahābāho bahubāhūrupādam
bahūdaraṁ bahudaṁṣṭrākarālaṁ-
dṛṣṭvā lokāḥ pravyathitāstathāham

Lord, seeing this stupendous and dreadful Form of Yours possessing numerous mouths and eyes, many arms, thighs and feet, many bellies and many teeth, the worlds are terror-struck; so am I. (23)

नभःस्पृशं दीप्तमनेकवर्णं-
व्यात्ताननं दीप्तविशालनेत्रम्।
दृष्ट्वा हि त्वां प्रव्यथितान्तरात्मा
धृतिं न विन्दामि शमं च विष्णो॥ २४॥

nabhaḥspṛśaṁ dīptamanekavarṇaṁ
vyāttānanaṁ dīptaviśālanetram
dṛṣṭvā hi tvāṁ pravyathitāntarātmā
dhṛtiṁ na vindāmi śamaṁ ca viṣṇo

Lord, seeing Your Form reaching the heavens, effulgent multi-coloured, having its mouth wide open and possessing large flaming eyes, I, with my inmost self frightened, have lost self-control and find no peace. (24)

दंष्ट्राकरालानि च ते मुखानि
दृष्ट्वैव कालानलसन्निभानि।
दिशो न जाने न लभे च शर्म
प्रसीद देवेश जगन्निवास॥ २५॥

daṁṣṭrākarālāni ca te mukhāni
dṛṣṭvaiva kālānalasannibhāni
diśo na jāne na labhe ca śarma
prasīda deveśa jagannivāsa

Seeing Your faces frightful on account of their teeth, and blazing like the fire at the time of universal destruction, I am utterly bewildered and find no happiness; therefore, have mercy on me, O Lord of celestials and Abode of the universe. (25)

अमी च त्वां धृतराष्ट्रस्य पुत्राः
सर्वे सहैवावनिपालसङ्घैः ।
भीष्मो द्रोणः सूतपुत्रस्तथासौ
सहास्मदीयैरपि योधमुख्यैः ॥ २६ ॥
वक्त्राणि ते त्वरमाणा विशन्ति
दंष्ट्राकरालानि भयानकानि ।
केचिद्विलग्ना दशनान्तरेषु
सन्दृश्यन्ते चूर्णितैरुत्तमाङ्गैः ॥ २७ ॥

amī ca tvāṁ dhṛtarāṣṭrasya putrāḥ
sarve sahaivāvanipālasaṅghaiḥ
bhīṣmo droṇaḥ sūtaputrastathāsau
sahāsmadīyairapi yodhamukhyaiḥ
vaktrāṇi te tvaramāṇā viśanti
daṁṣṭrākarālāni bhayānakāni
kecidvilagnā daśanāntareṣu
sandṛśyante cūrṇitairuttamāṅgaiḥ

All those sons of Dhṛtarāṣṭra with hosts of kings are entering You. Bhīṣma, Droṇa and yonder Karṇa, with the principal warriors on our side as well, are rushing headlong into Your fearful mouths looking all the more terrible on account of their teeth; some are seen stuck up in the gaps between Your teeth with their heads crushed. (26-27)

यथा नदीनां बहवोऽम्बुवेगाः
समुद्रमेवाभिमुखा द्रवन्ति ।
तथा तवामी नरलोकवीरा-
विशन्ति वक्त्राण्यभिविज्वलन्ति ॥ २८ ॥

yathā nadīnāṁ bahavo'mbuvegāḥ
samudramevābhimukhā dravanti
tathā tavāmī naralokavīrā-
viśanti vaktrāṇyabhivijvalanti

As the myriad streams of rivers rush towards the sea alone, so do those warriors of the mortal world enter Your flaming mouths. (28)

यथा प्रदीप्तं ज्वलनं पतङ्गा-
विशन्ति नाशाय समृद्धवेगाः।
तथैव नाशाय विशन्ति लोका-
स्तवापि वक्त्राणि समृद्धवेगाः॥ २९॥

yathā pradīptaṁ jvalanaṁ pataṅgā-
viśanti nāśāya samṛddhavegāḥ
tathaiva nāśāya viśanti lokā-
stavāpi vaktrāṇi samṛddhavegāḥ

As moths rush with great speed into the blazing fire for extinction out of their folly, even so all these people are with great rapidity entering Your mouths to meet their doom. (29)

लेलिह्यसे ग्रसमानः समन्ता-
ल्लोकान्समग्रान्वदनैर्ज्वलद्भिः।
तेजोभिरापूर्य जगत्समग्रं-
भासस्तवोग्राः प्रतपन्ति विष्णो॥ ३०॥

lelihyase grasamānaḥ samantā-
llokānsamagrānvadanairjvaladbhiḥ
tejobhirāpūrya jagatsamagraṁ-
bhāsastavogrāḥ pratapanti viṣṇo

Devouring through Your blazing mouths, You are licking all those people on all sides. Lord, Your fiery rays fill the whole universe with their fierce radiance and scorch it. (30)

आख्याहि मे को भवानुग्ररूपो-
नमोऽस्तु ते देववर प्रसीद।
विज्ञातुमिच्छामि भवन्तमाद्यं-
न हि प्रजानामि तव प्रवृत्तिम्॥ ३१॥

ākhyāhi me ko bhavānugrarūpo-
namo'stu te devavara prasīda
vijñātumicchāmi bhavantamādyaṁ-
na hi prajānāmi tava pravṛttim

Tell me who You are with a form so terrible? My obeisance to You, O best of gods; be kind to me. I wish to know You, the Primal Being, in particular; for I know not Your purpose. (31)

श्रीभगवानुवाच

कालोऽस्मि लोकक्षयकृत्प्रवृद्धो-
लोकान्समाहर्तुमिह प्रवृत्तः।
ऋतेऽपि त्वां न भविष्यन्ति सर्वे
येऽवस्थिताः प्रत्यनीकेषु योधाः॥ ३२॥

śrībhagavānuvāca

kālo'smi lokakṣayakṛtpravṛddho-
lokānsamāhartumiha pravṛttaḥ
ṛte'pi tvāṁ na bhaviṣyanti sarve
ye'vasthitāḥ pratyanīkeṣu yodhāḥ

Śrī Bhagavān said : I am mighty Kāla (the eternal Time-spirit), the destroyer of the worlds. I am out to exterminate these people. Even without you all those warriors, arrayed in the enemy's camp, shall die. (32)

तस्मात्त्वमुत्तिष्ठ यशो लभस्व
जित्वा शत्रून्भुङ्क्ष्व राज्यं समृद्धम्।
मयैवैते निहताः पूर्वमेव
निमित्तमात्रं भव सव्यसाचिन्॥ ३३॥

tasmāttvamuttiṣṭha yaśo labhasva
jitvā śatrūnbhuṅkṣva rājyaṁ samṛddham
mayaivaite nihatāḥ pūrvameva
nimittamātraṁ bhava savyasācin

Therefore, do you arise and win glory; conquering foes, enjoy the affluent kingdom. These warriors stand already slain by Me; be you only an instrument, Arjuna. (33)

द्रोणं च भीष्मं च जयद्रथं च
कर्णं तथान्यानपि योधवीरान्।
मया हतांस्त्वं जहि मा व्यथिष्ठा-
युध्यस्व जेतासि रणे सपत्नान्॥ ३४॥

droṇaṁ ca bhīṣmaṁ ca jayadrathaṁ ca
karṇaṁ tathānyānapi yodhavīrān
mayā hatāṁstvaṁ jahi mā vyathiṣṭhā-
yudhyasva jetāsi raṇe sapatnān

Do kill Droṇa and Bhīṣma and Jayadratha and Karṇa and other brave warriors, who already stand killed by Me; fear not. Fight and you will surely conquer the enemies in the war. (34)

सञ्जय उवाच

एतच्छ्रुत्वा वचनं केशवस्य
कृताञ्जलिर्वेपमानः किरीटी।
नमस्कृत्वा भूय एवाह कृष्णं-
सगद्गदं भीतभीतः प्रणम्य॥ ३५॥

sañjaya uvāca

etacchrutvā vacanaṁ keśavasya
kṛtāñjalirvepamānaḥ kirīṭī
namaskṛtvā bhūya evāha kṛṣṇaṁ-
sagadgadaṁ bhītabhītaḥ praṇamya

Sañjaya said : Hearing these words of Bhagavān Keśava, Arjuna tremblingly bowed to Him with joined palms, and bowing again in extreme terror spoke to Śrī Kṛṣṇa in faltering accents. (35)

अर्जुन उवाच

स्थाने हृषीकेश तव प्रकीर्त्या
जगत्प्रहृष्यत्यनुरज्यते च।
रक्षांसि भीतानि दिशो द्रवन्ति
सर्वे नमस्यन्ति च सिद्धसङ्घाः॥ ३६॥

arjuna uvāca

sthāne hṛṣīkeśa tava prakīrtyā
jagatprahṛṣyatyanurajyate ca
rakṣāṁsi bhītāni diśo dravanti
sarve namasyanti ca siddhasaṅghāḥ

Arjuna said : Lord, well it is, the universe exults and is filled with love by chanting Your names, virtues and glory; terrified Rākṣasas are fleeing in all directions, and all the hosts of Siddhas are bowing to You. (36)

कस्माच्च ते न नमेरन्महात्मन्
गरीयसे ब्रह्मणोऽप्यादिकर्त्रे।
अनन्त देवेश जगन्निवास
त्वमक्षरं सदसत्तत्परं यत्॥ ३७॥

kasmācca te na nameranmahātman
garīyase brahmaṇo'pyādikartre
ananta deveśa jagannivāsa
tvamakṣaraṁ sadasattatparaṁ yat

O Great soul, why should they not bow to you, who are the progenitor of Brahmā himself and the greatest of the great? O infinite Lord of celestials, Abode of the universe, You are that which is existent (Sat), that which is non-existent (Asat) and also that which is beyond both, viz., the indestructible Brahma. (37)

त्वमादिदेवः पुरुषः पुराण-
स्त्वमस्य विश्वस्य परं निधानम्।
वेत्तासि वेद्यं च परं च धाम
त्वया ततं विश्वमनन्तरूप॥ ३८॥

tvamādidevaḥ puruṣaḥ purāṇa-
stvamasya viśvasya paraṁ nidhānam
vettāsi vedyaṁ ca paraṁ ca dhāma
tvayā tataṁ viśvamanantarūpa

You are the primal Deity, the most ancient Person; You are the ultimate resort of this universe. You are both the knower and the knowable, and the highest abode. It is You who pervade the universe, assuming endless forms. (38)

वायुर्यमोऽग्निर्वरुणः शशाङ्कः
प्रजापतिस्त्वं प्रपितामहश्च।
नमो नमस्तेऽस्तु सहस्रकृत्वः
पुनश्च भूयोऽपि नमो नमस्ते॥ ३९॥

vāyuryamo'gnirvaruṇaḥ śaśāṅkaḥ
prajāpatistvaṁ prapitāmahaśca
namo namaste'stu sahasrakṛtvaḥ
punaśca bhūyo'pi namo namaste

You are Vāyu (the wind-god), Yama (the god of death), Agni (the god of fire), Varuṇa (the god of water), the moon-god, Brahmā (the Lord of creation), nay, the father of Brahmā himself. Hail, hail to You a thousand times; salutations, repeated salutations to You once again. (39)

नमः पुरस्तादथ पृष्ठतस्ते
नमोऽस्तु ते सर्वत एव सर्व।
अनन्तवीर्यामितविक्रमस्त्वं-
सर्वं समाप्नोषि ततोऽसि सर्वः॥ ४०॥

namaḥ purastādatha pṛṣṭhataste
namo'stu te sarvata eva sarva
anantavīryāmitavikramastvaṁ-
sarvaṁ samāpnoṣi tato'si sarvaḥ

O Lord of infinite prowess, my salutations to You from the front and from behind. O soul of all, my obeisance to You from all sides indeed. You, who possess infinite might, pervade all; therefore, You are all. (40)

सखेति मत्वा प्रसभं यदुक्तं-
हे कृष्ण हे यादव हे सखेति।
अजानता महिमानं तवेदं-
मया प्रमादात्प्रणयेन वापि॥ ४१॥
यच्चावहासार्थमसत्कृतोऽसि
विहारशय्यासनभोजनेषु।
एकोऽथवाप्यच्युत तत्समक्षं-
तत्क्षामये त्वामहमप्रमेयम्॥ ४२॥

sakheti matvā prasabhaṁ yaduktaṁ-
he kṛṣṇa he yādava he sakheti
ajānatā mahimānaṁ tavedaṁ-
mayā pramādātpraṇayena vāpi
yaccāvahāsārthamasatkṛto'si
vihāraśayyāsanabhojaneṣu
eko'thavāpyacyuta tatsamakṣaṁ-
tatkṣāmaye tvāmahamaprameyam

The way in which I have importunately called You, either through intimacy or thoughtlessly, "Ho Kṛṣṇa! Ho Yādava! Ho Comrade!" and so on, unaware of the greatness of Yours, and thinking You only to be a friend, and the way in which You have been slighted by me in jest, O sinless one, while at play, reposing, sitting or at meals, either alone or even in the presence of others—for all that I crave forgiveness from You, O Immeasurable. (41-42)

पितासि लोकस्य चराचरस्य
त्वमस्य पूज्यश्च गुरुर्गरीयान्।
न त्वत्समोऽस्त्यभ्यधिकः कुतोऽन्यो-
लोकत्रयेऽप्यप्रतिमप्रभाव ॥ ४३ ॥

pitāsi lokasya carācarasya
tvamasya pūjyaśca gururgarīyān
na tvatsamo'styabhyadhikaḥ kuto'nyo-
lokatraye'pyapratimaprabhāva

You are the father, nay, the greatest teacher of this moving and unmoving creation, and worthy of adoration. O Lord of incomparable might, in all the three worlds there is none else even equal to You; how, then, can anyone be superior to You? (43)

तस्मात्प्रणम्य प्रणिधाय कायं-
प्रसादये त्वामहमीशमीड्यम्।
पितेव पुत्रस्य सखेव सख्युः
प्रियः प्रियायार्हसि देव सोढुम्॥ ४४ ॥

tasmātpraṇamya praṇidhāya kāyaṁ
prasādaye tvāmahamīśamīḍyam
piteva putrasya sakheva sakhyuḥ
priyaḥ priyāyārhasi deva soḍhum

Therefore, Lord, prostrating my body at Your feet and bowing low I seek to propitiate You, the ruler of all and worthy of all praise. It behoves You to bear with me even as a father bears with his son, a friend with his friend and a husband with his beloved spouse. (44)

अदृष्टपूर्वं हृषितोऽस्मि दृष्ट्वा
भयेन च प्रव्यथितं मनो मे।
तदेव मे दर्शय देवरूपं-
प्रसीद देवेश जगन्निवास॥ ४५॥

adṛṣṭapūrvaṁ hṛṣito'smi dṛṣṭvā
bhayena ca pravyathitaṁ mano me
tadeva me darśaya devarūpaṁ-
prasīda deveśa jagannivāsa

Having seen Your wondrous form, which was never seen before, I feel transported with joy; at the same time my mind is tormented by fear. Pray reveal to me that divine form; the form of Viṣṇu with four-arms; O Lord of celestials, Abode of the universe, be gracious. (45)

किरीटिनं गदिनं चक्रहस्त-
मिच्छामि त्वां द्रष्टुमहं तथैव।
तेनैव रूपेण चतुर्भुजेन
सहस्रबाहो भव विश्वमूर्ते॥ ४६॥

kirīṭinaṁ gadinaṁ cakrahasta-
micchāmi tvāṁ draṣṭumahaṁ tathaiva
tenaiva rūpeṇa caturbhujena
sahasrabāho bhava viśvamūrte

I wish to see You adorned in the same way with a diadem on the head, and holding a mace and a discus in two of Your hands. O Lord with a thousand arms, O Universal Being, appear again in the same four-armed Form. (46)

श्रीभगवानुवाच

मया प्रसन्नेन तवार्जुनेदं-
रूपं परं दर्शितमात्मयोगात्।
तेजोमयं विश्वमनन्तमाद्यं-
यन्मे त्वदन्येन न दृष्टपूर्वम्॥ ४७॥

śrībhagavānuvāca

mayā prasannena tavārjunedaṁ-
rūpaṁ paraṁ darśitamātmayogāt
tejomayaṁ viśvamanantamādyaṁ-
yanme tvadanyena na dṛṣṭapūrvam

Śrī Bhagavān said : Arjuna! pleased with you I have shown you, through My power of Yoga, this supreme, effulgent, primal and infinite Cosmic Form, which has never been seen before by anyone other than you.(47)

न वेदयज्ञाध्ययनैर्न दानै-
र्नच क्रियाभिर्न तपोभिरुग्रैः।
एवंरूपः शक्य अहं नृलोके
द्रष्टुं त्वदन्येन कुरुप्रवीर॥ ४८॥

na vedayajñādhyayanairna dānai-
rnaca kriyābhirna tapobhirugraiḥ
evaṁrūpaḥ śakya ahaṁ nṛloke
draṣṭuṁ tvadanyena kurupravīra

Arjuna, in this mortal world I cannot be seen in this Form by anyone else than you, either through study of the Vedas or of rituals, or again through gifts, actions or austere penances. (48)

मा ते व्यथा मा च विमूढभावो-
दृष्ट्वा रूपं घोरमीदृङ्ममेदम्।
व्यपेतभीः प्रीतमनाः पुनस्त्वं-
तदेव मे रूपमिदं प्रपश्य॥ ४९॥

mā te vyathā mā ca vimūḍhabhāvo-
dṛṣṭvā rūpaṁ ghoramīdṛṅmamedam
vyapetabhīḥ prītamanāḥ punastvaṁ-
tadeva me rūpamidaṁ prapaśya

Seeing such a dreadful Form of Mine as this, do not be perturbed or perplexed; with a fearless and tranquil mind, behold once again the same four-armed Form of Mine (bearing the conch, discus, mace and lotus). (49)

सञ्जय उवाच

इत्यर्जुनं वासुदेवस्तथोक्त्वा
स्वकं रूपं दर्शयामास भूयः।
आश्वासयामास च भीतमेनं-
भूत्वा पुनः सौम्यवपुर्महात्मा॥ ५०॥

sañjaya uvāca

ityarjunaṁ vāsudevastathoktvā
svakaṁ rūpaṁ darśayāmāsa bhūyaḥ
āśvāsayāmāsa ca bhītamenaṁ-
bhūtvā punaḥ saumyavapurmahātmā

Sañjaya said : Having spoken thus to Arjuna, Bhagavān Vāsudeva again revealed to him His own four-armed Form; and then, assuming a genial form, the high-souled

Śrī Kṛṣṇa consoled the frightened Arjuna. (50)

अर्जुन उवाच

दृष्ट्वेदं मानुषं रूपं तव सौम्यं जनार्दन।
इदानीमस्मि संवृत्तः सचेताः प्रकृतिं गतः॥ ५१॥

arjuna uvāca

dṛṣṭvedaṁ mānuṣaṁ rūpaṁ tava saumyaṁ janārdana
idānīmasmi saṁvṛttaḥ sacetāḥ prakṛtiṁ gataḥ

Arjuna said : Kṛṣṇa, seeing this gentle human form of Yours I have regained my composure and am myself again. (51)

श्रीभगवानुवाच

सुदुर्दर्शमिदं रूपं दृष्टवानसि यन्मम।
देवा अप्यस्य रूपस्य नित्यं दर्शनकाङ्क्षिणः॥ ५२॥

śrībhagavānuvāca

sudurdarśamidaṁ rūpaṁ dṛṣṭavānasi yanmama
devā apyasya rūpasya nityaṁ darśanakāṅkṣiṇaḥ

Śrī Bhagavān said : This form of Mine (with four-arms) which you have just seen, is exceedingly difficult to behold. Even the gods are always eager to see this form. (52)

नाहं वेदैर्न तपसा न दानेन न चेज्यया।
शक्य एवंविधो द्रष्टुं दृष्टवानसि मां यथा॥ ५३॥

nāhaṁ vedairna tapasā na dānena na cejyayā
śakya evaṁvidho draṣṭuṁ dṛṣṭavānasi māṁ yathā

Neither by study of the Vedas nor by penance, nor again by charity, nor even by ritual can I be seen in this form (with four-arms) as you have seen Me. (53)

भक्त्या त्वनन्यया शक्य अहमेवंविधोऽर्जुन।
ज्ञातुं द्रष्टुं च तत्त्वेन प्रवेष्टुं च परन्तप॥ ५४॥

bhaktyā tvananyayā śakya ahamevaṁvidho'rjuna
jñātuṁ draṣṭuṁ ca tattvena praveṣṭuṁ ca parantapa

Through single-minded devotion, however, I can be seen in this form (with four-arms), nay, known in essence and even entered into, O valiant Arjuna. (54)

मत्कर्मकृन्मत्परमो मद्भक्तः सङ्गवर्जितः।
निर्वैरः सर्वभूतेषु यः स मामेति पाण्डव॥ ५५॥

matkarmakṛnmatparamo madbhaktaḥ saṅgavarjitaḥ
nirvairaḥ sarvabhūteṣu yaḥ sa māmeti pāṇḍava

Arjuna, he who performs all his duties for My sake, depends on Me, is devoted to Me; has no attachment, and is free from malice towards all beings, reaches Me. (55)

ॐ तत्सदिति श्रीमद्भगवद्गीतासूपनिषत्सु ब्रह्मविद्यायां
योगशास्त्रे श्रीकृष्णार्जुनसंवादे विश्वरूपदर्शनयोगो
नामैकादशोऽध्यायः॥ ११॥

Thus, in the Upaniṣad sung by the Lord, the Science of Brahma, the scripture of Yoga, the dialogue between Śrī Kṛṣṇa and Arjuna, ends the eleventh chapter entitled "The Yoga of the Vision of the Universal Form."

ॐ श्रीपरमात्मने नमः

अथ द्वादशोऽध्यायः

CHAPTER TWELVE

अर्जुन उवाच

एवं सततयुक्ता ये भक्तास्त्वां पर्युपासते।
ये चाप्यक्षरमव्यक्तं तेषां के योगवित्तमाः ॥ १ ॥

arjuna uvāca

evaṁ satatayuktā ye bhaktāstvāṁ paryupāsate
ye cāpyakṣaramavyaktaṁ teṣāṁ ke yogavittamāḥ

Arjuna said : The devotees exclusively and constantly devoted to You in the manner stated just earlier, adore You as possessed of form and attributes, and those who adore as the supreme Reality only the indestructible unmanifest Brahma (who is Truth, Knowledge and Bliss solidified)—of these two types of worshippers who are the best knowers of Yoga? (1)

श्रीभगवानुवाच

मय्यावेश्य मनो ये मां नित्ययुक्ता उपासते।
श्रद्धया परयोपेतास्ते मे युक्ततमा मताः ॥ २ ॥

śrībhagavānuvāca

mayyāveśya mano ye māṁ nityayuktā upāsate
śraddhayā parayopetāste me yuktatamā matāḥ

Śrī Bhagavān said : I consider them to be the best Yogīs, who endowed with supreme faith, and ever united through meditation with Me, worship Me with the mind centred on Me. (2)

ये त्वक्षरमनिर्देश्यमव्यक्तं पर्युपासते।
सर्वत्रगमचिन्त्यं च कूटस्थमचलं ध्रुवम्॥ ३॥
सन्नियम्येन्द्रियग्रामं सर्वत्र समबुद्धयः।
ते प्राप्नुवन्ति मामेव सर्वभूतहिते रताः॥ ४॥

ye tvakṣaramanirdeśyamavyaktaṁ paryupāsate
sarvatragamacintyaṁ ca kūṭasthamacalaṁ dhruvam
sanniyamyendriyagrāmaṁ sarvatra samabuddhayaḥ
te prāpnuvanti māmeva sarvabhūtahite ratāḥ

Those, however, who fully controlling all their senses and even-minded towards all, and devoted to the welfare of all beings, constantly adore as their very self the unthinkable, omnipresent, indestructible, indefinable, eternal, immovable; unmanifest and changeless Brahma, they too come to Me. (3-4)

क्लेशोऽधिकतरस्तेषामव्यक्तासक्तचेतसाम्।
अव्यक्ता हि गतिर्दुःखं देहवद्भिरवाप्यते॥ ५॥

kleśo'dhikatarasteṣāmavyaktāsaktacetasām
avyaktā hi gatirduḥkhaṁ dehavadbhiravāpyate

Of course, the strain is greater for those who have their mind attached to the Unmanifest, as attunement with the Unmanifest is attained with difficulty by the body-conscious people. (5)

ये तु सर्वाणि कर्माणि मयि सन्न्यस्य मत्पराः।
अनन्येनैव योगेन मां ध्यायन्त उपासते॥ ६॥

तेषामहं समुद्धर्ता मृत्युसंसारसागरात्।
भवामि नचिरात्पार्थ मय्यावेशितचेतसाम्॥ ७॥

ye tu sarvāṇi karmāṇi mayi sannyasya matparāḥ
ananyenaiva yogena māṁ dhyāyanta upāsate
teṣāmahaṁ samuddhartā mṛtyusaṁsārasāgarāt
bhavāmi nacirātpārtha mayyāveśitacetasām

On the other hand, those who depending exclusively on Me, and surrendering all actions to Me, worship Me (God with attributes), constantly meditating on Me with single-minded devotion. Them, Arjuna, I speedily deliver from the ocean of birth and death, their mind being fixed on Me. (6-7)

मय्येव मन आधत्स्व मयि बुद्धिं निवेशय।
निवसिष्यसि मय्येव अत ऊर्ध्वं न संशयः॥ ८॥

mayyeva mana ādhatsva mayi buddhiṁ niveśaya
nivasiṣyasi mayyeva ata ūrdhvaṁ na saṁśayaḥ

Therefore, fix your mind on Me, and establish your intellect in Me alone; thereafter you will abide solely in Me. There is no doubt about it. (8)

अथ चित्तं समाधातुं न शक्नोषि मयि स्थिरम्।
अभ्यासयोगेन ततो मामिच्छाप्तुं धनञ्जय॥ ९॥

atha cittaṁ samādhātuṁ na śaknoṣi mayi sthiram
abhyāsayogena tato māmicchāptuṁ dhanañjaya

If you cannot steadily fix the mind on Me, Arjuna, then seek to attain Me through the Yoga of practice. (9)

अभ्यासेऽप्यसमर्थोऽसि मत्कर्मपरमो भव।
मदर्थमपि कर्माणि कुर्वन्सिद्धिमवाप्स्यसि॥ १०॥

abhyāse'pyasamartho'si matkarmaparamo bhava
madarthamapi karmāṇi kurvansiddhimavāpsyasi

If you are unequal even to the pursuit of such practice, be intent to work for Me; you shall attain perfection (in the shape of My realization) even by performing actions for My sake. (10)

अथैतदप्यशक्तोऽसि कर्तुं मद्योगमाश्रितः।
सर्वकर्मफलत्यागं ततः कुरु यतात्मवान्॥ ११॥

athaitadapyaśakto'si kartuṁ madyogamāśritaḥ
sarvakarmaphalatyāgaṁ tataḥ kuru yatātmavān

If, taking recourse to the Yoga of My realization, you are unable even to do this, then, subduing your mind and intellect etc., relinquish the fruit of all actions. (11)

श्रेयो हि ज्ञानमभ्यासाज्ज्ञानाद्ध्यानं विशिष्यते।
ध्यानात्कर्मफलत्यागस्त्यागाच्छान्तिरनन्तरम्॥ १२॥

śreyo hi jñānamabhyāsājjñānāddhyānaṁ viśiṣyate
dhyānātkarmaphalatyāgastyāgācchāntiranantaram

Knowledge is better than practice (without discernment), meditation on God is superior to knowledge, and renunciation of the fruit of actions is even superior to meditation; for peace immediately follows from renunciation. (12)

अद्वेष्टा सर्वभूतानां मैत्रः करुण एव च।
निर्ममो निरहङ्कारः समदुःखसुखः क्षमी॥ १३॥
सन्तुष्टः सततं योगी यतात्मा दृढनिश्चयः।
मय्यर्पितमनोबुद्धिर्यो मद्भक्तः स मे प्रियः॥ १४॥

advestā sarvabhūtānāṁ maitraḥ karuṇa eva ca
nirmamo nirahaṅkāraḥ samaduḥkhasukhaḥ kṣamī
santuṣṭaḥ satataṁ yogī yatātmā dṛḍhaniścayaḥ
mayyarpitamanobuddhiryo madbhaktaḥ sa me priyaḥ

He who is free from malice towards all beings, friendly and compassionate, rid of 'I' and 'mine', balanced in joy and sorrow, forgiving by nature, ever-contented and mentally united with Me, nay, who has subdued his mind, senses and body, has a firm resolve, and has surrendered his mind and reason to Me—that devotee of Mine is dear to Me. (13-14)

यस्मान्नोद्विजते लोको लोकान्नोद्विजते च यः।
हर्षामर्षभयोद्वेगैर्मुक्तो यः स च मे प्रियः॥ १५॥

yasmānnodvijate loko lokānnodvijate ca yaḥ
harṣāmarṣabhayodvegairmukto yaḥ sa ca me priyaḥ

He who is not a source of annoyance to his fellow-creatures, and who in his turn does not feel vexed with his fellow-creatures, and who is free from delight and envy, perturbation and fear, is dear to Me. (15)

अनपेक्षः शुचिर्दक्ष उदासीनो गतव्यथः।
सर्वारम्भपरित्यागी यो मद्भक्तः स मे प्रियः॥ १६॥

anapekṣaḥ śucirdakṣa udāsīno gatavyathaḥ
sarvārambhaparityāgī yo madbhaktaḥ sa me priyaḥ

He who wants nothing, who is both internally and externally pure, is wise and impartial and has risen above all distractions, and who renounces the sense of doership in all undertakings—such a devotee of Mine is dear to Me. (16)

यो न हृष्यति न द्वेष्टि न शोचति न काङ्क्षति।
शुभाशुभपरित्यागी भक्तिमान्यः स मे प्रियः॥ १७॥

yo na hṛṣyati na dveṣṭi na śocati na kāṅkṣati
śubhāśubhaparityāgī bhaktimānyaḥ sa me priyaḥ

He who neither rejoices nor hates, nor grieves, nor desires, and who renounces both good and evil actions and is full of devotion, is dear to Me. (17)

समः शत्रौ च मित्रे च तथा मानापमानयोः।
शीतोष्णसुखदुःखेषु समः सङ्गविवर्जितः॥ १८॥
तुल्यनिन्दास्तुतिर्मौनी सन्तुष्टो येन केनचित्।
अनिकेतः स्थिरमतिर्भक्तिमान्मे प्रियो नरः॥ १९॥

samaḥ śatrau ca mitre ca tathā mānāpamānayoḥ
śītoṣṇasukhaduḥkheṣu samaḥ saṅgavivarjitaḥ
tulyanindāstutirmaunī santuṣṭo yena kenacit
aniketaḥ sthiramatirbhaktimānme priyo naraḥ

He who deals equally with friend and foe, and is the same in honour and ignominy, who is alike in heat and cold, pleasure and pain and other contrary experiences, and is free from attachment, he who takes praise and reproach alike, and is given to contemplation and is contented with any means of subsistence available, entertaining no sense of ownership and attachment in respect of his dwelling-place and is full of devotion to Me, that person is dear to Me. (18-19)

ये तु धर्म्यामृतमिदं यथोक्तं पर्युपासते।
श्रद्दधाना मत्परमा भक्तास्तेऽतीव मे प्रियाः ॥ २० ॥

ye tu dharmyāmṛtamidaṁ yathoktaṁ paryupāsate
śraddadhānā matparamā bhaktāste'tīva me priyāḥ

Those devotees, however, who partake in a disinterested way of this nectar of pious wisdom set forth above, endowed with faith and solely devoted to Me, they are extremely dear to Me. (20)

ॐ तत्सदिति श्रीमद्भगवद्गीतासूपनिषत्सु ब्रह्मविद्यायां
योगशास्त्रे श्रीकृष्णार्जुनसंवादे भक्तियोगो
नाम द्वादशोऽध्यायः ॥ १२ ॥

Thus, in the Upaniṣad sung by the Lord, the Science of Brahma, the scripture of Yoga, the dialogue between Śrī Kṛṣṇa and Arjuna, ends the twelfth chapter entitled "The Yoga of Devotion."

ॐ श्रीपरमात्मने नमः

अथ त्रयोदशोऽध्यायः
CHAPTER THIRTEEN

श्रीभगवानुवाच

इदं शरीरं कौन्तेय क्षेत्रमित्यभिधीयते।
एतद्यो वेत्ति तं प्राहुः क्षेत्रज्ञ इति तद्विदः॥ १॥

śrībhagavānuvāca

idaṁ śarīraṁ kaunteya kṣetramityabhidhīyate
etadyo vetti taṁ prāhuḥ kṣetrajña iti tadvidaḥ

Śrī Bhagavān said : This body, Arjuna is termed as the Field (Kṣetra) and he who knows it, is called the knower of the Field (Kṣetrajña) by the sages discerning the truth about both. (1)

क्षेत्रज्ञं चापि मां विद्धि सर्वक्षेत्रेषु भारत।
क्षेत्रक्षेत्रज्ञयोर्ज्ञानं यत्तज्ज्ञानं मतं मम॥ २॥

kṣetrajñaṁ cāpi māṁ viddhi sarvakṣetreṣu bhārata
kṣetrakṣetrajñayorjñānaṁ yattajjñānaṁ mataṁ mama

Know Myself to be the Kṣetrajña (individual soul) in all the Kṣetras (fields), Arjuna. And it is the knowledge of the field (Kṣetra) and knower (Kṣetrajña) (i.e., of Matter with its evolutes and the Spirit) which I consider as true knowledge. (2)

तत्क्षेत्रं यच्च यादृक्च यद्विकारि यतश्च यत्।
स च यो यत्प्रभावश्च तत्समासेन मे शृणु॥ ३॥

tatkṣetraṁ yacca yādṛkca yadvikāri yataśca yat
sa ca yo yatprabhāvaśca tatsamāsena me śṛṇu

What that Field (Kṣetra) is and what it is like, what are its modifications, and from what causes what effects have sprung, and also who its knower (Kṣetrajña) is, and what is His glory—hear all this from Me in brief. (3)

ऋषिभिर्बहुधा गीतं छन्दोभिर्विविधैः पृथक्।
ब्रह्मसूत्रपदैश्चैव हेतुमद्भिर्विनिश्चितैः॥ ४॥

ṛṣibhirbahudhā gītaṁ chandobhirvividhaiḥ pṛthak
brahmasūtrapadaiścaiva hetumadbhirviniścitaiḥ

The truth about the Kṣetra and the Kṣetrajña has been expounded by the seers in manifold ways; again, it has been separately stated in different Vedic chants and also in the conclusive and reasoned texts of the Brahmasūtras. (4)

महाभूतान्यहङ्कारो बुद्धिरव्यक्तमेव च।
इन्द्रियाणि दशैकं च पञ्च चेन्द्रियगोचराः॥ ५॥

mahābhūtānyahaṅkāro buddhiravyaktameva ca
indriyāṇi daśaikaṁ ca pañca cendriyagocarāḥ

The five elements, the ego, the intellect, the Unmanifest (Primordial Matter), the ten organs of perception and action, the mind, and the five objects of sense (sound, touch, colour, taste and smell). (5)

इच्छा द्वेषः सुखं दुःखं सङ्घातश्चेतना धृतिः।
एतत्क्षेत्रं समासेन सविकारमुदाहृतम्॥ ६॥

icchā dveṣaḥ sukhaṁ duḥkhaṁ saṅghātaścetanā dhṛtiḥ
etatkṣetraṁ samāsena savikāramudāhṛtam

Also desire, aversion, pleasure, pain, the physical body, consciousness, firmness: thus is the Kṣetra, with its evolutes, briefly stated. (6)

अमानित्वमदम्भित्वमहिंसा क्षान्तिरार्जवम्।
आचार्योपासनं शौचं स्थैर्यमात्मविनिग्रहः॥ ७॥

amānitvamadambhitvamahiṁsā kṣāntirārjavam
ācāryopāsanaṁ śaucaṁ sthairyamātmavinigrahaḥ

Absence of pride, freedom from hypocrisy, non-violence, forbearance, straightness of body, speech and mind, devout service of the preceptor, internal and external purity, steadfastness of mind and control of body, mind and the senses. (7)

इन्द्रियार्थेषु वैराग्यमनहङ्कार एव च।
जन्ममृत्युजराव्याधिदुःखदोषानुदर्शनम्॥ ८॥

indriyārtheṣu vairāgyamanahaṅkāra eva ca
janmamṛtyujarāvyādhiduḥkhadoṣānudarśanam

Dispassion towards the objects of enjoyment of this world and the next, and also absence of egotism, pondering again and again on the pain and evils inherent in birth, death, old age and disease; (8)

असक्तिरनभिष्वङ्गः पुत्रदारगृहादिषु।
नित्यं च समचित्तत्वमिष्टानिष्टोपपत्तिषु॥ ९॥

asaktiranabhiṣvaṅgaḥ putradāragṛhādiṣu
nityaṁ ca samacittatvamiṣṭāniṣṭopapattiṣu

Absence of attachment and the sense of oneness in respect of son, wife, home etc., and constant equipoise of mind both in favourable and unfavourable circumstances; (9)

मयि चानन्ययोगेन भक्तिरव्यभिचारिणी।
विविक्तदेशसेवित्वमरतिर्जनसंसदि ॥ १० ॥

mayi cānanyayogena bhaktiravyabhicāriṇī
viviktadeśasevitvamaratirjanasaṁsadi

Unflinching devotion to Me through exclusive attachment, living in secluded and holy places, and finding no delight in the company of worldly people; (10)

अध्यात्मज्ञाननित्यत्वं तत्त्वज्ञानार्थदर्शनम्।
एतज्ज्ञानमिति प्रोक्तमज्ञानं यदतोऽन्यथा ॥ ११ ॥

adhyātmajñānanityatvaṁ tattvajñānārthadarśanam
etajjñānamiti proktamajñānaṁ yadato'nyathā

Constancy in self-knowledge and seeing God as the object of true knowledge—all this is declared as knowledge, and what is other than this is called ignorance. (11)

ज्ञेयं यत्तत्प्रवक्ष्यामि यज्ज्ञात्वामृतमश्नुते।
अनादिमत्परं ब्रह्म न सत्तन्नासदुच्यते ॥ १२ ॥

jñeyaṁ yattatpravakṣyāmi yajjñātvāmṛtamaśnute
anādimatparaṁ brahma na sattannāsaducyate

I shall speak to you at length about that which ought

to be known, and knowing which one attains supreme Bliss. That supreme Brahma, who is the lord of beginningless entities, is said to be neither Sat (being) nor Asat (non-being). (12)

सर्वतःपाणिपादं तत्सर्वतोऽक्षिशिरोमुखम्।
सर्वतःश्रुतिमल्लोके सर्वमावृत्य तिष्ठति॥ १३॥

sarvataḥpāṇipādaṁ tatsarvato'kṣiśiromukham
sarvataḥśrutimalloke sarvamāvṛtya tiṣṭhati

It has hands and feet on all sides, eyes, head and mouth in all directions, and ears all-round; for it stands pervading all in the universe. (13)

सर्वेन्द्रियगुणाभासं सर्वेन्द्रियविवर्जितम्।
असक्तं सर्वभृच्चैव निर्गुणं गुणभोक्तृ च॥ १४॥

sarvendriyaguṇābhāsaṁ sarvendriyavivarjitam
asaktaṁ sarvabhṛccaiva nirguṇaṁ guṇabhoktṛ ca

Though perceiving all sense-objects, it is really speaking devoid of all senses. Nay, though unattached, it is the sustainer of all nonetheless; and though attributeless, it is the enjoyer of guṇas, the three modes of Prakṛti. (14)

बहिरन्तश्च भूतानामचरं चरमेव च।
सूक्ष्मत्वात्तदविज्ञेयं दूरस्थं चान्तिके च तत्॥ १५॥

bahirantaśca bhūtānāmacaraṁ carameva ca
sūkṣmatvāttadavijñeyaṁ dūrasthaṁ cāntike ca tat

It exists without and within all beings, and constitutes the animate and inanimate creation as well. And by reason of its subtlety, it is incomprehensible; it is close at hand and stands afar too. (15)

अविभक्तं च भूतेषु विभक्तमिव च स्थितम्।
भूतभर्तृ च तज्ज्ञेयं ग्रसिष्णु प्रभविष्णु च॥ १६॥

avibhaktaṁ ca bhūteṣu vibhaktamiva ca sthitam
bhūtabhartṛ ca tajjñeyaṁ grasiṣṇu prabhaviṣṇu ca

Though integral like space in its undivided aspect, it appears divided as it were in all animate and inanimate beings. And that Godhead, which is the only object worth knowing, is the sustainer of being (as Viṣṇu), the destroyer (as Rudra) and the creator of all (as Brahmā). (16)

ज्योतिषामपि तज्ज्योतिस्तमसः परमुच्यते।
ज्ञानं ज्ञेयं ज्ञानगम्यं हृदि सर्वस्य विष्ठितम्॥ १७॥

jyotiṣāmapi tajjyotistamasaḥ paramucyate
jñānaṁ jñeyaṁ jñānagamyaṁ hṛdi sarvasya viṣṭhitam

That supreme Brahma is said to be the light of all lights and entirely beyond Māyā. That godhead is knowledge itself, worth knowing, and worth attaining through real wisdom, and is particularly abiding in the heart of all. (17)

इति क्षेत्रं तथा ज्ञानं ज्ञेयं चोक्तं समासतः।
मद्भक्त एतद्विज्ञाय मद्भावायोपपद्यते॥ १८॥

iti kṣetraṁ tathā jñānaṁ jñeyaṁ coktaṁ samāsataḥ
madbhakta etadvijñāya madbhāvāyopapadyate

Thus the truth of the Kṣetra and knowledge, as well as of the object worth knowing, God has been briefly discussed; knowing this in reality, My devotee enters into My being. (18)

प्रकृतिं पुरुषं चैव विद्ध्यनादी उभावपि।
विकारांश्च गुणांश्चैव विद्धि प्रकृतिसम्भवान्॥ १९॥

prakṛtiṁ puruṣaṁ caiva viddhyanādī ubhāvapi
vikārāṁśca guṇāṁścaiva viddhi prakṛtisambhavān

Prakṛti and Puruṣa, know both these as beginningless. And know all modifications such as likes and dislikes etc., and all objects constituted of the three Guṇas as born of Prakṛti. (19)

कार्यकरणकर्तृत्वे हेतुः प्रकृतिरुच्यते।
पुरुषः सुखदुःखानां भोक्तृत्वे हेतुरुच्यते॥ २०॥

kāryakaraṇakartṛtve hetuḥ prakṛtirucyate
puruṣaḥ sukhaduḥkhānāṁ bhoktṛtve heturucyate

Prakṛti is said to be responsible for bringing forth the evolutes and the instruments; while the individual soul is declared to be the cause of experience of joys and sorrows. (20)

पुरुषः प्रकृतिस्थो हि भुङ्क्ते प्रकृतिजान्गुणान्।
कारणं गुणसङ्गोऽस्य सदसद्योनिजन्मसु॥ २१॥

puruṣaḥ prakṛtistho hi bhuṅkte prakṛtijānguṇān
kāraṇaṁ guṇasaṅgo'sya sadasadyonijanmasu

Only the Puruṣa in association with Prakṛti experiences

objects of the nature of the three Guṇas evolved from Prakṛti. And it is contact with these guṇas that is responsible for the birth of this soul in good and evil wombs. (21)

उपद्रष्टानुमन्ता च भर्ता भोक्ता महेश्वरः।
परमात्मेति चाप्युक्तो देहेऽस्मिन्पुरुषः परः॥ २२॥

upadraṣṭānumantā ca bhartā bhoktā maheśvaraḥ
paramātmeti cāpyukto dehe'sminpuruṣaḥ paraḥ

The Spirit dwelling in this body, is really the same as the Supreme. He has been spoken of as the Witness, the true Guide, the Sustainer of all, the Experiencer (as the embodied soul), the Overlord and the Absolute as well. (22)

य एवं वेत्ति पुरुषं प्रकृतिं च गुणैः सह।
सर्वथा वर्तमानोऽपि न स भूयोऽभिजायते॥ २३॥

ya evaṁ vetti puruṣaṁ prakṛtiṁ ca guṇaiḥ saha
sarvathā vartamāno'pi na sa bhūyo'bhijāyate

He who thus knows the Puruṣa (Spirit) and Prakṛti (Nature) together with the Guṇas—even though performing his duties in everyway, is never born again. (23)

ध्यानेनात्मनि पश्यन्ति केचिदात्मानमात्मना।
अन्ये साङ्ख्येन योगेन कर्मयोगेन चापरे॥ २४॥

dhyānenātmani paśyanti kecidātmānamātmanā
anye sāṅkhyena yogena karmayogena cāpare

Some by meditation behold the supreme Spirit in the heart with the help of their refined and sharp intellect; others realize it through the discipline of Knowledge, and still others, through the discipline of Action, i.e., Karmayoga. (24)

अन्ये त्वेवमजानन्तः श्रुत्वान्येभ्य उपासते।
तेऽपि चातितरन्त्येव मृत्युं श्रुतिपरायणाः॥ २५॥

anye tvevamajānantaḥ śrutvānyebhya upāsate
te'pi cātitarantyeva mṛtyuṁ śrutiparāyaṇāḥ

Other dull-witted persons, however, not knowing thus, worship even as they have heard from others; and even those who are thus devoted to what they have heard, are able to cross the ocean of mundane existence in the shape of death. (25)

यावत्सञ्जायते किञ्चित्सत्त्वं स्थावरजङ्गमम्।
क्षेत्रक्षेत्रज्ञसंयोगात्तद्विद्धि भरतर्षभ॥ २६॥

yāvatsañjāyate kiñcitsattvaṁ sthāvarajaṅgamam
kṣetrakṣetrajñasaṁyogāttadviddhi bharatarṣabha

Arjuna, whatsoever being, moving or unmoving, is born, know it as emanated through the union of Kṣetra (Matter) and the Kṣetrajña (Spirit). (26)

समं सर्वेषु भूतेषु तिष्ठन्तं परमेश्वरम्।
विनश्यत्स्वविनश्यन्तं यः पश्यति स पश्यति॥ २७॥

samaṁ sarveṣu bhūteṣu tiṣṭhantaṁ parameśvaram
vinaśyatsvavinaśyantaṁ yaḥ paśyati sa paśyati

He alone truly sees, who sees the supreme Lord as imperishable and abiding equally in all perishable beings, both animate and inanimate. (27)

समं पश्यन्हि सर्वत्र समवस्थितमीश्वरम्।
न हिनस्त्यात्मनात्मानं ततो याति परां गतिम्॥ २८॥

samaṁ paśyanhi sarvatra samavasthitamīśvaram
na hinastyātmanātmānaṁ tato yāti parāṁ gatim

For, by seeing the Supreme Lord equally present in all, he does not kill the Self by himself, and thereby attains the supreme state. (28)

प्रकृत्यैव च कर्माणि क्रियमाणानि सर्वशः।
यः पश्यति तथात्मानमकर्तारं स पश्यति॥ २९॥

prakṛtyaiva ca karmāṇi kriyamāṇāni sarvaśaḥ
yaḥ paśyati tathātmānamakartāraṁ sa paśyati

He who sees that all actions are performed in everyway by nature (Prakṛti) and the Self as the non-doer, he alone verily sees. (29)

यदा भूतपृथग्भावमेकस्थमनुपश्यति।
तत एव च विस्तारं ब्रह्म सम्पद्यते तदा॥ ३०॥

yadā bhūtapṛthagbhāvamekasthamanupaśyati
tata eva ca vistāraṁ brahma sampadyate tadā

The moment man perceives the diversified existence of beings as rooted in the one supreme Spirit, and the spreading forth of all beings from the same, that very moment he attains Brahma (who is Truth, Consciousness and Bliss solidified). (30)

अनादित्वान्निर्गुणत्वात्परमात्मायमव्ययः ।
शरीरस्थोऽपि कौन्तेय न करोति न लिप्यते॥ ३१॥

**anāditvānnirguṇatvātparamātmāyamavyayaḥ
śarīrastho'pi kaunteya na karoti na lipyate**

Arjuna, being without beginning and without attributes, this indestructible supreme Spirit, though dwelling in the body, in fact does nothing, nor gets contaminated. (31)

यथा सर्वगतं सौक्ष्म्यादाकाशं नोपलिप्यते।
सर्वत्रावस्थितो देहे तथात्मा नोपलिप्यते॥ ३२॥

**yathā sarvagataṁ saukṣmyādākāśaṁ nopalipyate
sarvatrāvasthito dehe tathātmā nopalipyate**

As the all-pervading ether is not contaminated by reason of its subtlety, though permeating the body, the Self is not affected by the attributes of the body due to Its attributeless character. (32)

यथा प्रकाशयत्येकः कृत्स्नं लोकमिमं रविः।
क्षेत्रं क्षेत्री तथा कृत्स्नं प्रकाशयति भारत॥ ३३॥

**yathā prakāśayatyekaḥ kṛtsnaṁ lokamimaṁ raviḥ
kṣetraṁ kṣetrī tathā kṛtsnaṁ prakāśayati bhārata**

Arjuna, as the one sun illumines this entire universe, so the one Ātmā (Spirit) illumines the whole Kṣetra (Field). (33)

क्षेत्रक्षेत्रज्ञयोरेवमन्तरं ज्ञानचक्षुषा।
भूतप्रकृतिमोक्षं च ये विदुर्यान्ति ते परम्॥ ३४॥

kṣetrakṣetrajñayorevamantaraṁ jñānacakṣuṣā
bhūtaprakṛtimokṣaṁ ca ye viduryānti te param

Those who thus perceive with the eye of wisdom the difference between the Kṣetra and Kṣetrajña, and the phenomenon of liberation from Prakṛti with her evolutes, reach the supreme eternal Spirit. (34)

ॐ तत्सदिति श्रीमद्भगवद्गीतासूपनिषत्सु ब्रह्मविद्यायां
योगशास्त्रे श्रीकृष्णार्जुनसंवादे क्षेत्रक्षेत्रज्ञविभागयोगो
नामत्रयोदशोऽध्यायः ॥ १३ ॥

Thus, in the Upaniṣad sung by the Lord, the Science of Brahma, the scripture of Yoga, the dialogue between Śrī Kṛṣṇa and Arjuna, ends the thirteenth chapter entitled "The Yoga of discrimination between the Field and the Knower of the Field."

ॐ श्रीपरमात्मने नमः

अथ चतुर्दशोऽध्यायः

CHAPTER FOURTEEN

श्रीभगवानुवाच

परं भूयः प्रवक्ष्यामि ज्ञानानां ज्ञानमुत्तमम्।
यज्ज्ञात्वा मुनयः सर्वे परां सिद्धिमितो गताः॥ १॥

śrībhagavānuvāca

paraṁ bhūyaḥ pravakṣyāmi jñānānāṁ jñānamuttamam
yajjñātvā munayaḥ sarve parāṁ siddhimito gatāḥ

Śrī Bhagavān said : I shall expound once more the supreme knowledge, the best of all knowledge, acquiring which all sages have attained highest perfection, being liberated from this mundane existence. (1)

इदं ज्ञानमुपाश्रित्य मम साधर्म्यमागताः।
सर्गेऽपि नोपजायन्ते प्रलये न व्यथन्ति च॥ २॥

idaṁ jñānamupāśritya mama sādharmyamāgatāḥ
sarge'pi nopajāyante pralaye na vyathanti ca

Those who, by practising this knowledge, have entered into My being, are not born again at the cosmic dawn, nor feel disturbed even during the cosmic night. (2)

मम योनिर्महद्ब्रह्म तस्मिन्गर्भं दधाम्यहम्।
सम्भवः सर्वभूतानां ततो भवति भारत॥ ३॥

mama yonirmahadbrahma tasmingarbhaṁ dadhāmyaham
sambhavaḥ sarvabhūtānāṁ tato bhavati bhārata

My primordial Nature, known as the great Brahma, is the womb of all creatures; in that womb I place the seed of all life. The creation of all beings follows from that union of Matter and Spirit, O Arjuna. (3)

सर्वयोनिषु कौन्तेय मूर्तयः सम्भवन्ति याः ।
तासां ब्रह्म महद्योनिरहं बीजप्रदः पिता ॥ ४ ॥

sarvayoniṣu kaunteya mūrtayaḥ sambhavanti yāḥ
tāsāṁ brahma mahadyoniraham̐ bījapradaḥ pitā

Of all embodied beings that appear in all the species of various kinds, Arjuna, Prakṛti or Nature is the conceiving Mother, while I am the seed-giving Father. (4)

सत्त्वं रजस्तम इति गुणाः प्रकृतिसम्भवाः ।
निबध्नन्ति महाबाहो देहे देहिनमव्ययम् ॥ ५ ॥

sattvaṁ rajastama iti guṇāḥ prakṛtisambhavāḥ
nibadhnanti mahābāho dehe dehinamavyayam

Sattva, Rajas and Tamas—these three Guṇas born of Nature tie down the imperishable soul to the body, Arjuna. (5)

तत्र सत्त्वं निर्मलत्वात्प्रकाशकमनामयम् ।
सुखसङ्गेन बध्नाति ज्ञानसङ्गेन चानघ ॥ ६ ॥

tatra sattvaṁ nirmalatvātprakāśakamanāmayam
sukhasaṅgena badhnāti jñānasaṅgena cānagha

Of these Sattva, being immaculate, is illuminating

and flawless, Arjuna; it binds through attachment to happiness and knowledge. (6)

रजो रागात्मकं विद्धि तृष्णासङ्गसमुद्भवम्।
तन्निबध्नाति कौन्तेय कर्मसङ्गेन देहिनम्॥ ७॥

rajo rāgātmakaṁ viddhi tṛṣṇāsaṅgasamudbhavam
tannibadhnāti kaunteya karmasaṅgena dehinam

Arjuna, know the quality of Rajas, which is of the nature of passion, as born of desire and attachment. It binds the soul through attachment to actions and their fruit. (7)

तमस्त्वज्ञानजं विद्धि मोहनं सर्वदेहिनाम्।
प्रमादालस्यनिद्राभिस्तन्निबध्नाति भारत॥ ८॥

tamastvajñānajaṁ viddhi mohanaṁ sarvadehinām
pramādālasyanidrābhistannibadhnāti bhārata

And know Tamas, the deluder of all those who look upon the body as their own self, as born of ignorance. It binds the soul through error, sloth and sleep, Arjuna. (8)

सत्त्वं सुखे सञ्जयति रजः कर्मणि भारत।
ज्ञानमावृत्य तु तमः प्रमादे सञ्जयत्युत॥ ९॥

sattvaṁ sukhe sañjayati rajaḥ karmaṇi bhārata
jñānamāvṛtya tu tamaḥ pramāde sañjayatyuta

Sattva draws one to joy and Rajas to action; while Tamas, clouding wisdom, impels one to error, sleep and sloth. (9)

रजस्तमश्चाभिभूय सत्त्वं भवति भारत।
रजः सत्त्वं तमश्चैव तमः सत्त्वं रजस्तथा॥ १०॥

rajastamaścābhibhūya sattvaṁ bhavati bhārata
rajaḥ sattvaṁ tamaścaiva tamaḥ sattvaṁ rajastathā

Overpowering Rajas and Tamas, Arjuna, Sattva prevails; overpowering Sattva and Tamas, Rajas prevails; even so, overpowering Sattva and Rajas, Tamas prevails. (10)

सर्वद्वारेषु देहेऽस्मिन्प्रकाश उपजायते।
ज्ञानं यदा तदा विद्याद्विवृद्धं सत्त्वमित्युत॥ ११॥

sarvadvāreṣu dehe'sminprakāśa upajāyate
jñānaṁ yadā tadā vidyādvivṛddhaṁ sattvamityuta

When light and discernment dawn in this body, as well as in the mind and senses, then one should know that Sattva is predominant. (11)

लोभः प्रवृत्तिरारम्भः कर्मणामशमः स्पृहा।
रजस्येतानि जायन्ते विवृद्धे भरतर्षभ॥ १२॥

lobhaḥ pravṛttirārambhaḥ karmaṇāmaśamaḥ spṛhā
rajasyetāni jāyante vivṛddhe bharatarṣabha

With the preponderance of Rajas, Arjuna, greed, activity, undertaking of action with an interested motive, restlessness and a thirst for enjoyment make their appearance. (12)

अप्रकाशोऽप्रवृत्तिश्च प्रमादो मोह एव च।
तमस्येतानि जायन्ते विवृद्धे कुरुनन्दन॥ १३॥

aprakāśo'pravṛttiśca pramādo moha eva ca
tamasyetāni jāyante vivṛddhe kurunandana

With the growth of Tamas, Arjuna, obtuseness of the mind and senses, disinclination to perform one's obligatory duties, frivolity and stupor—all these appear. (13)

यदा सत्त्वे प्रवृद्धे तु प्रलयं याति देहभृत्।
तदोत्तमविदां लोकानमलान्प्रतिपद्यते ॥ १४ ॥

yadā sattve pravṛddhe tu pralayaṁ yāti dehabhṛt
tadottamavidāṁ lokānamalānpratipadyate

When a man dies during the preponderance of Sattva, he obtains the stainless ethereal worlds (heaven etc.,) attained by men of noble deeds. (14)

रजसि प्रलयं गत्वा कर्मसङ्गिषु जायते।
तथा प्रलीनस्तमसि मूढयोनिषु जायते ॥ १५ ॥

rajasi pralayaṁ gatvā karmasaṅgiṣu jāyate
tathā pralīnastamasi mūḍhayoniṣu jāyate

Dying when Rajas predominates, he is born among those attached to action; even so the man who has expired during the preponderance of Tamas is reborn in the species of stupid creatures, such as insects and beasts etc. (15)

कर्मणः सुकृतस्याहुः सात्त्विकं निर्मलं फलम्।
रजसस्तु फलं दुःखमज्ञानं तमसः फलम् ॥ १६ ॥

karmaṇaḥ sukṛtasyāhuḥ sāttvikaṁ nirmalaṁ phalam
rajasastu phalaṁ duḥkhamajñānaṁ tamasaḥ phalam

The reward of a righteous act, they say, is Sāttvika i.e., faultless in the shape of joy, wisdom and dispassion etc., sorrow is declared to be the fruit of a Rājasika act and ignorance, the fruit of a Tāmasika act. (16)

सत्त्वात्सञ्जायते ज्ञानं रजसो लोभ एव च।
प्रमादमोहौ तमसो भवतोऽज्ञानमेव च॥ १७॥

sattvātsañjāyate jñānaṁ rajaso lobha eva ca
pramādamohau tamaso bhavato'jñānameva ca

Wisdom follows from Sattva, and greed, undoubtedly, from Rajas; likewise obstinate error, stupor and also ignorance follow from Tamas. (17)

ऊर्ध्वं गच्छन्ति सत्त्वस्था मध्ये तिष्ठन्ति राजसाः।
जघन्यगुणवृत्तिस्था अधो गच्छन्ति तामसाः॥ १८॥

ūrdhvaṁ gacchanti sattvasthā madhye tiṣṭhanti rājasāḥ
jaghanyaguṇavṛttisthā adho gacchanti tāmasāḥ

Those who abide in the quality of Sattva wend their way upwards; while those of a Rājasika disposition stay in the middle. And those of a Tāmasika temperament, enveloped as they are in the effects of Tamoguṇa, sink down. (18)

नान्यं गुणेभ्यः कर्तारं यदा द्रष्टानुपश्यति।
गुणेभ्यश्च परं वेत्ति मद्भावं सोऽधिगच्छति॥ १९॥

nānyaṁ guṇebhyaḥ kartāraṁ yadā draṣṭānupaśyati
guṇebhyaśca paraṁ vetti madbhāvaṁ so'dhigacchati

When the discerning person sees no one as doer

other than the three Guṇas, and realizes Me, the supreme Spirit standing entirely beyond these Guṇas, he enters into My being. (19)

गुणानेतानतीत्य त्रीन्देही देहसमुद्भवान्।
जन्ममृत्युजरादुःखैर्विमुक्तोऽमृतमश्नुते ॥ २० ॥

guṇānetānatītya trīndehī dehasamudbhavān
janmamṛtyujarāduḥkhairvimukto'mṛtamaśnute

Having transcended the aforesaid three Guṇas, which have caused the body, and freed from birth, death, old age and all kinds of sorrow, this soul attains supreme bliss. (20)

अर्जुन उवाच

कैर्लिङ्गैस्त्रीन्गुणानेतानतीतो भवति प्रभो।
किमाचारः कथं चैतांस्त्रीन्गुणानतिवर्तते ॥ २१ ॥

arjuna uvāca

kairliṅgaistrīnguṇānetānatīto bhavati prabho
kimācāraḥ kathaṁ caitāṁstrīnguṇānativartate

Arjuna said : What are the marks of him who has risen above the three Guṇas, and what is his conduct ? And how, Lord, does he rise above the three Guṇas ? (21)

श्रीभगवानुवाच

प्रकाशं च प्रवृत्तिं च मोहमेव च पाण्डव।
न द्वेष्टि सम्प्रवृत्तानि न निवृत्तानि काङ्क्षति ॥ २२ ॥

śrībhagavānuvāca

prakāśaṁ ca pravṛttiṁ ca mohameva ca pāṇḍava
na dveṣṭi sampravṛttāni na nivṛttāni kāṅkṣati

Śrī Bhagavān said : Arjuna, he who hates not light (which is born of Sattva) and activity (which is born of Rajas) and even stupor (which is born of Tamas), when prevalent, nor longs for them when they have ceased. (22)

उदासीनवदासीनो गुणैर्यो न विचाल्यते।
गुणा वर्तन्त इत्येव योऽवतिष्ठति नेङ्गते॥ २३॥

udāsīnavadāsīno guṇairyo na vicālyate
guṇā vartanta ityeva yo'vatiṣṭhati neṅgate

He who, sitting like a witness, is not disturbed by the Guṇas, and who, knowing that the Guṇas alone move among the Guṇas, remains established in identity with God, and never falls off from that state. (23)

समदुःखसुखः स्वस्थः समलोष्टाश्मकाञ्चनः।
तुल्यप्रियाप्रियो धीरस्तुल्यनिन्दात्मसंस्तुतिः॥ २४॥

samaduḥkhasukhaḥ svasthaḥ samaloṣṭāśmakāñcanaḥ
tulyapriyāpriyo dhīrastulyanindātmasaṁstutiḥ

He who is ever established in the Self, takes pain and pleasure alike, regards a clod of earth, a stone and a piece of gold as equal in value, is possessed of wisdom, accepts the pleasant as well as the unpleasant in the same spirit, and views censure and praise alike. (24)

मानापमानयोस्तुल्यस्तुल्यो मित्रारिपक्षयोः।
सर्वारम्भपरित्यागी गुणातीतः स उच्यते॥ २५॥

mānāpamānayostulyastulyo mitrāripakṣayoḥ
sarvārambhaparityāgī guṇātītaḥ sa ucyate

He who is equipoised in honour or ignominy, is alike towards a friend or an enemy, and has renounced the sense of doership in all undertakings, is said to have risen above the three guṇas. (25)

मां च योऽव्यभिचारेण भक्तियोगेन सेवते।
स गुणान्समतीत्यैतान्ब्रह्मभूयाय कल्पते॥ २६॥

māṁ ca yo'vyabhicāreṇa bhaktiyogena sevate
sa guṇānsamatītyaitānbrahmabhūyāya kalpate

He too who, constantly worships Me through the Yoga of exclusive devotion—transcending these three Guṇas, he becomes eligible for attaining Brahma. (26)

ब्रह्मणो हि प्रतिष्ठाहममृतस्याव्ययस्य च।
शाश्वतस्य च धर्मस्य सुखस्यैकान्तिकस्य च॥ २७॥

brahmaṇo hi pratiṣṭhāhamamṛtasyāvyayasya ca
śāśvatasya ca dharmasya sukhasyaikāntikasya ca

For, I am the substratum of the imperishable Brahma, of immortality, of the eternal Dharma and of Absolute bliss. (27)

ॐ तत्सदिति श्रीमद्भगवद्गीतासूपनिषत्सु ब्रह्मविद्यायां
योगशास्त्रे श्रीकृष्णार्जुनसंवादे गुणत्रयविभागयोगो
नाम चतुर्दशोऽध्यायः॥ १४॥

Thus, in the Upaniṣad sung by the Lord, the Science of Brahma, the scripture of Yoga, the dialogue between Śrī Kṛṣṇa and Arjuna, ends the fourteenth chapter entitled "The Yoga of Division of three Guṇas."

ॐ श्रीपरमात्मने नमः

अथ पञ्चदशोऽध्यायः

CHAPTER FIFTEEN

श्रीभगवानुवाच

ऊर्ध्वमूलमधःशाखमश्वत्थं प्राहुरव्ययम्।
छन्दांसि यस्य पर्णानि यस्तं वेद स वेदवित्॥ १॥

śrībhagavānuvāca

ūrdhvamūlamadhaḥśākhamaśvattham prāhuravyayam
chandāṁsi yasya parṇāni yastaṁ veda sa vedavit

Śrī Bhagavān said : He who knows the Pīpala tree (in the form of creation); which is said to be imperishable with its roots in the Primeval Being (God), whose stem is represented by Brahmā (the Creator), and whose leaves are the Vedas, is a knower of the purport of the Vedas. (1)

अधश्चोर्ध्वं प्रसृतास्तस्य शाखा
गुणप्रवृद्धा विषयप्रवालाः।
अधश्च मूलान्यनुसन्ततानि
कर्मानुबन्धीनि मनुष्यलोके॥ २॥

adhaścordhvaṁ prasṛtāstasya śākhā
guṇapravṛddhā viṣayapravālāḥ
adhaśca mūlānyanusantatāni
karmānubandhīni manuṣyaloke

Fed by the three Guṇas and having sense-objects for

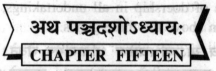

their tender leaves, the branches of the aforesaid tree (in the shape of the different orders of creation) extend both downwards and upwards; and its roots, which bind the soul according to its actions in the human body, are spread in all regions, higher as well as lower. (2)

न रूपमस्येह तथोपलभ्यते
नान्तो न चादिर्न च सम्प्रतिष्ठा।
अश्वत्थमेनं सुविरूढमूल-
मसङ्गशस्त्रेण दृढेन छित्त्वा॥ ३॥

na rūpamasyeha tathopalabhyate
nānto na cādirna ca sampratiṣṭhā
aśvatthamenaṁ suvirūḍhamūla-
masaṅgaśastreṇa dṛḍhena chittvā

The nature of this tree of creation does not on mature thought turn out what it is represented to be; for it has neither beginning nor end, nor even stability. Therefore, felling this Pīpala tree, which is most firmly rooted, with the formidable axe of dispassion. (3)

ततः पदं तत्परिमार्गितव्यं-
यस्मिन्गता न निवर्तन्ति भूयः।
तमेव चाद्यं पुरुषं प्रपद्ये
यतः प्रवृत्तिः प्रसृता पुराणी॥ ४॥

tataḥ padaṁ tatparimārgitavyaṁ-
yasmingatā na nivartanti bhūyaḥ
tameva cādyaṁ puruṣaṁ prapadye
yataḥ pravṛttiḥ prasṛtā purāṇī

Thereafter a man should diligently seek for that supreme state, viz., God, having attained to which they return no more to this world; and having fully resolved that he stands dedicated to that Primeval Being (God Nārāyaṇa) Himself, from whom the flow of this beginningless creation has progressed, he should dwell and meditate on Him. (4)

निर्मानमोहा जितसङ्गदोषा-
अध्यात्मनित्या विनिवृत्तकामाः ।
द्वन्द्वैर्विमुक्ताः सुखदुःखसञ्ज्ञै-
र्गच्छन्त्यमूढाः पदमव्ययं तत् ॥ ५ ॥

nirmānamohā jitasaṅgadoṣā-
adhyātmanityā vinivṛttakāmāḥ
dvandvairvimuktāḥ sukhaduḥkhasañjñai-
rgacchantyamūḍhāḥ padamavyayaṁ tat

They who are free from pride and delusion, who have conquered the evil of attachment, and are in eternal union with God, whose cravings have altogether ceased and who are completely immune from all pairs of opposites going by the names of pleasure and pain, and are undeluded, attain that supreme immortal state. (5)

न तद्भासयते सूर्यो न शशाङ्को न पावकः ।
यद्गत्वा न निवर्तन्ते तद्धाम परमं मम ॥ ६ ॥

na tadbhāsayate sūryo na śaśāṅko na pāvakaḥ
yadgatvā na nivartante taddhāma paramaṁ mama

Neither the sun nor the moon nor fire can illumine that supreme self-effulgent state, attaining to which they never return to this world; that is My supreme abode. (6)

ममैवांशो जीवलोके जीवभूतः सनातनः।
मनःषष्ठानीन्द्रियाणि प्रकृतिस्थानि कर्षति ॥ ७ ॥

mamaivāṁśo jīvaloke jīvabhūtaḥ sanātanaḥ
manaḥṣaṣṭhānīndriyāṇi prakṛtisthāni karṣati

The eternal Jīvātmā in this body is a fragment of My own being; and it is That alone which draws around itself the mind and the five senses, which abide in Prakṛti. (7)

शरीरं यदवाप्नोति यच्चाप्युत्क्रामतीश्वरः।
गृहीत्वैतानि संयाति वायुर्गन्धानिवाशयात् ॥ ८ ॥

śarīraṁ yadavāpnoti yaccāpyutkrāmatīśvaraḥ
gṛhītvaitāni saṁyāti vāyurgandhānivāśayāt

Even as the wind wafts scents from their seat, so too the Jīvātmā, which is the controller of the body etc., taking the mind and the senses from the body which it leaves behind forthwith migrates to the body which it acquires. (8)

श्रोत्रं चक्षुः स्पर्शनं च रसनं घ्राणमेव च।
अधिष्ठाय मनश्चायं विषयानुपसेवते ॥ ९ ॥

śrotraṁ cakṣuḥ sparśanaṁ ca rasanaṁ ghrāṇameva ca
adhiṣṭhāya manaścāyaṁ viṣayānupasevate

It is while dwelling in the senses of hearing, sight, touch, taste and smell, as well as in the mind, that this

Jīvātmā enjoys the objects of senses. (9)

उत्क्रामन्तं स्थितं वापि भुञ्जानं वा गुणान्वितम्।
विमूढा नानुपश्यन्ति पश्यन्ति ज्ञानचक्षुषः॥ १०॥

utkrāmantaṁ sthitaṁ vāpi bhuñjānaṁ vā guṇānvitam
vimūḍhā nānupaśyanti paśyanti jñānacakṣuṣaḥ

The ignorant know not the soul departing from, or dwelling in the body, or enjoying the objects of senses, i.e., even when it is connected with the three Guṇas; only those endowed with the eyes of wisdom are able to realize it. (10)

यतन्तो योगिनश्चैनं पश्यन्त्यात्मन्यवस्थितम्।
यतन्तोऽप्यकृतात्मानो नैनं पश्यन्त्यचेतसः॥ ११॥

yatanto yoginaścainaṁ paśyantyātmanyavasthitam
yatanto'pyakṛtātmāno nainaṁ paśyantyacetasaḥ

Striving Yogīs too are able to realise this self enshrined in their heart. The ignorant, however, whose heart has not been purified, know not this self in spite of their best endeavours. (11)

यदादित्यगतं तेजो जगद्भासयतेऽखिलम्।
यच्चन्द्रमसि यच्चाग्नौ तत्तेजो विद्धि मामकम्॥ १२॥

yadādityagataṁ tejo jagadbhāsayate'khilam
yaccandramasi yaccāgnau tattejo viddhi māmakam

The radiance in the sun that illumines the entire world, and that which shines in the moon and that which shines in the fire too, know that radiance to be Mine. (12)

गामाविश्य च भूतानि धारयाम्यहमोजसा।
पुष्णामि चौषधीः सर्वाः सोमो भूत्वा रसात्मकः ॥ १३ ॥

gāmāviśya ca bhūtāni dhārayāmyahamojasā
puṣṇāmi cauṣadhīḥ sarvāḥ somo bhūtvā rasātmakaḥ

And permeating the soil, it is I who support all creatures by My vital energy, and becoming the sapful moon, I nourish all plants. (13)

अहं वैश्वानरो भूत्वा प्राणिनां देहमाश्रितः।
प्राणापानसमायुक्तः पचाम्यन्नं चतुर्विधम् ॥ १४ ॥

ahaṁ vaiśvānaro bhūtvā prāṇināṁ dehamāśritaḥ
prāṇāpānasamāyuktaḥ pacāmyannaṁ caturvidham

Taking the form of fire, as Vaiśvānara, lodged in the body of all creatures and united with the Prāṇa (exhalation) and Apāna (inhalation) breaths, it is I who digest and assimilate the four kinds of food. (14)

सर्वस्य चाहं हृदि सन्निविष्टो-
मत्तः स्मृतिर्ज्ञानमपोहनं च।
वेदैश्च सर्वैरहमेव वेद्यो-
वेदान्तकृद्वेदविदेव चाहम् ॥ १५ ॥

sarvasya cāhaṁ hṛdi sanniviṣṭo-
mattaḥ smṛtirjñānamapohanaṁ ca
vedaiśca sarvairahameva vedyo-
vedāntakṛdvedavideva cāham

It is I who remain seated in the heart of all creatures as the inner controller of all; and it is I who am the source of memory, knowledge and the ratiocinative faculty. Again, I am the only object worth knowing through the Vedas; I alone am the father of Vedānta and the knower of the Vedas too. (15)

द्वाविमौ पुरुषौ लोके क्षरश्चाक्षर एव च।
क्षरः सर्वाणि भूतानि कूटस्थोऽक्षर उच्यते॥ १६॥

dvāvimau puruṣau loke kṣaraścākṣara eva ca
kṣaraḥ sarvāṇi bhūtāni kūṭastho'kṣara ucyate

The perishable and the imperishable too—these are the two kinds of Puruṣas in this world. Of these, the bodies of all beings are spoken of as the perishable; while the Jīvātmā or the embodied soul is called imperishable. (16)

उत्तमः पुरुषस्त्वन्यः परमात्मेत्युदाहृतः।
यो लोकत्रयमाविश्य बिभर्त्यव्यय ईश्वरः॥ १७॥

uttamaḥ puruṣastvanyaḥ paramātmetyudāhṛtaḥ
yo lokatrayamāviśya bibhartyavyaya īśvaraḥ

Yet, the Supreme Person is other than these, who, having encompassed all the three worlds, upholds and maintains all, and has been spoken of as the imperishable Lord and the Supreme Spirit. (17)

यस्मात्क्षरमतीतोऽहमक्षरादपि चोत्तमः।
अतोऽस्मि लोके वेदे च प्रथितः पुरुषोत्तमः॥ १८॥

yasmātkṣaramatīto'hamakṣarādapi cottamaḥ
ato'smi loke vede ca prathitaḥ puruṣottamaḥ

Since I am wholly beyond the perishable world of matter or Kṣetra, and am superior even to the imperishable soul, Jīvātmā, hence I am known as the Puruṣottama, the Supreme Self, in the world as well as in the Vedas. (18)

यो मामेवमसम्मूढो जानाति पुरुषोत्तमम्।
स सर्वविद्भजति मां सर्वभावेन भारत॥ १९॥

yo māmevamasammūḍho jānāti puruṣottamam
sa sarvavidbhajati māṁ sarvabhāvena bhārata

Arjuna, the wise man who thus realizes Me as the Supreme Person—knowing all, he constantly worships Me (the all-pervading Lord) with his whole being. (19)

इति गुह्यतमं शास्त्रमिदमुक्तं मयानघ।
एतद्बुद्ध्वा बुद्धिमान्स्यात्कृतकृत्यश्च भारत॥ २०॥

iti guhyatamaṁ śāstramidamuktaṁ mayānagha
etadbuddhvā buddhimānsyātkṛtakṛtyaśca bhārata

Arjuna, this most esoteric teaching has thus been imparted by Me; grasping it in essence man becomes wise and his mission in life is accomplished. (20)

ॐ तत्सदिति श्रीमद्भगवद्गीतासूपनिषत्सु ब्रह्मविद्यायां
योगशास्त्रे श्रीकृष्णार्जुनसंवादे पुरुषोत्तमयोगो
नाम पञ्चदशोऽध्यायः॥ १५॥

Thus, in the Upaniṣad sung by the Lord, the Science of Brahma, the scripture of Yoga, the dialogue between Śrī Kṛṣṇa and Arjuna, ends the fifteenth chapter entitled "The Yoga of the Supreme Person."

ॐ श्रीपरमात्मने नमः

अथ षोडशोऽध्यायः

CHAPTER SIXTEEN

श्रीभगवानुवाच

अभयं सत्त्वसंशुद्धिर्ज्ञानयोगव्यवस्थितिः।
दानं दमश्च यज्ञश्च स्वाध्यायस्तप आर्जवम्॥ १॥

śrībhagavānuvāca

abhayaṁ sattvasaṁśuddhirjñānayogavyavasthitiḥ
dānaṁ damaśca yajñaśca svādhyāyastapa ārjavam

Absolute fearlessness, perfect purity of mind, constant fixity in the Yoga of meditation for the sake of Self-realization, and even so charity in its Sāttvika form, control of the senses, worship of God and other deities as well as of one's elders including the performance of Agnihotra (pouring oblations into the sacred fire) and other sacred duties, study and teaching of the Vedas and other sacred books as well as the chanting of God's names and praises, suffering hardships for the discharge of one's sacred obligations and straightness of mind as well as of the body and senses. (1)

अहिंसा सत्यमक्रोधस्त्यागः शान्तिरपैशुनम्।
दया भूतेष्वलोलुप्त्वं मार्दवं ह्रीरचापलम्॥ २॥

ahiṁsā satyamakrodhastyāgaḥ śāntirapaiśunam
dayā bhūteṣvaloluptvaṁ mārdavaṁ hrīracāpalam

Non-violence in thought, word and deed, truthfulness and geniality of speech, absence of anger even on provocation, disclaiming doership in respect of actions, quietude or composure of mind, abstaining from malicious gossip, compassion towards all creatures, absence of attachment to the objects of senses even during their contact with the senses, mildness, a sense of shame in transgressing against the scriptures or usage, and abstaining from frivolous pursuits; (2)

तेजः क्षमा धृतिः शौचमद्रोहो नातिमानिता।
भवन्ति सम्पदं दैवीमभिजातस्य भारत॥ ३॥

tejaḥ kṣamā dhṛtiḥ śaucamadroho nātimānitā
bhavanti sampadaṁ daivīmabhijātasya bhārata

Sublimity, forbearance, fortitude, external purity, bearing enmity to none and absence of self-esteem—these are the marks of him, who is born with the divine gifts, Arjuna. (3)

दम्भो दर्पोऽभिमानश्च क्रोधः पारुष्यमेव च।
अज्ञानं चाभिजातस्य पार्थ सम्पदमासुरीम्॥ ४॥

dambho darpo'bhimānaśca krodhaḥ pāruṣyameva ca
ajñānaṁ cābhijātasya pārtha sampadamāsurīm

Hypocrisy, arrogance and pride, and anger, sternness and ignorance too—these are the marks of him, who is born with demoniac properties. (4)

दैवी सम्पद्विमोक्षाय निबन्धायासुरी मता।
मा शुचः सम्पदं दैवीमभिजातोऽसि पाण्डव॥ ५॥

daivī sampadvimokṣāya nibandhāyāsurī matā
mā śucaḥ sampadaṁ daivīmabhijāto'si pāṇḍava

The divine endowment has been recognized as conductive to liberation, and the demoniac one as leading to bondage. Grieve not, Arjuna, for you are born with the divine propensities. (5)

द्वौ भूतसर्गौ लोकेऽस्मिन्दैव आसुर एव च।
दैवो विस्तरशः प्रोक्त आसुरं पार्थ मे शृणु॥ ६॥

dvau bhūtasargau loke'smindaiva āsura eva ca
daivo vistaraśaḥ prokta āsuraṁ pārtha me śṛṇu

There are only two types of men in this world, Arjuna, the one possessing a divine nature and the other possessing a demoniac disposition. Of these, the type possessing divine nature has been dealt with at length; now hear in detail from Me about the type possessing demoniac disposition. (6)

प्रवृत्तिं च निवृत्तिं च जना न विदुरासुराः।
न शौचं नापि चाचारो न सत्यं तेषु विद्यते॥ ७॥

pravṛttiṁ ca nivṛttiṁ ca janā na vidurāsurāḥ
na śaucaṁ nāpi cācāro na satyaṁ teṣu vidyate

Men possessing a demoniac disposition know not what is right activity and what is right abstinence from activity. Hence they possess neither purity (external or internal) nor good conduct nor even truthfulness. (7)

असत्यमप्रतिष्ठं ते जगदाहुरनीश्वरम्।
अपरस्परसम्भूतं किमन्यत्कामहैतुकम्॥ ८॥

asatyamapratiṣṭhaṁ te jagadāhuranīśvaram
aparasparasambhūtaṁ kimanyatkāmahaitukam

Men possessing a demoniac disposition say this world is without any foundation, absolutely unreal and godless, brought forth by mutual union of the male and female and hence conceived in lust; what else than this? (8)

एतां दृष्टिमवष्टभ्य नष्टात्मानोऽल्पबुद्धयः।
प्रभवन्त्युग्रकर्माणः क्षयाय जगतोऽहिताः॥ ९॥

etāṁ dṛṣṭimavaṣṭabhya naṣṭātmāno'lpabuddhayaḥ
prabhavantyugrakarmāṇaḥ kṣayāya jagato'hitāḥ

Clinging to this false view these slow-witted men of a vile disposition and terrible deeds, enemies of mankind, prove equal only to the destruction of the universe. (9)

काममाश्रित्य दुष्पूरं दम्भमानमदान्विताः।
मोहाद्गृहीत्वासद्ग्राहान्प्रवर्तन्तेऽशुचिव्रताः॥ १०॥

kāmamāśritya duṣpūraṁ dambhamānamadānvitāḥ
mohādgṛhītvāsadgrāhānpravartante'śucivratāḥ

Cherishing insatiable desires and embracing false doctrines through ignorance, these men of impure conduct move in this world, full of hypocrisy, pride and arrogance. (10)

चिन्तामपरिमेयां च प्रलयान्तामुपाश्रिताः।
कामोपभोगपरमा एतावदिति निश्चिताः॥ ११॥

cintāmaparimeyāṁ ca pralayāntāmupāśritāḥ
kāmopabhogaparamā etāvaditi niścitāḥ

Giving themselves up to innumerable cares ending only with death, they remain devoted to the enjoyment of sensuous pleasures and are positive in their belief that this is the highest limit of joy. (11)

आशापाशशतैर्बद्धाः कामक्रोधपरायणाः।
ईहन्ते कामभोगार्थमन्यायेनार्थसञ्चयान्॥ १२॥

āśāpāśaśatairbaddhāḥ kāmakrodhaparāyaṇāḥ
īhante kāmabhogārthamanyāyenārthasañcayān

Held in bondage by hundreds of ties of expectation and wholly giving themselves up to lust and anger, they strive to amass by unfair means hoards of money and other objects for the enjoyment of sensuous pleasures. (12)

इदमद्य मया लब्धमिमं प्राप्स्ये मनोरथम्।
इदमस्तीदमपि मे भविष्यति पुनर्धनम्॥ १३॥

idamadya mayā labdhamimaṁ prāpsye manoratham
idamastīdamapi me bhaviṣyati punardhanam

They say to themselves, "This much has been secured by me today and now I shall realize this ambition. So much wealth is already with me and yet again this shall be mine. (13)

असौ मया हतः शत्रुर्हनिष्ये चापरानपि।
ईश्वरोऽहमहं भोगी सिद्धोऽहं बलवान्सुखी॥ १४॥

asau mayā hataḥ śatrurhaniṣye cāparānapi
īśvaro'hamahaṁ bhogī siddho'haṁ balavānsukhī

That enemy has been slain by me and I shall kill those others too. I am the lord of all, the enjoyer of all power, I am endowed with all supernatural powers, and am mighty and happy. (14)

आढ्योऽभिजनवानस्मि कोऽन्योऽस्ति सदृशो मया।
यक्ष्ये दास्यामि मोदिष्य इत्यज्ञानविमोहिताः ॥ १५ ॥
अनेकचित्तविभ्रान्ता मोहजालसमावृताः।
प्रसक्ताः कामभोगेषु पतन्ति नरकेऽशुचौ ॥ १६ ॥

āḍhyo'bhijanavānasmi ko'nyo'sti sadṛśo mayā
yakṣye dāsyāmi modiṣya ityajñānavimohitāḥ
anekacittavibhrāntā mohajālasamāvṛtāḥ
prasaktāḥ kāmabhogeṣu patanti narake'śucau

"I am wealthy and own a large family; who else is equal to me? I will sacrifice to gods, will give alms, I will make merry," Thus blinded by ignorance, enveloped in the mesh of delusion and addicted to the enjoyment of sensuous pleasures, their mind bewildered by numerous thoughts, these men of devilish disposition fall into the foulest hell. (15-16)

आत्मसम्भाविताः स्तब्धा धनमानमदान्विताः।
यजन्ते नामयज्ञैस्ते दम्भेनाविधिपूर्वकम् ॥ १७ ॥

ātmasambhāvitāḥ stabdhā dhanamānamadānvitāḥ
yajante nāmayajñaiste dambhenāvidhipūrvakam

Intoxicated by wealth and honour, those self-conceited and haughty men worship God through sacrifices only in name for ostentation, without following the sacred rituals. (17)

अहङ्कारं बलं दर्पं कामं क्रोधं च संश्रिताः।
मामात्मपरदेहेषु प्रद्विषन्तोऽभ्यसूयकाः॥ १८॥

ahaṅkāraṁ balaṁ darpaṁ kāmaṁ krodhaṁ ca saṁśritāḥ
māmātmaparadeheṣu pradviṣanto'bhyasūyakāḥ

Given over to egotism, brute force, arrogance, lust and anger etc. and calumniating others, they despise Me (the inner controller of all), dwelling in their own bodies as well as in those of others. (18)

तानहं द्विषतः क्रूरान्संसारेषु नराधमान्।
क्षिपाम्यजस्रमशुभानासुरीष्वेव योनिषु॥ १९॥

tānahaṁ dviṣataḥ krūrānsaṁsāreṣu narādhamān
kṣipāmyajasramaśubhānāsurīṣveva yoniṣu

These haters, sinful, cruel and vilest among men, I cast again and again into demoniacal wombs in this world. (19)

आसुरीं योनिमापन्ना मूढा जन्मनि जन्मनि।
मामप्राप्यैव कौन्तेय ततो यान्त्यधमां गतिम्॥ २०॥

āsurīṁ yonimāpannā mūḍhā janmani janmani
māmaprāpyaiva kaunteya tato yāntyadhamāṁ gatim

Failing to reach Me, Arjuna, these stupid souls are

born life after life in demoniac wombs and then verily sink down to a still lower plane. (20)

त्रिविधं नरकस्येदं द्वारं नाशनमात्मनः।
कामः क्रोधस्तथा लोभस्तस्मादेतत्त्रयं त्यजेत्॥ २१॥

trividhaṁ narakasyedaṁ dvāraṁ nāśanamātmanaḥ
kāmaḥ krodhastathā lobhastasmādetattrayaṁ tyajet

Desire, anger and greed–these triple gates of hell, bring about the downfall of the soul. Therefore, one should shun all these three. (21)

एतैर्विमुक्तः कौन्तेय तमोद्वारैस्त्रिभिर्नरः।
आचरत्यात्मनः श्रेयस्ततो याति परां गतिम्॥ २२॥

etairvimuktaḥ kaunteya tamodvāraistribhirnaraḥ
ācaratyātmanaḥ śreyastato yāti parāṁ gatim

Freed from these three gates of hell, man works for his own salvation and thereby attains the supreme goal, i.e. God. (22)

यः शास्त्रविधिमुत्सृज्य वर्तते कामकारतः।
न स सिद्धिमवाप्नोति न सुखं न परां गतिम्॥ २३॥

yaḥ śāstravidhimutsṛjya vartate kāmakārataḥ
na sa siddhimavāpnoti na sukhaṁ na parāṁ gatim

Discarding the injunctions of the scriptures, he who acts in an arbitrary way according to his own sweet will, such a person neither attains perfection, nor the supreme goal, nor even happiness. (23)

तस्माच्छास्त्रं प्रमाणं ते कार्याकार्यव्यवस्थितौ ।
ज्ञात्वा शास्त्रविधानोक्तं कर्म कर्तुमिहार्हसि ॥ २४ ॥

tasmācchāstraṁ pramāṇaṁ te kāryākāryavyavasthitau
jñātvā śāstravidhānoktaṁ karma kartumihārhasi

Therefore, the scripture alone is your guide in determining what should be done and what should not be done. Knowing this, you ought to perform only such action as is ordained by the scriptures. (24)

ॐ तत्सदिति श्रीमद्भगवद्गीतासूपनिषत्सु ब्रह्मविद्यायां
योगशास्त्रे श्रीकृष्णार्जुनसंवादे दैवासुरसम्पद्विभागयोगो
नाम षोडशोऽध्यायः ॥ १६ ॥

Thus, in the Upaniṣad sung by the Lord, the Science of Brahma, the scripture of Yoga, the dialogue between Śrī Kṛṣṇa and Arjuna, ends the sixteenth chapter entitled "The Yoga of Division between the Divine and the Demoniacal Properties."

ॐ श्रीपरमात्मने नमः

अथ सप्तदशोऽध्यायः

CHAPTER SEVENTEEN

अर्जुन उवाच

ये शास्त्रविधिमुत्सृज्य यजन्ते श्रद्धयान्विताः।
तेषां निष्ठा तु का कृष्ण सत्त्वमाहो रजस्तमः॥ १॥

arjuna uvāca

ye śāstravidhimutsṛjya yajante śraddhayānvitāḥ
teṣāṁ niṣṭhā tu kā kṛṣṇa sattvamāho rajastamaḥ

Arjuna said: Those, endowed with faith, who worship gods and others, disregarding the injunctions of the scriptures, where do they stand, Kṛṣṇa—in Sattva, Rajas or Tamas? (1)

श्रीभगवानुवाच

त्रिविधा भवति श्रद्धा देहिनां सा स्वभावजा।
सात्त्विकी राजसी चैव तामसी चेति तां शृणु॥ २॥

śrībhagavānuvāca

trividhā bhavati śraddhā dehināṁ sā svabhāvajā
sāttvikī rājasī caiva tāmasī ceti tāṁ śṛṇu

Śrī Bhagavān said: That untutored innate faith of men is of three kinds—Sāttvika, Rājasika and Tāmasika. Hear of it from Me. (2)

सत्त्वानुरूपा सर्वस्य श्रद्धा भवति भारत।
श्रद्धामयोऽयं पुरुषो यो यच्छ्रद्धः स एव सः ॥ ३ ॥

sattvānurūpā sarvasya śraddhā bhavati bhārata
śraddhāmayo'yaṁ puruṣo yo yacchraddhaḥ sa eva saḥ

The faith of all men conforms to their mental disposition, Arjuna. Faith constitutes a man; whatever the nature of his faith, verily he is that. (3)

यजन्ते सात्त्विका देवान्यक्षरक्षांसि राजसाः।
प्रेतान्भूतगणांश्चान्ये यजन्ते तामसा जनाः ॥ ४ ॥

yajante sāttvikā devānyakṣarakṣāṁsi rājasāḥ
pretānbhūtagaṇāṁścānye yajante tāmasā janāḥ

Men of Sāttvika disposition worship gods; those of Rājasika temperament worship demigods, the demons; while others, who are of Tāmasika disposition, worship the spirits of the dead and ghosts. (4)

अशास्त्रविहितं घोरं तप्यन्ते ये तपो जनाः।
दम्भाहङ्कारसंयुक्ताः कामरागबलान्विताः ॥ ५ ॥

aśāstravihitaṁ ghoraṁ tapyante ye tapo janāḥ
dambhāhaṅkārasaṁyuktāḥ kāmarāgabalānvitāḥ

Men who practise dire penance of an arbitrary type not sanctioned by the scriptures, and who are full of hypocrisy and egotism and are obsessed with desire, attachment and pride of power; (5)

कर्शयन्तः शरीरस्थं भूतग्राममचेतसः।
मां चैवान्तःशरीरस्थं तान्विद्ध्यासुरनिश्चयान् ॥ ६ ॥

karśayantaḥ śarīrasthaṁ bhūtagrāmamacetasaḥ
māṁ caivāntaḥśarīrasthaṁ tānviddhyāsuraniścayān

And who emaciate the elements constituting their body as well as Me, the Supreme Spirit, dwelling in their heart—know these senseless people to have a demoniac disposition. (6)

आहारस्त्वपि सर्वस्य त्रिविधो भवति प्रियः ।
यज्ञस्तपस्तथा दानं तेषां भेदमिमं शृणु ॥ ७ ॥

āhārastvapi sarvasya trividho bhavati priyaḥ
yajñastapastathā dānaṁ teṣāṁ bhedamimaṁ śṛṇu

Food also, which is agreeable to different men according to their innate disposition is of three kinds. And likewise sacrifice, penance and charity too are of three kinds each; hear their distinction as follows. (7)

आयुःसत्त्वबलारोग्यसुखप्रीतिविवर्धनाः ।
रस्याः स्निग्धाः स्थिरा हृद्या आहाराः सात्त्विकप्रियाः ॥ ८ ॥

āyuḥsattvabalārogyasukhaprītivivardhanāḥ
rasyāḥ snigdhāḥ sthirā hṛdyā āhārāḥ sāttvikapriyāḥ

Foods which promote longevity, intelligence, vigour, health, happiness and cheerfulness, and which are juicy, succulent, substantial and naturally agreeable, are liked by men of Sāttvika nature. (8)

कट्वम्ललवणात्युष्णतीक्ष्णरूक्षविदाहिनः ।
आहारा राजसस्येष्टा दुःखशोकामयप्रदाः ॥ ९ ॥

kaṭvamlalavaṇātyuṣṇatīkṣṇarūkṣavidāhinaḥ
āhārā rājasasyeṣṭā duḥkhaśokāmayapradāḥ

Foods which are bitter, sour, salty, overhot, pungent, dry and burning, and which cause suffering, grief and sickness, are dear to the Rājasika. (9)

यातयामं गतरसं पूति पर्युषितं च यत्।
उच्छिष्टमपि चामेध्यं भोजनं तामसप्रियम्॥ १०॥

yātayāmaṁ gatarasaṁ pūti paryuṣitaṁ ca yat
ucchiṣṭamapi cāmedhyaṁ bhojanaṁ tāmasapriyam

Food which is ill-cooked or not fully ripe, insipid, putrid, stale and polluted, and which is impure too, is dear to men of Tāmasika disposition. (10)

अफलाकाङ्क्षिभिर्यज्ञो विधिदृष्टो य इज्यते।
यष्टव्यमेवेति मनः समाधाय स सात्त्विकः॥ ११॥

aphalākāṅkṣibhiryajño vidhidṛṣṭo ya ijyate
yaṣṭavyameveti manaḥ samādhāya sa sāttvikaḥ

The sacrifice which is offered, as ordained by scriptural injunctions, by men who expect no return and who believe that such sacrifices must be performed, is Sāttvika in character. (11)

अभिसन्धाय तु फलं दम्भार्थमपि चैव यत्।
इज्यते भरतश्रेष्ठ तं यज्ञं विद्धि राजसम्॥ १२॥

abhisandhāya tu phalaṁ dambhārthamapi caiva yat
ijyate bharataśreṣṭha taṁ yajñaṁ viddhi rājasam

That sacrifice, however, which is offered for the sake of mere show or even with an eye to its fruit, know it to be Rājasika, Arjuna. (12)

विधिहीनमसृष्टान्नं मन्त्रहीनमदक्षिणम्।
श्रद्धाविरहितं यज्ञं तामसं परिचक्षते॥ १३॥

vidhihīnamasṛṣṭānnaṁ mantrahīnamadakṣiṇam
śraddhāvirahitaṁ yajñaṁ tāmasaṁ paricakṣate

A sacrifice, which is not in conformity with scriptural injunctions, in which no food is offered, and no sacrificial fees are paid, which is without sacred chant of hymns and devoid of faith, is said to be Tāmasika. (13)

देवद्विजगुरुप्राज्ञपूजनं शौचमार्जवम्।
ब्रह्मचर्यमहिंसा च शारीरं तप उच्यते॥ १४॥

devadvijagurupräjñapūjanaṁ śaucamārjavam
brahmacaryamahiṁsā ca śārīraṁ tapa ucyate

Worship of gods, the Brāhmaṇas, one's elders and great souls, purity, straightforwardness, continence and non-violence–this is called penance of the body. (14)

अनुद्वेगकरं वाक्यं सत्यं प्रियहितं च यत्।
स्वाध्यायाभ्यसनं चैव वाङ्मयं तप उच्यते॥ १५॥

anudvegakaraṁ vākyaṁ satyaṁ priyahitaṁ ca yat
svādhyāyābhyasanaṁ caiva vāṅmayaṁ tapa ucyate

Words which cause no annoyance to others and are truthful, agreeable and beneficial, as well as the study of the Vedas and other Śāstras and the practice of the chanting of Divine Name–this is known as penance of speech. (15)

मनःप्रसादः सौम्यत्वं मौनमात्मविनिग्रहः।
भावसंशुद्धिरित्येतत्तपो मानसमुच्यते॥ १६॥

manaḥprasādaḥ saumyatvaṁ maunamātmavinigrahaḥ
bhāvasaṁśuddhirityetattapo mānasamucyate

Cheerfulness of mind, placidity, habit of contemplation on God, control of the mind and perfect purity of inner feelings—all this is called austerity of the mind. (16)

श्रद्धया परया तप्तं तपस्तत्त्रिविधं नरैः।
अफलाकाङ्क्षिभिर्युक्तैः सात्त्विकं परिचक्षते॥ १७॥

śraddhayā parayā taptaṁ tapastattrividhaṁ naraiḥ
aphalākāṅkṣibhiryuktaiḥ sāttvikaṁ paricakṣate

This threefold penance performed with supreme faith by Yogīs expecting no return is called Sāttvika. (17)

सत्कारमानपूजार्थं तपो दम्भेन चैव यत्।
क्रियते तदिह प्रोक्तं राजसं चलमध्रुवम्॥ १८॥

satkāramānapūjārthaṁ tapo dambhena caiva yat
kriyate tadiha proktaṁ rājasaṁ calamadhruvam

The austerity which is performed for the sake of renown, honour or adoration, as well as for any other selfish gain, either in all sincerity or by way of ostentation, and yields an uncertain and momentary fruit, has been spoken of here as Rājasika. (18)

मूढग्राहेणात्मनो यत्पीडया क्रियते तपः।
परस्योत्सादनार्थं वा तत्तामसमुदाहृतम्॥ १९॥

mūḍhagrāheṇātmano yatpīḍayā kriyate tapaḥ
parasyotsādanārthaṁ vā tattāmasamudāhṛtam

Penance which is resorted to out of foolish notion and is accompanied by self-mortification, or is intended to harm others, such penance has been declared as Tāmasika. (19)

दातव्यमिति यद्दानं दीयतेऽनुपकारिणे।
देशे काले च पात्रे च तद्दानं सात्त्विकं स्मृतम्॥ २०॥

dātavyamiti yaddānaṁ dīyate'nupakāriṇe
deśe kāle ca pātre ca taddānaṁ sāttvikaṁ smṛtam

A gift which is bestowed with a sense of duty on one from whom no return is expected, at appropriate time and place, and to a deserving person, that gift has been declared as Sāttvika. (20)

यत्तु प्रत्युपकारार्थं फलमुद्दिश्य वा पुनः।
दीयते च परिक्लिष्टं तद्दानं राजसं स्मृतम्॥ २१॥

yattu pratyupakārārthaṁ phalamuddiśya vā punaḥ
dīyate ca parikliṣṭaṁ taddānaṁ rājasaṁ smṛtam

A gift which is bestowed in a grudging spirit and with the object of getting a service in return or in the hope of obtaining a reward, is called Rājasika. (21)

अदेशकाले यद्दानमपात्रेभ्यश्च दीयते।
असत्कृतमवज्ञातं तत्तामसमुदाहृतम्॥ २२॥

adeśakāle yaddānamapātrebhyaśca dīyate
asatkṛtamavajñātaṁ tattāmasamudāhṛtam

A gift which is made without good grace and in a disdainful spirit out of time and place and to undeserving persons, is said to be Tāmasika. (22)

ॐ तत्सदिति निर्देशो ब्रह्मणस्त्रिविधः स्मृतः।
ब्राह्मणास्तेन वेदाश्च यज्ञाश्च विहिताः पुरा॥ २३॥

oṁ tatsaditi nirdeśo brahmaṇastrividhaḥ smṛtaḥ
brāhmaṇāstena vedāśca yajñāśca vihitāḥ purā

OṀ, TAT and SAT—this has been declared as the triple appellation of Brahma, who is Truth, Consciousness and Bliss. By that were the Brāhmaṇas and the Vedas as well as sacrifices created at the cosmic dawn. (23)

तस्मादोमित्युदाहृत्य यज्ञदानतपःक्रियाः।
प्रवर्तन्ते विधानोक्ताः सततं ब्रह्मवादिनाम्॥ २४॥

tasmādomityudāhṛtya yajñadānatapaḥkriyāḥ
pravartante vidhānoktāḥ satataṁ brahmavādinām

Therefore, acts of sacrifice, charity and austerity, as enjoined by sacred precepts, are always commenced by noble persons, used to the recitation of Vedic chants, with the invocation of the divine name 'OṀ'. (24)

तदित्यनभिसन्धाय फलं यज्ञतपःक्रियाः।
दानक्रियाश्च विविधाः क्रियन्ते मोक्षकाङ्क्षिभिः॥ २५॥

tadityanabhisandhāya phalaṁ yajñatapaḥkriyāḥ
dānakriyāśca vividhāḥ kriyante mokṣakāṅkṣibhiḥ

With the idea that all this belongs to God, who is denoted by the appellation TAT, acts of sacrifice and austerity as well as acts of charity of various kinds, are performed by the seekers of liberation, expecting no return for them. (25)

सद्भावे साधुभावे च सदित्येतत्प्रयुज्यते।
प्रशस्ते कर्मणि तथा सच्छब्दः पार्थ युज्यते॥ २६॥

sadbhāve sādhubhāve ca sadityetatprayujyate
praśaste karmaṇi tathā sacchabdaḥ pārtha yujyate

The name of God, SAT, is used in the sense of reality and goodness. And the word SAT is also used in the sense of a praiseworthy, auspicious action, Arjuna. (26)

यज्ञे तपसि दाने च स्थितिः सदिति चोच्यते।
कर्म चैव तदर्थीयं सदित्येवाभिधीयते॥ २७॥

yajñe tapasi dāne ca sthitiḥ saditi cocyate
karma caiva tadarthīyaṁ sadityevābhidhīyate

And steadfastness in sacrifice, austerity and charity is likewise spoken of as 'SAT' and action for the sake of God is verily termed as 'SAT'. (27)

अश्रद्धया हुतं दत्तं तपस्तप्तं कृतं च यत्।
असदित्युच्यते पार्थ न च तत्प्रेत्य नो इह॥ २८॥

aśraddhayā hutaṁ dattaṁ tapastaptaṁ kṛtaṁ ca yat
asadityucyate pārtha na ca tatpretya no iha

An oblation which is offered, a gift given, an austerity practised, and whatever good deed is performed, if it is without faith, it is termed as naught i.e. 'asat'; therefore, it is of no avail here or hereafter. (28)

ॐ तत्सदिति श्रीमद्भगवद्गीतासूपनिषत्सु ब्रह्मविद्यायां
योगशास्त्रे श्रीकृष्णार्जुनसंवादे श्रद्धात्रयविभागयोगो
नाम सप्तदशोऽध्यायः ॥ १७ ॥

Thus, in the Upaniṣad sung by the Lord, the Science of Brahma, the scripture of Yoga, the dialogue between Śrī Kṛṣṇa and Arjuna, ends the seventeenth chapter entitled "The Yoga of the Division of the Threefold Faith."

ॐ श्रीपरमात्मने नमः

अथाष्टादशोऽध्यायः

CHAPTER EIGHTEEN

अर्जुन उवाच

सन्न्यासस्य महाबाहो तत्त्वमिच्छामि वेदितुम्।
त्यागस्य च हृषीकेश पृथक्केशिनिषूदन॥ १॥

arjuna uvāca

sannyāsasya mahābāho tattvamicchāmi veditum
tyāgasya ca hṛṣīkeśa pṛthakkeśiniṣūdana

Arjuna said: O mighty-armed Śrī Kṛṣṇa, O inner controller of all, O Slayer of Keśi, I wish to know severally the truth of Sannyāsa as also of Tyāga. (1)

श्रीभगवानुवाच

काम्यानां कर्मणां न्यासं सन्न्यासं कवयो विदुः।
सर्वकर्मफलत्यागं प्राहुस्त्यागं विचक्षणाः॥ २॥

śrībhagavānuvāca

kāmyānāṁ karmaṇāṁ nyāsaṁ sannyāsaṁ kavayo viduḥ
sarvakarmaphalatyāgaṁ prāhustyāgaṁ vicakṣaṇāḥ

Śrī Bhagavān said : Some sages understand Sannyāsa as the giving up of all actions motivated by desire; and the wise declare that Tyāga consists in relinquishing the fruit of all actions. (2)

त्याज्यं दोषवदित्येके कर्म प्राहुर्मनीषिणः।
यज्ञदानतपःकर्म न त्याज्यमिति चापरे॥ ३॥

tyājyaṁ doṣavadityeke karma prāhurmanīṣiṇaḥ
yajñadānatapaḥkarma na tyājyamiti cāpare

Some wise men declare that all actions contain a measure of evil, and are therefore worth giving up; while others say that acts of sacrifice, charity and penance are not to be given up. (3)

निश्चयं शृणु मे तत्र त्यागे भरतसत्तम।
त्यागो हि पुरुषव्याघ्र त्रिविधः सम्प्रकीर्तितः॥ ४॥

niścayaṁ śṛṇu me tatra tyāge bharatasattama
tyāgo hi puruṣavyāghra trividhaḥ samprakīrtitaḥ

Of Sannyāsa and Tyāga, first hear My conclusion on the subject of renunciation (Tyāga), Arjuna; for renunciation, O tiger among men, has been declared to be of three kinds—Sāttvika, Rājasika and Tāmasika. (4)

यज्ञदानतपःकर्म न त्याज्यं कार्यमेव तत्।
यज्ञो दानं तपश्चैव पावनानि मनीषिणाम्॥ ५॥

yajñadānatapaḥkarma na tyājyaṁ kāryameva tat
yajño dānaṁ tapaścaiva pāvanāni manīṣiṇām

Acts of sacrifice, charity and penance are not worth giving up; they must be performed. For sacrifice, charity and penance—all these are purifiers of wise men. (5)

एतान्यपि तु कर्माणि सङ्गं त्यक्त्वा फलानि च।
कर्तव्यानीति मे पार्थ निश्चितं मतमुत्तमम्॥ ६॥

etānyapi tu karmāṇi saṅgaṁ tyaktvā phalāni ca
kartavyānīti me pārtha niścitaṁ matamuttamam

Hence these acts of sacrifice, charity and penance, and all other acts of duty too, must be performed without attachment and expectation of reward : this is My well considered and supreme verdict, Arjuna. (6)

नियतस्य तु सन्न्यासः कर्मणो नोपपद्यते।
मोहात्तस्य परित्यागस्तामसः परिकीर्तितः ॥ ७ ॥

niyatasya tu sannyāsaḥ karmaṇo nopapadyate
mohāttasya parityāgastāmasaḥ parikīrtitaḥ

(Prohibited acts and those that are motivated by desire should no doubt be given up). But it is not advisable to abandon a prescribed duty. Such abandonment through ignorance has been declared as Tāmasika. (7)

दुःखमित्येव यत्कर्म कायक्लेशभयात्त्यजेत्।
स कृत्वा राजसं त्यागं नैव त्यागफलं लभेत् ॥ ८ ॥

duḥkhamityeva yatkarma kāyakleśabhayāttyajet
sa kṛtvā rājasaṁ tyāgaṁ naiva tyāgaphalaṁ labhet

Should anyone give up his duties for fear of physical strain, thinking that all actions are verily painful–practising such Rājasika form of renunciation, he does not reap the fruit of renunciation. (8)

कार्यमित्येव यत्कर्म नियतं क्रियतेऽर्जुन।
सङ्गं त्यक्त्वा फलं चैव स त्यागः सात्त्विको मतः ॥ ९ ॥

kāryamityeva yatkarma niyataṁ kriyate'rjuna
saṅgaṁ tyaktvā phalaṁ caiva sa tyāgaḥ sāttviko mataḥ

A prescribed duty which is performed simply because it has to be performed, giving up attachment and fruit, that alone has been recognized as the Sāttvika form of renunciation. (9)

न द्वेष्ट्यकुशलं कर्म कुशले नानुषज्जते।
त्यागी सत्त्वसमाविष्टो मेधावी छिन्नसंशयः॥ १०॥

na dveṣṭyakuśalaṁ karma kuśale nānuṣajjate
tyāgī sattvasamāviṣṭo medhāvī chinnasaṁśayaḥ

He who has neither aversion for action which is leading to bondage nor attachment to that which is conducive to blessedness-imbued with the quality of goodness, he has all his doubts resolved, is intelligent and a man of true renunciation. (10)

न हि देहभृता शक्यं त्यक्तुं कर्माण्यशेषतः।
यस्तु कर्मफलत्यागी स त्यागीत्यभिधीयते॥ ११॥

na hi dehabhṛtā śakyaṁ tyaktuṁ karmāṇyaśeṣataḥ
yastu karmaphalatyāgī sa tyāgītyabhidhīyate

Since all actions cannot be given up in their entirety by anyone possessing a body, he alone who renounces the fruit of actions is called a man of renunciation. (11)

अनिष्टमिष्टं मिश्रं च त्रिविधं कर्मणः फलम्।
भवत्यत्यागिनां प्रेत्य न तु सन्न्यासिनां क्वचित्॥ १२॥

aniṣṭamiṣṭaṁ miśraṁ ca trividhaṁ karmaṇaḥ phalam bhavatyatyāgināṁ pretya na tu sannyāsināṁ kvacit

Agreeable, disagreeable and mixed–threefold, indeed, is the fruit that accrues after death from the actions of the unrenouncing. But there is none whatsoever for those who have renounced. (12)

पञ्चैतानि महाबाहो कारणानि निबोध मे।
साङ्ख्ये कृतान्ते प्रोक्तानि सिद्धये सर्वकर्मणाम्॥ १३॥

pañcaitāni mahābāho kāraṇāni nibodha me sāṅkhye kṛtānte proktāni siddhaye sarvakarmaṇām

In the branch of learning known as Sāṅkhya, which prescribes means for neutralizing all actions, the five factors have been mentioned as contributory to the accomplishment of all actions; know them all from Me, Arjuna. (13)

अधिष्ठानं तथा कर्ता करणं च पृथग्विधम्।
विविधाश्च पृथक्चेष्टा दैवं चैवात्र पञ्चमम्॥ १४॥

adhiṣṭhānaṁ tathā kartā karaṇaṁ ca pṛthagvidham vividhāśca pṛthakceṣṭā daivaṁ caivātra pañcamam

The following are the factors operating towards the accomplishment of actions, viz., the body and the doer, the organs of different kinds and the different functions of manifold kinds; and the fifth is Daiva or destiny. (14)

शरीरवाङ्मनोभिर्यत्कर्म प्रारभते नरः।
न्याय्यं वा विपरीतं वा पञ्चैते तस्य हेतवः॥ १५॥

śarīravāṅmanobhiryatkarma prārabhate naraḥ
nyāyyaṁ vā viparītaṁ vā pañcaite tasya hetavaḥ

These five are the contributory causes of whatever actions, right or wrong, man performs with the mind, speech and body. (15)

तत्रैवं सति कर्तारमात्मानं केवलं तु यः।
पश्यत्यकृतबुद्धित्वान्न स पश्यति दुर्मतिः॥ १६॥

tatraivaṁ sati kartāramātmānaṁ kevalaṁ tu yaḥ
paśyatyakṛtabuddhitvānna sa paśyati durmatiḥ

Notwithstanding this, however, he who, having an impure mind, regards the absolute, taintless Self alone as the doer, that man of perverse understanding does not view aright. (16)

यस्य नाहङ्कृतो भावो बुद्धिर्यस्य न लिप्यते।
हत्वापि स इमाँल्लोकान्न हन्ति न निबध्यते॥ १७॥

yasya nāhaṅkṛto bhāvo buddhiryasya na lipyate
hatvāpi sa imāँllokānna hanti na nibadhyate

He whose mind is free from the sense of doership, and whose reason is not affected by worldly objects and activities, does not really kill, even having killed all these people, nor does any sin accrue to him. (17)

ज्ञानं ज्ञेयं परिज्ञाता त्रिविधा कर्मचोदना।
करणं कर्म कर्तेति त्रिविधः कर्मसङ्ग्रहः॥ १८॥

jñānaṁ jñeyaṁ parijñātā trividhā karmacodanā
karaṇaṁ karma karteti trividhaḥ karmasaṅgrahaḥ

The Knower, knowledge and the object of knowledge—these three motivate action. Even so, the doer, the organs and activity—these are the three constituents of action. (18)

ज्ञानं कर्म च कर्ता च त्रिधैव गुणभेदतः।
प्रोच्यते गुणसङ्ख्याने यथावच्छृणु तान्यपि॥ १९॥

jñānaṁ karma ca kartā ca tridhaiva guṇabhedataḥ
procyate guṇasaṅkhyāne yathāvacchṛṇu tānyapi

In the branch of knowledge dealing with the Guṇas or modes of Prakṛti, knowledge and action as well as the doer have been declared to be of three kinds acccording to the Guṇa which predominates in each; hear them too duly from Me. (19)

सर्वभूतेषु येनैकं भावमव्ययमीक्षते।
अविभक्तं विभक्तेषु तज्ज्ञानं विद्धि सात्त्विकम्॥ २०॥

sarvabhūteṣu yenaikaṁ bhāvamavyayamīkṣate
avibhaktaṁ vibhakteṣu tajjñānaṁ viddhi sāttvikam

That by which man perceives one imperishable divine existence as undivided and equally present in all individual beings, know that knowledge to be Sāttvika. (20)

पृथक्त्वेन तु यज्ज्ञानं नानाभावान्पृथग्विधान्।
वेत्ति सर्वेषु भूतेषु तज्ज्ञानं विद्धि राजसम्॥ २१॥

pṛthaktvena tu yajjñānaṁ nānābhāvānpṛthagvidhān
vetti sarveṣu bhūteṣu tajjñānaṁ viddhi rājasam

The knowledge by which man cognizes many

existences of various kinds, as apart from one another, in all beings, know that knowledge to be Rājasika. (21)

यत्तु कृत्स्नवदेकस्मिन्कार्ये सक्तमहैतुकम्।
अतत्त्वार्थवदल्पं च तत्तामसमुदाहृतम्॥ २२॥

yattu kṛtsnavadekasminkārye saktamahaitukam
atattvārthavadalpaṁ ca tattāmasamudāhṛtam

Again, that knowledge which clings to one body as if it were the whole, and which is irrational, has no real grasp of truth and is trivial, has been declared as Tāmasika. (22)

नियतं सङ्गरहितमरागद्वेषतः कृतम्।
अफलप्रेप्सुना कर्म यत्तत्सात्त्विकमुच्यते॥ २३॥

niyataṁ saṅgarahitamarāgadveṣataḥ kṛtam
aphalaprepsunā karma yattatsāttvikamucyate

That action which is ordained by the scriptures and is not accompanied by the sense of doership, and has been done without any partiality or prejudice by one who seeks no return, is called Sāttvika. (23)

यत्तु कामेप्सुना कर्म साहङ्कारेण वा पुनः।
क्रियते बहुलायासं तद्राजसमुदाहृतम्॥ २४॥

yattu kāmepsunā karma sāhaṅkāreṇa vā punaḥ
kriyate bahulāyāsaṁ tadrājasamudāhṛtam

That action however, which involves much strain and is performed by one who seeks enjoyments or by a man full of egotism, has been spoken of as Rājasika. (24)

अनुबन्धं क्षयं हिंसामनवेक्ष्य च पौरुषम्।
मोहादारभ्यते कर्म यत्तत्तामसमुच्यते॥ २५॥

anubandhaṁ kṣayaṁ hiṁsāmanavekṣya ca pauruṣam
mohādārabhyate karma yattattāmasamucyate

That action which is undertaken through sheer ignorance, without regard to consequences or loss to oneself, injury to others and one's own resourcefulness, is declared as Tāmasika. (25)

मुक्तसङ्गोऽनहंवादी धृत्युत्साहसमन्वितः।
सिद्ध्यसिद्ध्योर्निर्विकारः कर्ता सात्त्विक उच्यते॥ २६॥

muktasaṅgo'nahaṁvādī dhṛtyutsāhasamanvitaḥ
siddhyasiddhyornirvikāraḥ kartā sāttvika ucyate

Free from attachment, unegoistic, endowed with firmness and zeal and unswayed by success and failure—such a doer is said to be Sāttvika. (26)

रागी कर्मफलप्रेप्सुर्लुब्धो हिंसात्मकोऽशुचिः।
हर्षशोकान्वितः कर्ता राजसः परिकीर्तितः॥ २७॥

rāgī karmaphalaprepsurlubdho hiṁsātmako'śuciḥ
harṣaśokānvitaḥ kartā rājasaḥ parikīrtitaḥ

The doer who is full of attachment, seeks the fruit of actions and is greedy, and who is oppressive by nature and of impure conduct, and is affected by joy and sorrow, has been called Rājasika. (27)

अयुक्तः प्राकृतः स्तब्धः शठोऽनैष्कृतिकोऽलसः।
विषादी दीर्घसूत्री च कर्ता तामस उच्यते॥ २८॥

ayuktaḥ prākṛtaḥ stabdhaḥ śaṭho'naiṣkṛtiko'lasaḥ
viṣādī dīrghasūtrī ca kartā tāmasa ucyate

Lacking piety and self-control, uncultured, arrogant, deceitful, inclined to rob others of their livelihood, slothful, despondent and procrastinating—such a doer is called Tāmasika. (28)

बुद्धेर्भेदं धृतेश्चैव गुणतस्त्रिविधं शृणु।
प्रोच्यमानमशेषेण पृथक्त्वेन धनञ्जय॥ २९॥

buddherbhedaṁ dhṛteścaiva guṇatastrividhaṁ śṛṇu
procyamānamaśeṣeṇa pṛthaktvena dhanañjaya

Now hear, Arjuna, the threefold divison, based on the predominance of each Guṇa, of understanding (Buddhi) and firmness (Dhṛti), which I shall explain in detail, one by one. (29)

प्रवृत्तिं च निवृत्तिं च कार्याकार्ये भयाभये।
बन्धं मोक्षं च या वेत्ति बुद्धिः सा पार्थ सात्त्विकी॥ ३०॥

pravṛttiṁ ca nivṛttiṁ ca kāryākārye bhayābhaye
bandhaṁ mokṣaṁ ca yā vetti buddhiḥ sā pārtha sāttvikī

The intellect which correctly determines the paths of activity and renunciation, what ought to be done and what should not be done, what is fear and what is fearlessness, and what is bondage and what is liberation, that intellect is Sāttvika. (30)

यया धर्ममधर्मं च कार्यं चाकार्यमेव च।
अयथावत्प्रजानाति बुद्धिः सा पार्थ राजसी॥ ३१॥

yayā dharmamadharmaṁ ca kāryaṁ cākāryameva ca
ayathāvatprajānāti buddhiḥ sā pārtha rājasī

The intellect by which man does not truly perceive what is Dharma and what is Adharma, what ought to be done and what should not be done—that intellect is Rājasika. (31)

अधर्मं धर्ममिति या मन्यते तमसावृता।
सर्वार्थान्विपरीतांश्च बुद्धिः सा पार्थ तामसी॥ ३२॥

adharmaṁ dharmamiti yā manyate tamasāvṛtā
sarvārthānviparītāṁśca buddhiḥ sā pārtha tāmasī

The intellect which imagines even Adharma to be Dharma, and sees all other things upside-down—wrapped in ignorance, that intellect is Tāmasika, Arjuna. (32)

धृत्या यया धारयते मनःप्राणेन्द्रियक्रियाः।
योगेनाव्यभिचारिण्या धृतिः सा पार्थ सात्त्विकी॥ ३३॥

dhṛtyā yayā dhārayate manaḥprāṇendriyakriyāḥ
yogenāvyabhicāriṇyā dhṛtiḥ sā pārtha sāttvikī

The unwavering firmness by which man controls through the Yoga of meditation the functions of the mind, the vital airs and the senses—that firmness, Arjuna, is Sāttvika. (33)

यया तु धर्मकामार्थान्धृत्या धारयतेऽर्जुन।
प्रसङ्गेन फलाकाङ्क्षी धृतिः सा पार्थ राजसी॥ ३४॥

yayā tu dharmakāmārthāndhṛtyā dhārayate'rjuna
prasaṅgena phalākāṅkṣī dhṛtiḥ sā pārtha rājasī

The firmness (Dhṛti), however, by which the man seeking a reward for his actions clutches with extreme fondness virtues, earthly possessions and worldly enjoyments—that firmness (Dhṛti) is said to be Rājasika, Arjuna. (34)

यया स्वप्नं भयं शोकं विषादं मदमेव च।
न विमुञ्चति दुर्मेधा धृतिः सा पार्थ तामसी॥ ३५॥

yayā svapnaṁ bhayaṁ śokaṁ viṣādaṁ madameva ca
na vimuñcati durmedhā dhṛtiḥ sā pārtha tāmasī

The firmness (Dhṛti) by which an evil-minded person does not give up sleep, fear, anxiety, sorrow and vanity as well, that firmness is Tāmasika. (35)

सुखं त्विदानीं त्रिविधं शृणु मे भरतर्षभ।
अभ्यासाद्रमते यत्र दुःखान्तं च निगच्छति॥ ३६॥
यत्तदग्रे विषमिव परिणामेऽमृतोपमम्।
तत्सुखं सात्त्विकं प्रोक्तमात्मबुद्धिप्रसादजम्॥ ३७॥

sukhaṁ tvidānīṁ trividhaṁ śṛṇu me bharatarṣabha
abhyāsādramate yatra duḥkhāntaṁ ca nigacchati
yattadagre viṣamiva pariṇāme'mṛtopamam
tatsukhaṁ sāttvikaṁ proktamātmabuddhiprasādajam

Now hear from Me the threefold joy too. That in which the striver finds enjoyment through practice of adoration, meditation and service to God etc., and whereby he reaches the end of sorrow—such a joy, though appearing as poison in the beginning, tastes like nectar in the end; hence that joy, born as it is of the placidity of mind brought about by meditation on God, has been declared as Sāttvika. (36-37)

विषयेन्द्रियसंयोगाद्यत्तदग्रेऽमृतोपमम् ।
परिणामे विषमिव तत्सुखं राजसं स्मृतम् ॥ ३८ ॥

viṣayendriyasaṁyogādyattadagre'mṛtopamam
pariṇāme viṣamiva tatsukhaṁ rājasaṁ smṛtam

The delight which follows from the contact of the senses with their objects is eventually poison-like, though appearing at first as nectar; hence it has been spoken of as Rājasika. (38)

यदग्रे चानुबन्धे च सुखं मोहनमात्मनः ।
निद्रालस्यप्रमादोत्थं तत्तामसमुदाहृतम् ॥ ३९ ॥

yadagre cānubandhe ca sukhaṁ mohanamātmanaḥ
nidrālasyapramādotthaṁ tattāmasamudāhṛtam

That which stupefies the self during its enjoyment as well as in the end—derived from sleep, indolence and obstinate error, such delight has been called Tāmasika. (39)

न तदस्ति पृथिव्यां वा दिवि देवेषु वा पुनः ।
सत्त्वं प्रकृतिजैर्मुक्तं यदेभिः स्यात्त्रिभिर्गुणैः ॥ ४० ॥

na tadasti pṛthivyāṁ vā divi deveṣu vā punaḥ
sattvaṁ prakṛtijairmuktaṁ yadebhiḥ syāttribhirguṇaiḥ

There is no being on earth, or even among the gods in heaven or anywhere else, who is free from these three Guṇas, born of Prakṛti. (40)

ब्राह्मणक्षत्रियविशां शूद्राणां च परन्तप।
कर्माणि प्रविभक्तानि स्वभावप्रभवैर्गुणैः॥ ४१॥

brāhmaṇakṣatriyaviśāṁ śūdrāṇāṁ ca parantapa
karmāṇi pravibhaktāni svabhāvaprabhavairguṇaiḥ

The duties of the Brāhmaṇas, the Kṣatriyas and the Vaiśyas, as well as of the Śūdras have been assigned according to their inborn qualities, Arjuna. (41)

शमो दमस्तपः शौचं क्षान्तिरार्जवमेव च।
ज्ञानं विज्ञानमास्तिक्यं ब्रह्मकर्म स्वभावजम्॥ ४२॥

śamo damastapaḥ śaucaṁ kṣāntirārjavameva ca
jñānaṁ vijñānamāstikyaṁ brahmakarma svabhāvajam

Subjugation of the mind and senses, enduring hardships for the discharge of one's sacred obligations, external and internal purity, forgiving the faults of others, straightness of mind, senses and behaviour, belief in the Vedas and other scriptures, God and life after death etc., study and teaching of the Vedas and other scriptures and realization of the truth relating to God—all these constitute the natural duties of a Brāhmaṇa. (42)

शौर्यं तेजो धृतिर्दाक्ष्यं युद्धे चाप्यपलायनम्।
दानमीश्वरभावश्च क्षात्रं कर्म स्वभावजम्॥ ४३॥

śauryaṁ tejo dhṛtirdākṣyaṁ yuddhe cāpyapalāyanam
dānamīśvarabhāvaśca kṣātraṁ karma svabhāvajam

Heroism, fearlessness, firmness, diligence and dauntlessness in battle, bestowing gifts, and lordliness—

all these constitute the natural duty of a Kṣatriya. (43)

कृषिगौरक्ष्यवाणिज्यं वैश्यकर्म स्वभावजम्।
परिचर्यात्मकं कर्म शूद्रस्यापि स्वभावजम्॥ ४४॥

kṛṣigaurakṣyavāṇijyaṁ vaiśyakarma svabhāvajam
paricaryātmakaṁ karma śūdrasyāpi svabhāvajam

Agriculture, rearing of cows and honest exchange of merchandise—these constitute the natural duty of a Vaiśya (a member of the trading class). And service of the other classes is the natural duty even of a Śūdra (a member of the labouring class). (44)

स्वे स्वे कर्मण्यभिरतः संसिद्धिं लभते नरः।
स्वकर्मनिरतः सिद्धिं यथा विन्दति तच्छृणु॥ ४५॥

sve sve karmaṇyabhirataḥ saṁsiddhiṁ labhate naraḥ
svakarmanirataḥ siddhiṁ yathā vindati tacchṛṇu

Keenly devoted to his own natural duty, man attains the highest perfection in the shape of God-realization. Hear the mode of performance whereby the man engaged in his inborn duty reaches that highest consummation. (45)

यतः प्रवृत्तिर्भूतानां येन सर्वमिदं ततम्।
स्वकर्मणा तमभ्यर्च्य सिद्धिं विन्दति मानवः॥ ४६॥

yataḥ pravṛttirbhūtānāṁ yena sarvamidaṁ tatam
svakarmaṇā tamabhyarcya siddhiṁ vindati mānavaḥ

By worshipping Him from whom all beings come into being and by whom the whole universe is pervaded, through the performance of his own natural duties, man attains the highest perfection. (46)

श्रेयान्स्वधर्मो विगुणः परधर्मात्स्वनुष्ठितात्।
स्वभावनियतं कर्म कुर्वन्नाप्नोति किल्बिषम्॥ ४७॥

śreyānsvadharmo viguṇaḥ paradharmātsvanuṣṭhitāt
svabhāvaniyataṁ karma kurvannāpnoti kilbiṣam

Better is one's own duty, though devoid of merit, than the duty of another well-performed; for performing the duty ordained by his own nature man does not incur sin. (47)

सहजं कर्म कौन्तेय सदोषमपि न त्यजेत्।
सर्वारम्भा हि दोषेण धूमेनाग्निरिवावृताः॥ ४८॥

sahajaṁ karma kaunteya sadoṣamapi na tyajet
sarvārambhā hi doṣeṇa dhūmenāgnirivāvṛtāḥ

Therefore, Arjuna, one should not relinquish one's innate duty, even though it has a measure of evil; for all undertakings are beset by some evil, as is the fire covered by smoke. (48)

असक्तबुद्धिः सर्वत्र जितात्मा विगतस्पृहः।
नैष्कर्म्यसिद्धिं परमां सन्न्यासेनाधिगच्छति॥ ४९॥

asaktabuddhiḥ sarvatra jitātmā vigataspṛhaḥ
naiṣkarmyasiddhiṁ paramāṁ sannyāsenādhigacchati

He whose intellect is unattached everywhere, whose thirst for enjoyment has altogether disappeared and who has subdued his mind, reaches through Sāṅkhyayoga (the path of Knowledge) the consummation of actionlessness. (49)

सिद्धिं प्राप्तो यथा ब्रह्म तथाप्नोति निबोध मे।
समासेनैव कौन्तेय निष्ठा ज्ञानस्य या परा॥ ५०॥

siddhiṁ prāpto yathā brahma tathāpnoti nibodha me
samāsenaiva kaunteya niṣṭhā jñānasya yā parā

Arjuna, know from Me only briefly the process through which man having attained actionlessness, which is the highest consummation of Jñānayoga (the path of Knowledge), reaches Brahma. (50)

बुद्ध्या विशुद्धया युक्तो धृत्यात्मानं नियम्य च।
शब्दादीन्विषयांस्त्यक्त्वा रागद्वेषौ व्युदस्य च॥ ५१॥
विविक्तसेवी लघ्वाशी यतवाक्कायमानसः।
ध्यानयोगपरो नित्यं वैराग्यं समुपाश्रितः॥ ५२॥
अहङ्कारं बलं दर्पं कामं क्रोधं परिग्रहम्।
विमुच्य निर्ममः शान्तो ब्रह्मभूयाय कल्पते॥ ५३॥

buddhyā viśuddhayā yukto dhṛtyātmānaṁ niyamya ca
śabdādīnviṣayāṁstyaktvā rāgadveṣau vyudasya ca
viviktasevī laghvāśī yatavākkāyamānasaḥ
dhyānayogaparo nityaṁ vairāgyaṁ samupāśritaḥ
ahaṅkāraṁ balaṁ darpaṁ kāmaṁ krodhaṁ parigraham
vimucya nirmamaḥ śānto brahmabhūyāya kalpate

Endowed with an untarnished intellect and partaking of a light, Sāttvika and regulated diet, living in a lonely and undefiled place having rejected sound and other objects of sense, having controlled the mind, speech and body by restraining the mind and senses through firmness of a Sāttvika type, taking a resolute stand on dispassion, after having completely got rid of attraction and aversion and remaining ever devoted to the Yoga of meditation having given up egotism, violence, arrogance, lust, anger and luxuries, devoid of the feeling of meum and tranquil of heart—such a man becomes qualified for oneness with Brahma, who is Truth, Consciousness and Bliss. (51—53)

ब्रह्मभूतः प्रसन्नात्मा न शोचति न काङ्क्षति।
समः सर्वेषु भूतेषु मद्भक्तिं लभते पराम्॥ ५४॥

brahmabhūtaḥ prasannātmā na śocati na kāṅkṣati
samaḥ sarveṣu bhūteṣu madbhaktiṁ labhate parām

Established in identity with Brahma (who is Truth, Consciousness and Bliss solidified), and cheerful in mind, the Sāṅkhyayogī no longer grieves nor craves for anything. The same to all beings, such a Yogī attains supreme devotion to Me. (54)

भक्त्या मामभिजानाति यावान्यश्चास्मि तत्त्वतः।
ततो मां तत्त्वतो ज्ञात्वा विशते तदनन्तरम्॥ ५५॥

bhaktyā māmabhijānāti yāvānyaścāsmi tattvataḥ
tato māṁ tattvato jñātvā viśate tadanantaram

Through that supreme devotion he comes to know Me in reality, what and who I am; and thereby knowing

Me truly, he forthwith merges into My being. (55)

सर्वकर्माण्यपि सदा कुर्वाणो मद्व्यपाश्रयः।
मत्प्रसादादवाप्नोति शाश्वतं पदमव्ययम्॥ ५६॥

sarvakarmāṇyapi sadā kurvāṇo madvyapāśrayaḥ
matprasādādavāpnoti śāśvataṁ padamavyayam

The Karmayogī, however, who depends on Me, attains by My grace the eternal, imperishable state, even though performing all actions. (56)

चेतसा सर्वकर्माणि मयि सन्न्यस्य मत्परः।
बुद्धियोगमुपाश्रित्य मच्चित्तः सततं भव॥ ५७॥

cetasā sarvakarmāṇi mayi sannyasya matparaḥ
buddhiyogamupāśritya maccittaḥ satataṁ bhava

Mentally dedicating all your actions to Me, and taking recourse to Yoga in the form of even-mindedness, be solely devoted to Me and constantly fix your mind on Me. (57)

मच्चित्तः सर्वदुर्गाणि मत्प्रसादात्तरिष्यसि।
अथ चेत्त्वमहङ्कारान्न श्रोष्यसि विनङ्क्ष्यसि॥ ५८॥

maccittaḥ sarvadurgāṇi matprasādāttariṣyasi
atha cettvamahaṅkārānna śroṣyasi vinaṅkṣyasi

With your mind thus devoted to Me, you shall overcome all difficulties by My grace. But if from self conceit you do not care to listen to Me, you will be lost. (58)

यदहङ्कारमाश्रित्य न योत्स्य इति मन्यसे।
मिथ्यैष व्यवसायस्ते प्रकृतिस्त्वां नियोक्ष्यति॥ ५९॥

yadahaṅkāramāśritya na yotsya iti manyase
mithyaiṣa vyavasāyaste prakṛtistvāṁ niyokṣyati

If, taking your stand on egotism, you think, "I will not fight," vain is this resolve of yours; nature will drive you to the act. (59)

स्वभावजेन कौन्तेय निबद्धः स्वेन कर्मणा।
कर्तुं नेच्छसि यन्मोहात्करिष्यस्यवशोऽपि तत्॥ ६०॥

svabhāvajena kaunteya nibaddhaḥ svena karmaṇā
kartuṁ necchasi yanmohātkariṣyasyavaśo'pi tat

That action, too which you are not willing to undertake through ignorance you will perforce perform, bound by your own duty born of your nature. (60)

ईश्वरः सर्वभूतानां हृद्देशेऽर्जुन तिष्ठति।
भ्रामयन्सर्वभूतानि यन्त्रारूढानि मायया॥ ६१॥

īśvaraḥ sarvabhūtānāṁ hṛddeśe'rjuna tiṣṭhati
bhrāmayansarvabhūtāni yantrārūḍhāni māyayā

Arjuna, God abides in the heart of all creatures, causing them to revolve according to their Karma by His illusive power (māyā) as though mounted on a machine. (61)

तमेव शरणं गच्छ सर्वभावेन भारत।
तत्प्रसादात्परां शान्तिं स्थानं प्राप्स्यसि शाश्वतम्॥ ६२॥

tameva śaraṇaṁ gaccha sarvabhāvena bhārata
tatprasādātparāṁ śāntiṁ sthānaṁ prāpsyasi śāśvatam

Take refuge in Him alone with all your being, Arjuna. By His mere grace you will attain supreme peace and the eternal abode. (62)

इति ते ज्ञानमाख्यातं गुह्याद्गुह्यतरं मया।
विमृश्यैतदशेषेण यथेच्छसि तथा कुरु॥ ६३॥

iti te jñānamākhyātaṁ guhyādguhyataraṁ mayā
vimṛśyaitadaśeṣeṇa yathecchasi tathā kuru

Thus, has this wisdom, more profound than all profundities, been imparted to you by Me; deeply pondering over it, now do as you like. (63)

सर्वगुह्यतमं भूयः शृणु मे परमं वचः।
इष्टोऽसि मे दृढमिति ततो वक्ष्यामि ते हितम्॥ ६४॥

sarvaguhyatamaṁ bhūyaḥ śṛṇu me paramaṁ vacaḥ
iṣṭo'si me dṛḍhamiti tato vakṣyāmi te hitam

Hear, again, My supremely profound words, the most esoteric of all truths; as you are extremely dear to Me, therefore, I shall give you this salutary advice for your own good. (64)

मन्मना भव मद्भक्तो मद्याजी मां नमस्कुरु।
मामेवैष्यसि सत्यं ते प्रतिजाने प्रियोऽसि मे॥ ६५॥

manmanā bhava madbhakto madyājī māṁ namaskuru
māmevaiṣyasi satyaṁ te pratijāne priyo'si me

Give your mind to Me, be devoted to Me, worship

Me and bow to Me. Doing so you will come to Me alone, I truly promise you; for you are exceptionally dear to Me. (65)

सर्वधर्मान्परित्यज्य मामेकं शरणं व्रज।
अहं त्वा सर्वपापेभ्यो मोक्षयिष्यामि मा शुचः॥ ६६॥

sarvadharmānparityajya māmekaṁ śaraṇaṁ vraja
ahaṁ tvā sarvapāpebhyo mokṣayiṣyāmi mā śucaḥ

Resigning all your duties to Me, the all-powerful and all supporting Lord, take refuge in Me alone; I shall absolve you of all sins, worry not. (66)

इदं ते नातपस्काय नाभक्ताय कदाचन।
न चाशुश्रूषवे वाच्यं न च मां योऽभ्यसूयति॥ ६७॥

idaṁ te nātapaskāya nābhaktāya kadācana
na cāśuśrūṣave vācyaṁ na ca māṁ yo'bhyasūyati

This secret gospel of the Gītā should never be imparted to a man who lacks in austerity, nor to him who is wanting in devotion, nor even to him who is not willing to hear; and in no case to him who finds fault with Me. (67)

य इमं परमं गुह्यं मद्भक्तेष्वभिधास्यति।
भक्तिं मयि परां कृत्वा मामेवैष्यत्यसंशयः॥ ६८॥

ya imaṁ paramaṁ guhyaṁ madbhakteṣvabhidhāsyati
bhaktiṁ mayi parāṁ kṛtvā māmevaiṣyatyasaṁśayaḥ

He who, offering the highest love to Me, preaches the most profound gospel of the Gītā among My devotees, shall come to Me alone; there is no doubt about it. (68)

न च तस्मान्मनुष्येषु कश्चिन्मे प्रियकृत्तमः।
भविता न च मे तस्मादन्यः प्रियतरो भुवि॥ ६९॥

na ca tasmānmanuṣyeṣu kaścinme priyakṛttamaḥ
bhavitā na ca me tasmādanyaḥ priyataro bhuvi

Among men there is none who does Me a more loving service than he; nor shall anyone be dearer to Me on the entire globe than he. (69)

अध्येष्यते च य इमं धर्म्यं संवादमावयोः।
ज्ञानयज्ञेन तेनाहमिष्टः स्यामिति मे मतिः॥ ७०॥

adhyeṣyate ca ya imaṁ dharmyaṁ saṁvādamāvayoḥ
jñānayajñena tenāhamiṣṭaḥ syāmiti me matiḥ

Whosoever studies this sacred dialogue of ours in the form of the Gītā, by him too shall I be worshipped with Yajña of Knowledge; such is My conviction. (70)

श्रद्धावाननसूयश्च शृणुयादपि यो नरः।
सोऽपि मुक्तः शुभाँल्लोकान्प्राप्नुयात्पुण्यकर्मणाम्॥ ७१॥

śraddhāvānanasūyaśca śṛṇuyādapi yo naraḥ
so'pi muktaḥ śubhām̐llokānprāpnuyātpuṇyakarmaṇām

The man who listens the holy Gītā with reverence, being free from malice, he too, liberated from sin, shall reach the propitious worlds of the pious and righteous. (71)

कच्चिदेतच्छ्रुतं पार्थ त्वयैकाग्रेण चेतसा।
कच्चिदज्ञानसम्मोहः प्रनष्टस्ते धनञ्जय॥ ७२॥

kaccidetacchrutaṁ pārtha tvayaikāgreṇa cetasā
kaccidajñānasammohaḥ pranaṣṭaste dhanañjaya

Have you, O Arjuna, heard this gospel of the Gītā attentively? And has your delusion born of ignorance been destroyed, O Dhanañjaya, conqueror of riches? (72)

अर्जुन उवाच

नष्टो मोहः स्मृतिर्लब्धा त्वत्प्रसादान्मयाच्युत।
स्थितोऽस्मि गतसन्देहः करिष्ये वचनं तव॥ ७३॥

arjuna uvāca

naṣṭo mohaḥ smṛtirlabdhā tvatprasādānmayācyuta
sthito'smi gatasandehaḥ kariṣye vacanaṁ tava

Arjuna said: Kṛṣṇa, by Your grace my delusion has been destroyed and I have gained wisdom. I am free of all doubt. I shall do your bidding. (73)

सञ्जय उवाच

इत्यहं वासुदेवस्य पार्थस्य च महात्मनः।
संवादमिममश्रौषमद्भुतं रोमहर्षणम्॥ ७४॥

sañjaya uvāca

ityahaṁ vāsudevasya pārthasya ca mahātmanaḥ
saṁvādamimamaśrauṣamadbhutaṁ romaharṣaṇam

Sañjaya said: Thus I heard the mysterious and thrilling conversation between Śrī Kṛṣṇa and the high-souled Arjuna, O son of Kuntī. (74)

व्यासप्रसादाच्छ्रुतवानेतद्गुह्यमहं परम्।
योगं योगेश्वरात्कृष्णात्साक्षात्कथयतः स्वयम्॥ ७५॥

vyāsaprasādācchrutavānetadguhyamahaṁ param
yogaṁ yogeśvarātkṛṣṇātsākṣātkathayataḥ svayam

Having been blessed with the divine vision by the grace of Śrī Vyāsa, I heard in person this supremely esoteric gospel from the Lord of Yoga, Śrī Kṛṣṇa Himself, imparting it to Arjuna. (75)

राजन्संस्मृत्य संस्मृत्य संवादमिममद्भुतम्।
केशवार्जुनयोः पुण्यं हृष्यामि च मुहुर्मुहुः॥ ७६॥

rājansaṁsmṛtya saṁsmṛtya saṁvādamimamadbhutam
keśavārjunayoḥ puṇyaṁ hṛṣyāmi ca muhurmuhuḥ

Remembering, over and over, that sacred and mystic conversation between Bhagavān Śrī Kṛṣṇa and Arjuna, O King! I rejoice again and yet again. (76)

तच्च संस्मृत्य संस्मृत्य रूपमत्यद्भुतं हरेः।
विस्मयो मे महान्राजन्हृष्यामि च पुनः पुनः॥ ७७॥

tacca saṁsmṛtya saṁsmṛtya rūpamatyadbhutaṁ hareḥ
vismayo me mahānrājanhṛṣyāmi ca punaḥ punaḥ

Remembering also, again and again, that most wonderful Form of Śrī Kṛṣṇa, great is my wonder and I rejoice over and over again. (77)

यत्र योगेश्वरः कृष्णो यत्र पार्थो धनुर्धरः।
तत्र श्रीर्विजयो भूतिर्ध्रुवा नीतिर्मतिर्मम॥ ७८॥

yatra yogeśvaraḥ kṛṣṇo yatra pārtho dhanurdharaḥ
tatra śrīrvijayo bhūtirdhruvā nītirmatirmama

Wherever there is Bhagavān Śrī Kṛṣṇa, the Lord of Yoga, and wherever there is Arjuna, the wielder of the Gāṇḍīva bow, goodness, victory, glory and unfailing righteousness will surely be there : such is My conviction. (78)

ॐ तत्सदिति श्रीमद्भगवद्गीतासूपनिषत्सु ब्रह्मविद्यायां
योगशास्त्रे श्रीकृष्णार्जुनसंवादे मोक्षसन्न्यासयोगो
नामाष्टादशोऽध्यायः॥ १८॥

Thus, in the Upaniṣad sung by the Lord, the Science of Brahma, the scripture of Yoga, the dialogue between Śrī Kṛṣṇa and Arjuna, ends the eighteenth chapter entitled "The Yoga of Liberation through the Path of Knowledge and Self-Surrender."

Oṁ Tat Sat

आरती

जय भगवद्गीते, जय भगवद्गीते।
हरि-हिय-कमल-विहारिणि, सुन्दर सुपुनीते॥ जय०
कर्म-सुमर्म-प्रकाशिनि, कामासक्तिहरा।
तत्त्वज्ञान-विकाशिनि, विद्या ब्रह्म परा॥ जय०
निश्चल-भक्ति-विधायिनि, निर्मल मलहारी।
शरण-रहस्य-प्रदायिनि, सब विधि सुखकारी॥ जय०
राग-द्वेष-विदारिणि, कारिणि मोद सदा।
भव-भय-हारिणि, तारिणि, परमानन्दप्रदा॥ जय०
आसुरभाव-विनाशिनि, नाशिनि तम-रजनी।
दैवी सद्गुणदायिनि, हरि-रसिका सजनी॥ जय०
समता-त्याग सिखावनि, हरि-मुखकी बानी।
सकल शास्त्रकी स्वामिनि, श्रुतियोंकी रानी॥ जय०
दया-सुधा बरसावनि मातु! कृपा कीजै।
हरिपद-प्रेम दान कर अपनो कर लीजै॥ जय०

Our English Publications

457 **Śrīmad Bhagavadgītā—Tattva-Vivecanī** (With Sanskrit text, English Translation and Detailed Commentary) (By Jayadayal Goyandka)

[1080 / 1081 **Śrīmad Bhagavadgītā—Sādhaka-Sañjīvanī** (With Sanskrit Text, Roman Transliteration, English Translation and Detailed Commentary) (By Swami Ramsukhdas) Set of two volumes

534 **Śrīmad Bhagavadgītā** (Sanskrit Text and English Translation) (Hard Bound Edition) Pocket Size

[452 / 453 **Śrīmad Vālmīki-Rāmāyaṇa** (With Sanskrit Text and English Translation) Set of two volumes

1318 **Śrī Rāmacaritamānasa** (With Hindi Text, Roman Transliteration and English Translation)

786 **Śrī Rāmacaritamānasa** Medium Size

[564 / 565 **Śrīmad Bhāgavata** (With Sanskrit Text and English Translation) Set of two volumes

783 **Abortion Right or Wrong You Decide?** (By Gopi Nath Agrawal)

BY JAYADAYAL GOYANDKA

477 Gems of Truth [Vol. I]
478 Gems of Truth [Vol. II]
479 Sure Steps to God-Realization
481 Way to Divine Bliss
482 What is Dharma? What is God?
480 Instructive Eleven Stories
520 Secret of Jñānayoga
521 Secret of Premayoga
522 Secret of Karmayoga
523 Secret of Bhaktiyoga
694 Dialogue with the Lord During Meditation
1125 Five Divine Abodes
658 Secrets of Gītā
1013 Gems of Satsaṅga

BY HANUMAN PRASAD PODDAR

484 Look Beyond the Veil
622 How to Attain Eternal Happiness?
483 Turn to God
485 Path to Divinity
847 Gopīs' Love for Śrī Kṛṣṇa
620 The Divine Name and Its Practice
486 Wavelets of Bliss & the Divine Message

BY SWAMI RAMSUKHDAS

619 Ease in God-Realization
471 Benedictory Discourses
473 Art of Living
472 How to Lead A Household Life
570 Let us Know the Truth
638 Sahaja Sādhanā
621 Invaluable Advice
497 Truthfulness of Life
669 The Divine Name
552 Way to Attain the Supreme Bliss
562 Ancient Idealism for Modernday Living

SPECIAL EDITION

1411 **Śrīmad Bhagavadgītā—Roman Gītā** (With English Translation & Transliteration) (Book Size)

1391 **Śrīmad Bhagavadgītā** (Sanskrit Text and English Translation) Pocket Size

1413 **All is God**-by Swami Ramsukhdas
1406 **Gītā-Mādhurya** (")
1407 **Drops of Nectar** (")
1438 **Discovery of Truth & Immortality** (")
1414 **Story of Mīrā Bāī** -by Bankey Behari

website : **www.gitapress.org** | e-mail:**booksales@gitapress.org**

H